ASTROLOGICALLY SPEAKING

Astrologically Speaking

by

INGRID LIND, D.F.Astrol.S

Life Patron of the Astrological Association and the Faculty of
Astrological Studies

L. N. FOWLER & CO. LTD.
1201/3 HIGH ROAD, CHADWELL HEATH,
ROMFORD RM6 4DH

85243 366 2

Printed and bound in Great Britain at
The Camelot Press Ltd, Southampton

"Here is a man striding towards his home. I cannot say if he is going towards quarrel or love. I can ask myself only this. 'What kind of a man is he?' And when I know that, only then shall I know by what lodestone he is impelled, and where he is bound. For in the end man always gravitates in the direction commanded by the lodestone in him."

Antoine de Saint-Exupéry
(*Flight to Arras,* Heinemann, 1942)

Astrology, studied in depth, can furnish a blueprint of ingredients that go to make up any whole that is relatable to a moment in space and time. Understanding of this blueprint takes years of study. Given full knowledge of the ingredients – the signs and planets – the natural cleavage lines of the circle are only known when the rising degree and resultant angles are known, and only as fitting in to the framework of this precisely calculated cross can the functioning of an individual circle be read.

CONTENTS

8

INTRODUCTION

by Sir George Trevelyan, Bt., M.A.

Many people now recognise that Astrology is a gateway to knowledge opening on to an endless ocean of wisdom. It has been debased into mere fortune telling and the modern rational intellect has often scorned it. The Greek Mystery temples had carved above their portals 'Man know thyself and thou shalt know the Universe'. The corollary is: 'Man, if thou wouldst find thyself, seek in the Universe.' For there in the stellar regions is the archetype of the human soul and personality. So great a mystery cannot and should not be treated lightly. Many laymen get bogged down in the mass of data presented in astrological volumes.

Here is a book which will indeed help. Ingrid Lind is one of the leading astrologers in our time with thirty years of experience, but she is also a counsellor, helping people by sympathetic understanding and advice in the trials of life. Now a new movement for psychological counselling is developing and this is highly significant. A spiritual awakening is taking place in our time, involving a breakthrough into a holistic world-view which reaches far beyond the limitations of the materialistic outlook. This emergence of new dimensions of understanding of course brings many difficulties. But modern psychiatric science rarely, as yet, recognises the spiritual nature of man or the reality of his higher self. Therefore people in need of help often hesitate to get involved with a psychologist and seek elsewhere for help. Thus a body of counsellors is emerging to meet this very need, often with qualification in what is called Trans-personal Psychology. Many in the field now realise that true astrology can be of immense significance in clarifying and interpreting trends and potentialities in the soul and life pattern, and so are convinced that astrology should become a most valuable adjunct to psychological counselling.

Ingrid Lind is a counsellor of deep human sympathy, understanding and experience, but she can also bring her profound knowledge of astrology to bear on personal problems. This book, *Astrologically Speaking* will open for many an understanding of the invisible influences

9

working out in the destiny of each individual. Indeed there can be no human problem which is not touched by the knowledge. Many are now bewildered and have lost the sense of meaning in life. This is restored when we stretch our vision into the vast oneness of the living universe and see the human soul as a spiritual entity, eternal and imperishable, undergoing a long training through many lives on earth to reach an ultimate perfection in union with the Divine. Ingrid Lind's book will help many to win again this sense of meaning and with it joy and hope. Those who already possess astrological knowledge will find illumination on many aspects of this field of knowledge as applied in human life.

AUTHOR'S PREFACE

Specialists have been described as being those who tend to know more and more about less and less.

Today's book markets are reaching saturation point with New Age subjects; so will the reading public soon be knowing less and less about more and more?

Astrology finds its way into magazines and national dailies.

Everyone knows of the existence of the signs of the zodiac. Few, however, have any knowledge of astrology at its deeper levels or what it can disclose in the way of knowledge of the main energy factors and the balance and integration of a personality. This wide subject is creeping back into academic circles in what could be described, if tentatively, as a resurgence of interest such as prevailed among men of the calibre of Paracelsus, Copernicus, Francis Bacon, Isaac Newton and others.

The sceptic asks *why* an astronomical sky arrangement, as seen from a given place at a given time, should have anything to do with terrestrial beings or events.

I admit I began serious study of astrology (after years of hearing about it from an old aunt) with the idea of finding out if it were not mostly nonsense. Thirty years of non-stop astrological work later, I am totally convinced that no serious enquirer can practise with a large number of accurately calculated charts without finding that these represent the person (or subject) concerned with quite extraordinary accuracy. Nobody who has got over his elementary misconceptions about the subject and who works, as I do, as a consultant, can have any doubt at all that there is an active relation between the life and character of the individual and the sky-pattern when he was born.

You may learn from this book, but it does not set out full technicalities. It is in no way a 'how to do it' book. It is written in the hope of amplifying the knowledge of the lay reader and student alike. The last word can never be said about any sign or planetary energy. I know that I learn daily from client and colleague. What I write springs from years of experience and embodies, to some extent, the philosophy that the years have brought.

This book is written, then, for everyone who wants to know more about astrology and astrological practice without the time or inclination to pursue these thoroughly.

Thanks are due to those whose questions after talks to the general public have given me insight into what people want to know.

To friends and colleagues in the astrological world who don't need any information from me, I say, "I hope you will enjoy sharing in some of my experiences as a consultant."

There are many types of consultant. My own interest lies in the study of the human personality. What does it mean to study and practise astrology from the psychological angle? I must point out that the word 'psyche' means 'soul'. People who shy away from any mention of the soul seem quite happy to accept it in the context of psychology. The word psychosomatic is commonly used in medicine, but few doctors will tell you that your psychsomatic illness could be as accurately described as a 'soul sickness'.

A psychologist who is candidly anti-religious may quite reasonably avoid the word 'soul' because of its religious association.

No astrologer could be accused of religious orthodoxy, which is perhaps why I feel no hesitation in stating what I believe to be a fact for everyone. This is that man is primarily a soul, which in the course of time incarnates in many bodies.

This belief is most certainly *not* held by all astrologers. So, as well as being unorthodox in my religious beliefs I am also a law unto myself in the astrological world.

PART I

The Nature of Astrology

1. WHAT IS ASTROLOGY?

The purpose of this book is to present a point of view regarding astrology which may be acceptable to critical judgement and commonsense.

There are circles in which the very word 'astrologer' raises a laugh and the more thoughtless among our public characters will not hesitate either to score with a cheap jeer or dismiss the whole subject with contempt. This is largely the fault of so-called astrologers, for much nonsense has been uttered in the name of astrology; but it should really now be impossible for an educated person or one in an official position to misinform his audience that there can be nothing in it because astrologers have not heard of the precession of the equinox. Hipparchus, who discovered precession, was himself an astrologer.

At any rate the art, for it is an art as well as a science, has been practised throughout recorded history; and I am pretty certain that some astrologers in the far past were more learned and accomplished than many now living, though then as now the art of astrology was susceptible of development and use at any level – and it is easy to see the possibilities of malignant or merely foolish application. It is perhaps something of this kind that calls up in our minds the picture of men in strange hats drawing magic circles, whereas the technique no doubt grew naturally out of man's need for some practical method of judging times and seasons. Mapping of the 'stars' for this purpose may well have led to the observation of certain correspondences between certain phenomena in the heavens and events on earth, with the further consequence that those who could afford it – kings and princes – besides seeking advice on such matters as agriculture, began to consult astrologers regarding their personal fortunes. However this may be, astrology was practised by the Chaldeans, the Babylonians, the Egyptians, the Indians, the Chinese, the Greeks, the Romans, the Arabs and the Europeans.* Kepler believed that the Creator had made man in such a way that he might conquer the

---

* A list of astrologers of the past includes men respected for branches of learning other than astrology such as Paracelsus, Copernicus, Tycho Brahe the astronomer, Francis Bacon and many others who cannot be dismissed as fools or charlatans.

stars with that in him which transcends them; and this is precisely my own belief. Isaac Newton is said to have defended astrology when Halley pooh-poohed the subject with the remark, "Sir, I have studied it. You have not." I do not know if this conversation did in fact take place; but the same answer could be made to more recent pundits whose criticisms evidently derive from hearsay.

Our hope, then, fortified by a considerable experience of map-casting, interpretation and personal discussion with those who are perplexed by various difficulties of character and circumstance, is to offer some remarks which may serve to clarify the subject and remove some common fallacies which excite derision.

Let us say to begin with, from a psychological angle, that astrology is an art of interpretation which exhibits the correspondences between a man's character, and to some extent his circumstances, with the planetary situation disclosed in the planetary pattern at the moment of birth. To practise this art, the astrologer need have no innate gift such as clairvoyance, although it is a fact that some astrologers possess it, just as some doctors know what is wrong with a patient before subjecting him to clinical investigation.

This is far indeed from the 'astrology' of the popular newspapers and periodicals which purports to forecast personal trends for the day or week on the basis of the Sun-sign alone (the only item of astrological information that can be obtained without calculation and resource to almanacs), with the result that large numbers of people, knowing that their Sun is in Aries, Taurus or some other sign, read their personal fate in statements that in fact apply to about one-twelfth of the human race. For example, if an astrologer were to announce that all those born under Cancer were to meet a crocodile, this would be an exaggeration; but it would be true for a few of the many millions of Cancerians found in various parts of the world. Astrology does not divide people into twelve types destined to suffer the same fate at the same time; and it is because of an impression that this is what it amounts to that those who have not been into the subject dismiss it with a laugh. Astrology is not a matter of superstition and witchcraft but an art calling for exact calculation and interpretation carried out in a detached and scientific spirit.

The sceptic asks why an astronomical chart or sky-picture as seen from a given place at a given time should be supposed to have anything whatever to do with the life and fate of a man or any other creature (and indeed the birth moment may be that of a ship, a building, an industrial company, a horse, dormouse, man or nation). I may say that I have had hours of misgiving. When I began serious study of the subject after some years of casual interest, it was not without the idea of finding out if it were not mostly nonsense after all. What did I find? I found much that was vague, controversial and unsatisfactory: but much more that was reliable as well as deeply interesting and waiting to be rescued from its,

14

at that time (in the early fifties), obscure position. No serious astrologer can practise with a large number of accurately calculated charts without finding that they represent the person concerned, his character and potentials, with quite extraordinary accuracy; and nobody who has got over the elementary misconceptions about the subject and works as a consultant can have any doubt at all that there is an active relation between the life and character of an individual and the sky-pattern when he was born. It is a common experience for the consultant to cast the map of a person he has not yet seen or spoken to, draw his conclusions without psychic aids, and find, when the interview takes place, that much to the client's surprise an accurate and comprehensive picture of character and life trends has been worked out.

2. THE USES OF ASTROLOGY

Specific instances of the uses of astrology are to be found in Part III but in general let me say that astrology is not primarily an art of prediction. It is true that an astrologer can see the general pattern of a man's life and by inspection of certain factors and circumstances interpret the trend in a given field of experience; and it is true that astrologers do make exact forecasts; but in general this is a matter of luck in picking the right event from a number of possibilities, aided perhaps by a strong intuitive gift.

It is of course useless, and it may be disastrous, to draw any conclusion from the sole fact that your Sun is in this sign or the other; that you are 'Taurus' or your daughter 'Aries'. We can all know our Sun-sign by the date of our birth and many people suppose that this is astrology, whereas in fact it is a gross over-simplification. Those therefore who profess to read trends (or characters) on the basis of the Sun-sign alone and announce that romance is looming up for all those born under Leo, or that travel is inopportune for them, are lending themselves to fraud. Is it not unlikely that about one-twelfth of the world's population will meet much the same experience in the course of the day?

This is not to say that competent astrologers who write considered articles on the aspects to a given sign are not doing perfectly straight-forward work; but they would be the first to admit that their reading affects but one part of any one person's complex birth chart – namely, the aspects to the Sun. An example may make this clearer.

When beneficent Jupiter passes through a sign, the popular readings for the sign in question promise the benefits and expansions which are associated with this planet. But if Jupiter in your own chart is weak or if your personal progressed aspects are limiting in effect, you are unlikely to reap much good from Jupiter passing through your Sun-sign, although a friend born in the same month with happy progressions and a fortunate natal chart feels much benefit. You may remark that if the stars worked for your friend, they didn't for you. In fact they worked accurately for both of you.

Again, it is wrong to suppose that an aspect between two planets, say Mars and Mercury, can result in an actual event. All planets can be

16

described as energy factors, Mars being particularly involved in Energy, Heat, Activation; Mercury stands for Communication (through speech, writing or physical transport as well as inner transmission and the nervous system). A harmonious link-up of these two in the natal chart would certainly activate communication in some sense and by careful study of the chart, or, better still, consultation with the native and his circumstances, a pretty accurate guess can be made as to the field in which the combined force would operate. As regards A. it might stimulate athletic prowess. B, on the other hand, might be an intellectual and the same stimulus would spur him to writing, so that when the aspect was touched off he would meet success in that field. If A or B is intellectual as well as athletic the force could operate in both fields. For some reason, some planetary energies 'work' more strongly for one person than for another; and the significance of major transits can only be assessed after the astrologer has made enquiries about important events that have passed, noting the planetary set-up that obtained at the time.

Thus, knowledge concerning the client's life and circumstances can help a great deal in suggesting the type of experience that planetary changes are likely to bring; and in the writer's view this is the safe and correct use of astrology for predictive purposes.

Obviously, it is by no means enough that the consultative astrologer should work entirely by post. Unless one talks with clients, checking statements, verifying details, following indications, one is not unlikely to misread the facts, especially if facile, traditional interpretations are made use of. To give an example:

The Sun coming by progression to the position of the natal Venus is traditionally a happy event. Alan Leo wrote of it as follows:

The Sun in conjunction with the planet Venus gives light and life to all that is signified by this most benefic planet. The native will now come into very close contact with those to whom he will be drawn by sympathy and affection, and his prospects will look brighter and happier than they have done for some time. He will enjoy the blissful feeling of gratified emotions, which will thus be expanded for greater indulgence in pleasure and the pursuit of happiness, all things tending to bring increased ability to live in the better and more hopeful and cheerful side of the nature. The native will come into new and congenial society, will make new friends, and will gain in many ways through others and through his own attitude towards them. It is a very splendid solar influence, especially in regard to the cultivation of the feelings and higher emotions. This position often denotes marriage.

A client of mine had a similar aspect at the age of eleven. Clearly this did not involve marriage; and when I asked if it had been a pleasant year with new contacts and so forth, she answered, rather to my chagrin, that it had been dreadful; her father had run off with another woman and abandoned his wife and family. But on reflection I found a certain logic in this. In a child's chart the Sun can stand for the father, who had certainly had a Venusian experience in which the child was sufficiently involved for the event to be shown or forecast in the progressed chart.* Since then I have avoided textbook interpretations of progressed aspects and have recourse to the basic principles.

In the above case it could have been said that in her eleventh year this girl's Sun activates her natal Venus. At the appropriate age this would mean stimulation of the affections and marriage, or making of friends or important contacts is likely. As this is not likely at the age of eleven it is possible that some such event involves one of the parents. From the point of view of character rather than events an eleven-year-old could become more conscious of art or beauty: and matters regarding love or co-operation will be high-lighted.

I should mention that this method of prediction, based on what is called the progressed chart, involves a calculation which brings the natal chart up to date and shows trends for the year in question. Most astrologers use what are known as secondary directions and transits (see glossary of terms) when asked for detailed advice on a given problem at a given time; but unlike the reading of transits, which can be done at a glance, secondaries involve a complicated and lengthy process unsuitable for treatment here in what is in no sense a textbook.

My personal view, as a consultant, on this subject, is that astrological advice that is given in great detail and quantity should be taken with due reserve. There are, I find, those who take the whole thing *au grand serieux* and ask for progressed charts with day-to-day instructions as to the most insignificant acts. But cosmic patterns are not readily or usefully to be interpreted in relation to the question of changing one's hair style or making a journey to Spain. Moreover, if it is suggested that certain results will follow inevitably from a given planetary situation reliance is really being had on the fact that a large number of people react automatically to conditions and the client is being credited with no disposition or power to use his own inner strengths. It is indeed wise to allow in our plans for basic elements in our make-up and circumstances; but it is unhealthy in the extreme to substitute the rule of the 'stars' for our own will, and especially to try and escape what is coming to us by cosmic law.

This brings me to what the true uses of astrology seem to me to be.

The popular view of astrology seems to involve a kind of fatalism or determinism and close study of it does indeed lead us to conclude that a man is much less free than he imagines. But there is nothing in it whatever that excuses us from effort on the ground that 'the stars' are responsible. On the contrary, analysis of the chart shows us just where our effort should lie. It helps us towards self-consciousness, to self-government, to a sense of responsibility towards all life. For the life-

---

* Note to astrologers: The chart natally showed Venus in difficult aspect to the Sun.

pattern is not inalterable. The 'stars' do not constitute a separate and sometimes malignant force that arbitrarily controls us. The birth-chart is a portrait of our character, potentialities and to some extent our surroundings; and we are undoubtedly conditioned to an extent by circumstances, even the circumstances of character, into which we were thrust, or which we chose for ourselves, at birth: but we do not come off a production line; we are not machines designed to act in a given way for a given time. We are free, within limits, to react, free within God's will, within cosmic law, to make our life into something more than an automatism, into an ascending, or indeed a descending spiral. I use this term because when I study charts I see how the opportunities that the birth-chart indicates are offered again and again during the life and some accept and improve on them while others remain inert. The chart will disclose a certain weakness, shall we say? Each time a major planet touches off the exact degree of such weakness it is as it were underlined, accentuated, and opportunity is given to deal with it. To give an example: in your chart Mars has strong but difficult aspects and you are quick-tempered. Thus, as the degree of your natal Mars is touched off by progression or transit things will flare up, not always through your own action, which will stir your combative qualities; and this will happen again and again until you can wake up to the fact that you can refuse to react automatically. For we are always free within limits to react in our own way to the events that we are faced with. Just as the athlete trains nerve and muscle to cope with a given effort imposed on the body, so we can train our characters to cope with difficulties which seem to recur until we transcend them. And these difficulties are no more than externalisations of our own characteristics. For instance, the murderer's violent tendencies would show in his chart; but what happens is that he uses them in a moment of crisis at the lowest level, whereas the same forces might have earned him a V.C. So, while the chart shows a man's possibilities what he does is another story and it is not possible to see in the chart how an individual has reacted or will react, to circumstances. Twins with identical charts often react differently within the same framework. Social background plays an important part. Where one child is born in a palace, another born in a hovel at the same moment will also command, though in a different sphere. Where one boy will exercise his aggressive qualities in a street gang his contemporary could be a Judo expert. An evolved or fully educated person is less likely than others to react automatically, since rather than a sense of helplessness or compulsion there is a feeling that forces are at work which can be used well or ill. As we grow self-conscious and learn as far as is possible to act independently, we shall discover that true progress leads us back in full consciousness to the place in the wholeness which we once occupied as primitive automatisms.

There is no need, by the way, to accept the doctrine of reincarnation in this connection; but for those who do, the chart indicates where the reincarnating entity failed or succeeded in earlier lives. Assets such as talent, good fortune, good looks, have been earned. So have misfortune and disaster. I hope to show more fully in the following pages that the laws of cause and effect, of intelligible sequence, obtain at all levels, from cosmic levels to the ripples in a pond. What we sow we reap and I want to develop the theme that each of us has earned by some precedent if unknown set of acts or omissions the chart to which he is born. It is open to investigation whether this goes, as I think it does, for races as well as individuals. It is certain that an evolved country promises rosier opportunities than one where conditions are backward.

It is surely both useful and desirable that men should become more aware of themselves (unless of course this leads to brooding introspection). We may be friendless and not realise that something in our own nature causes it and can be amended. We may be accident-prone and not understand that it is because we invite calamity. And perhaps we do not realise our potentialities and neglect a talent that could give us joy. Again, a Birth-chart and character-reading help a parent to handle his child during the formative years and after. It is important, of course that wise use should be made of knowledge gained by this means – and it is for the parent who possesses it to make necessary and reasonable allowance, in the light of his own tendencies, for difference in temperament. For example, a fiery, impulsive child will not see why a sensitive, emotional parent is hurt by an outspoken remark, while a slow, gentle child will feel bustled and upset if urged on by a parent who is quick and impatient. These all-important differences in 'tempo' are dealt with more fully in Part III, pp. 188–197. They are responsible for much unhappiness. As they are fundamental and cannot be modified by urging or strict training it is wrong if parents realising what the child's tempo is, struggle to change what is fundamental in the child's make-up to suit their own view or convenience. In the earlier years it is for the parent to use self-knowledge, self-abnegation and tact. Consultation with a reliable astrologer can bring added comprehension to the task; and if serious misunderstanding is to be avoided and a child perhaps driven into a channel where he will not thrive it is clearly desirable that recourse should be had to this means of information while the child is still in its first infancy. Thus, astrology can help us to know our characters and the characters of those with whom we are in responsible contact, with the result that we are at any rate in a better position to recognise our own motives and control ourselves. As the Taoist said: 'A man who knows he is a fool is not a great fool.' And, incidentally, it is quite possible for a man to modify his own character in such a way that, among other results, he tends to attract events of a more favourable type than before.

3. DANGERS AND SAFEGUARDS

Dangers

There is perhaps no branch of knowledge or art that cannot be turned to unwise or dangerous use. The astrologer has great responsibility in this respect, especially in regard to the credulous, gullible or weak; and human failure in this respect will play its part as in other professions. There are so-called astrologers who wield power over their clients by pretending that they alone can save them from disaster and that without guidance from 'the stars' mistakes will certainly be made. Evil is not too strong a word for anyone who exerts power for his own ends.

Even newspaper 'horoscopes' can do harm if they make suggestions, attractive or sinister, which the weak take too seriously. The reader will perhaps hardly believe that anyone could regard them as more than a joke, but it is a fact that thousands are affected by them in some degree. As a matter of fact, the horoscopes in women's magazines are for the most part carefully and thoughtfully worded so as to cause no alarm, with no 'commands' and a good deal of perfectly reasonable encouragement; but there are 'strips' that give baleful warnings as well as thoroughly unjustified promises. One has only to imagine the effect on some rather silly young woman who reads on her wedding day that it is unwise to start a new project or who studies gloomy forebodings on the day her baby is born. It is easy to see that some wholesale, gross forecast could affect a decision for the worse, one way or another, in all sorts of connections. I have had letters from people who grieved over the fact that they were 'Scorpio' or 'Capricorn', as they had read that such people were ill-tempered, unhappy, ill-fated or something of the kind. Many regard such 'astrology' as innocent fun – but in my view it is pernicious to make such a suggestion as that to have the Sun in a given sign is enough to blight your enterprises if not your life. It is saddening, when one practises astrology at a serious level, to find what a lot of people there are who believe such nonsense, and disappointing that those who present, by way of entertainment, what purport to be astrological programmes on radio or television, do so with such misconception and in such a style as to be offensive to anyone who has found that astrology can

21

be of real value to life and conduct. But as long as people enjoy reading the 'strips' or watching programmes which are presented as though Sun-sign astrology were all that the public could appreciate, a certain number will go to the so-called astrologers, the fortune-tellers, in the hope of being told something agreeable. This ensures a livelihood for some whose astrological qualifications are non-existent.

Safeguards
What safeguards are possible?

First, no heed whatever should be paid to any astrological work that is not based on an accurately calculated chart of the relevant time, date and place. As this takes time and training, it will cost money. If an advertisement offers a relatively low-priced reading it is unlikely to be a really personal study. Computer readings furnish a surprising amount of accurately calculated information, but when it comes to interpretation this cannot compare with the work of an adequately trained astrologer.

The Correspondence Courses listed in the Appendix provide training for astrologers. Clearly not everyone who passes an examination proves to be a genius in his subject and the gaining of the Diploma of any of the three schools mentioned shows only that the holder has made a sustained effort to qualify. None of these diplomas are handed out lightly and are the fruit of years of study and at least fifteen hours of written exams.

4. A BASIS FOR BELIEF

Why, apart from daily experience that it works or at least that it can bring self-knowledge and a measure of insight into one mode of working of the solar system, should anyone 'believe in' astrology? Can it be supposed that there are planetary forces, including, by astrological convention, those of the Sun and Moon, which as it were impinge on a man, not only at the birth moment but throughout life? Why should it be the case that the pattern subsisting at our moment of birth, with the chart as a picture of it, remains the pattern within which we act and react, with a margin of free-will to govern our reactions?

First of all, if it is certain that at given times the pull of the Sun and the Moon are reflected in the tides of the sea, is it so strange that people as well should be affected, if in more subtle ways, by a complex of planetary movements, including those of the sun and moon? It cannot be ignored that radio weather is affected by planetary aspects. As long ago as 1951 a comprehensive account of this was to be seen in *Man and Time*. (Papers from the Eranos Yearbooks, 3; London: Routledge, under the heading 'Transformations of Science in Our Time' by Max Knoll.) This article stated how the traditional 'bad' aspects of astrology, namely the quadratic aspects, conjunctions and oppositions increase proton radiation and cause electromagnetic storms. The 'good' aspects, trines and sextiles, produce uniform radio weather.

The late Dr. C. G. Jung mentions this in his book *The Interpretation of Nature and the Psyche* (Routledge, 1955) and suggests that these facts provide a possible causal basis for astrology.

It seems likely then, unless one holds the extraordinary point of view that man's life is totally unconnected with the universe that contains him, that men may be regarded as minute, cell-like parts of a system, affected by changes in its total condition, increasing or decreasing with it in tension.

I suppose that the basic assumption, and one that has been made by all competent investigators from the Sages to modern physicists, is that all life is one and there is no event in one part of the cosmos without repercussion in every other. The universe amounts to a pattern of correlations, most of the elements in the picture remaining as yet unknown to us. Thus if the visible or invisible macrocosm is a pattern of growth and development, we may look on the birth chart of an individual – the crystallisation of a moment in time as it were – as showing where he, microcosm, stands and what he can do in shaping the life of the whole. As a cell in the human body is a living part of the totality, so all life is part of the cosmic life and each one of us is sensitive to the macrocosmic patterns and tensions and in a microcosmic way contributes. Each thought and action in short makes a ripple of effect. Thus a man remains part of the whole all his life, sensitive to that conjuncture in which he was born, one with a moment in time which is for ever significant for him, part of that unity whose purpose he can further and whose will he can thwart within limits set. There is no living and no so-called dead thing that does not belong and vibrate with the whole, changing, expanding in time, but shaped by the moment that gave it birth. Astrology, then, can provide a means whereby we can glimpse the life-pattern as it applies to ourselves or to life in general.

Mystics are aware of this, Traherne knew

> That all my mind was wholly everywhere,
> The utmost star
> Though seen from far,
> Was present in the apple of my eye.

('My Spirit'. *Oxford Book of English Mystical Verse*)

A.E. writes

> One thing in all things I have seen,

and

> At last, at last, the meaning caught –
> The spirit wears its diadem;
> It shakes the wondrous plumes of thought
> And trails the stars along with them.

('Unity'. *Oxford Book of English Mystical Verse*)

And once again the same thought from Francis Thompson

> Where is the land of Luthany,
> Where is the tract of Elenore?
> I am bound therefore.

> Pierce thy heart to find the key;
> With thee take
> Only what none else would keep . . .

> When to the new eyes of thee
> All things by immortal power,
> Near or far,

Hiddenly
To each other linkèd are,
That thou canst not stir a flower
Without troubling of a star . . .
        Seek no more,
O seek no more/
Pass the gates of Luthany, tread the region Elenore.

('The Mistress of Vision'. *Oxford Book of English Mystical Verse*)

Astronomers have suggested that our universe was at one time a single body and that it has since split into a central Sun with encircling planets and their own moons. Whether this is a physical fact or not it is surely a metaphysical one, symbolising the unity of all creation. If the fact is grasped that all life is one and all living things interdependent, it is less difficult to accept as a fact that we are combined in the cosmic pattern. Why it should be that the birth moment agrees with our individual pattern I can't say, except that it seems logical to see some significance in the starting time; but when it is realised that each moment in time when charted reveals a pattern that is different from any that has gone before, we are in a position to say to each child who comes into the world, "This is your opportunity. Make what you can of it."

PART II

Ingredients of the Astrological Chart

This section on the *ingredients* of an astrological chart is written in as *un-technical* way as possible while dealing with technicalities.

Further clarification of unfamiliar words – or astrological use of familiar words – will be found in the Glossary.

1. THE NATAL CHART

This chapter contains some technical information with diagrams which is necessary for the understanding of the subject. It is as short as possible; but it was thought that the reader would wish to know what a chart looks like and what the terms used in making and reading it mean. It does not set out to show how to calculate or interpret: advice is offered on text-books at the end of the book in the section entitled Recommended Reading.

The following diagrams, then (Figs. 1, 2, 3, and 4), show a chart or part of a chart, as it appears when the necessary calculations have been made on the basis of the three indispensable items of information, namely, time, date, and place of birth or of starting moment in the case of the chart of some enterprise or inanimate object. An accurate, detailed chart *cannot* be drawn without this information.

As to place, it is of course the latitude and longitude that matters: the place where birth was registered, for instance, irrelevant. If your child was born at sea, the information could be ascertained from the captain of the ship and an accurate map set up. The geographical longitude, or rather its equivalent in time, is needed if we are to obtain the local as opposed to the Greenwich sidereal time (which is quoted in the almanac or ephemeris for noon of each day). It is this local sidereal time that furnishes the degree of zodiac rising at the time of birth and enables the chart of the sky to be correctly oriented.

In practice, most people know the date and place of their birth, but very few can give the exact time. The chart will only be exact and the reading detailed if the time is known to the nearest minute (astrologers

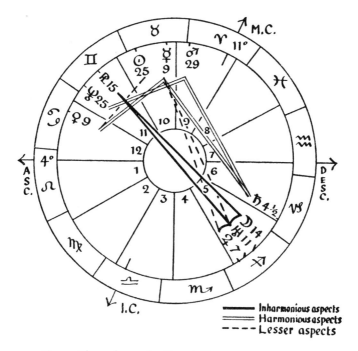

Fig. 1. Chart drawn by Equal House System

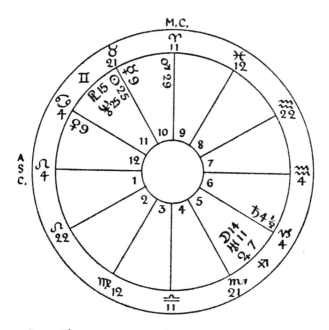

Fig. 2. Same Chart set out according to the Placidean House System

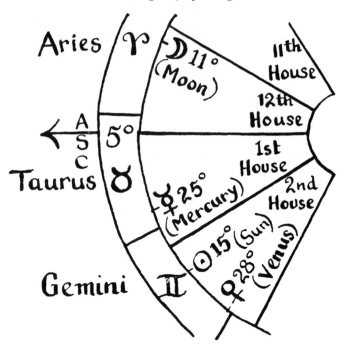

Fig. 3

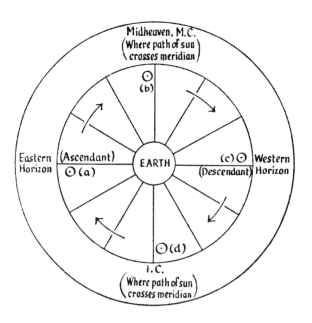

Fig. 4

28

KEY TO CHARTS

☉	Sun	♈	Aries
☽	Moon	♉	Taurus
☿	Mercury	♊	Gemini
♀	Venus	♋	Cancer
♂	Mars	♌	Leo
♃	Jupiter	♍	Virgo
♄	Saturn	♎	Libra
♅	Uranus	♏	Scorpio
♆	Neptune	♐	Sagittarius
♇ or ⯓	Pluto	♑	Capricorn
		♒	Aquarius
		♓	Pisces

have been known to time their child's first cry with a stop-watch). If this piece of information is not forthcoming, instead of studying the chart of his client the astrologer is in fact studying that of someone else born a little earlier or a little later.

Fortunately, the astrologer is able to achieve useful results by a process of approximation on such broader facts as are unaffected. As we have said, the chart purports to give an accurate sky-picture for the moment and place of birth and it can only do this on the basis of exact data. Nevertheless, many factors that have to be entered on it are capable of interpretation regardless of exact time, although the reading will then apply to others born on the same day anywhere in the world. For character-reading, a time accurate to within half an hour will suffice if the discrepancy involves no change of Sign; but a matter of one minute *can* change the degree rising from, say, 29° 50′ Scorpio to 0° Sagittarius, thus producing uncertainty as to the Ascendant.

Note on Chart (Fig. 1)

It may very roughly be said that the circle represents the band of sky marked by the path of the Sun and planets as they rise, set and circle below the horizon to rise again next day. When talking about astrology many people, confusing the planets with the stars, seem to think they can be seen almost anywhere in the sky; but of course this is not so. You can locate the planetary path, or Ecliptic, by noticing the path of the Sun throughout the year, the Sun being seen against a different distant star background every month. In April, for instance, it is seen against the bit of zodiac called Aries (note that it is the bit of zodiac *called* Aries and not the constellation Aries, owing to the precession of the equinoctial point) and whenever you look at the Sun during April whether it is rising, overhead or setting, you are looking at the bit of zodiac in question. If you were born at sunrise, your Sun-sign and Rising-sign are identical and astrologically speaking your personality will be doubly of that Sign.

Fig. 3 shows a segment of a chart near the rising degree or East point. 5° Taurus is rising. Sun is in 15° Gemini in the second house. Moon is in 11° Aries in the twelfth house. Mercury and Venus (known as the inferior planets because they are the only two nearer to the Sun than Earth is) are always in a Sign near that of the Sun. In this example Mercury is in 25° Taurus in the first house and Venus in 28° Gemini in the second house. Taking this as a personal chart, the individual concerned would have been born between midnight and sunrise. Note position of Sun and compare with examples in Fig. 4, which shows (*a*) Sun charted for birth at sunrise, (*b*) Sun charted for birth *near* midday, (*c*) Sun charted for birth at sunset, (*d*) Sun charted for birth *near* midnight.

2. THE SIGNS OF THE ZODIAC

The arrangement of this chapter has caused me some difficulty. From a character point of view the Planets, standing as they do for principles or impulses expressed in the personality, should take first place. Remembering, however, that for most people the Signs of the zodiac are the starting point and perhaps the only familiar piece of astrological knowledge, I am dealing with these first.

It will be explained in more detail in the section on Planets (pages 77–107) that from the point of view of the birth chart and character analysis the various planetary impulses will be expressed with ease or difficulty in the personality according to certain modifying factors.

The first modifying factor to be considered is the Sign of the zodiac in which a given Planet is found.

One has only to study descriptions of each to recognise points of similarity between certain Signs and certain Planets: in fact to describe Arien qualities is to speak of Mars and to discuss Taurean characteristics is to depict a strongly Venusian type. This is why astrologers say that certain Planets 'rule' certain Signs. Without question, the qualities of a Planet in its own Sign manifest markedly in the chart and the life.

Moreover, a Planet seems ill at ease in a Sign that is out of sympathy with it; just as, for instance, a person brought up in a happy, easy-going home where he is free to express himself will be ill at ease if he is transplanted to an office or other surroundings where the whole atmosphere seems alien. If he is not in tune with the new way of life or thinking, everything he does will lack confidence. In short, a Planet in an uncongenial Sign corresponds with a state or lack in an individual.

Table 1 (page 33) shows a list of Planets with the Signs they 'rule' and also the Signs with which they have sympathy rather than resemble.

Physically, a Sign of the zodiac is 30° of the circle of the Ecliptic against which, from a geocentric or earth point of view, the Sun, Moon and all the Planets appear to travel within a prescribed band. In ancient days this stellar background against which the movements of the Planets could be observed was divided and named. Thus a planet could be identified as being visible against the head of the Bull or the tail of the Scorpion, the constellations lying in the Ecliptic being used to identify positions in the zodiacal circle.

The usage of counting longitudes from the *vernal point* (known as 0° Aries) was introduced in all probability by Hipparchus as a consequence of his discovery of precession. Ptolemy uses it throughout the Almagest. There is no historical evidence of any 30° division of the zodiac until the fifth century. Thus the idea of 'Signs' of equal lengths (the constellations are of varying lengths) was introduced to effect regularity in measurement.

Some people imagine that the formation of the stars in the constellations gave rise to their names and the attempt to see animals or objects outlined. If this be the only origin of the names it is strange that the characteristics of the Signs have so much bearing on the symbol. At all events nobody knows when the Signs were given their names. Astrological symbols are to be found on ruins as ancient as those of Easter Island.

Another question that cannot be answered is *why* different effects should be produced when planets are in one segment of the zodiac or another, but even a small amount of study will show that this is in fact the case.

Although there are many excellent accounts of what each Sign of the Zodiac (Aries, Taurus and so on) means in terms of character, I well remember my own confusion as a student, trying to reconcile contradictions when it came to the classification of each Sign under the headings of Qualities or Elements (see Key-word meanings, page 265). It seemed nonsense when I read in one paragraph that all Fire Signs were 'ardent' and 'keen' and in the next that one of them, Leo, was 'fixed'. But worse was to come. All Water Signs, we were taught, were 'emotional' and 'sensitive' and therefore, it was presumed, 'introvert'; but we went on to read that one of them, Cancer, was also 'Cardinal' or outgoing and active. It was not until I was working constantly at analysis, and had as it were to dig my own way to the foundations, that I made the, to me, illuminating discovery that the Qualities and Elements have each their clear and separate meanings which combine, like ingredients in a cake, to produce the sometimes complex characteristics of a Sign.

In the following Sign-analyses, therefore, I have given the ingredients at the top of each, and tried to show how it is just the seemingly nonsensical contradictions that make the complexity of some of the Signs. It is interesting to note that the order in which the Signs are traditionally given, significantly corresponds to a progress from primitive unity and simplicity to complexity.

Table 1 Rulerships and Affinities

Sun and Moon	rule or have affinity with	Leo and Cancer respectively
Mercury	rules or has affinity with	Virgo and Gemini
Venus	rules or has affinity with	Libra and Taurus
Mars	rules or has affinity with	Scorpio and Aries
Jupiter	rules or has affinity with	Sagittarius and Pisces
Saturn	rules or has affinity with	Capricorn and Aquarius

It is interesting to note that in the above table by listing the planets in their order of distance from the Sun, the order of the signs (down the first column and up the second) conforms to their positions in the zodiac.

Uranus has no rulership but has affinity with Aquarius
Neptune has no rulership but has affinity with Pisces
Pluto is too recently discovered to be sure about but there seems some affinity with Scorpio.

In astrological language the Planets are said to be 'exalted' in certain Signs. This really means that the principle of the Planets finds freedom of expression in a Sign with which it is in sympathy. The opposite Sign to the 'exaltation' is known as the 'fall' and the action of the planet is said to be debilitated in this Sign and also in the Sign *opposite* the one 'ruled'. My own feeling is that these descriptions are a bit arbitrary and a little common sense is needed, as clearly the principle of energy (Mars) *can* be put to good or bad use in any direction. In the same way, the Sun vivifies and strenghtens wherever it is placed and cannot be said to have a weak or perverted manifestation through any Sign. I therefore leave it out of the following Table, but for those who are interested, its traditional exaltation is in Aries.

Table 2

		Exaltation		*Fall*
Moon	in	Taurus	in	Scorpio
Mercury		Virgo		Pisces
Venus		Pisces		Virgo
Mars		Capricorn		Cancer
Jupiter		Cancer		Capricorn
Saturn		Libra		Aries

To illustrate Planet/Sign sympathy or antipathy, Jupiter, principle of expansion and joviality, works strongly in its own sign of Sagittarius, where it is right at home, but in the opposite Sign, Gemini, it is less at ease, confined within intellectual concepts, forced to work with mind rather than intuition so that there is danger of expansion in mere verbiage. When this planet is in Cancer (its 'exaltation') the expansive force is used productively in sympathetic, protective, kindly qualities and all the warmth and generosity of the Jupiter-nature flourishes. Once again, in the opposite Sign to the 'exaltation', namely Capricorn, there will be cold, disciplined ambition; and the force of expansion or exaggeration can in this case inflate such ambition until it becomes a power-complex. Thus, even the Jovial nature can degenerate into false bonhomie and the gift for hospitality be used for social climbing.

Mars in its own sign, Aries, can hardly go unnoticed in a personality, so strongly and confidently, if not aggressively, does the principle of energy and initiative manifest; but in the opposite sign, Libra, a gentle Venus Sign, this principle is not at all at home. How can energy and aggressiveness flourish in such an atmosphere? Indeed they cannot and people with Mars in Libra often seem unable to take decisions, since what should be a driving principle of action only serves to strengthen the Libran habit of vacillation and putting off the evil day. But just as Jupiter is not at home in Capricorn, Mars in this position works well; the energy expands in practical effort and productiveness and the fiery impulse is checked by the commonsense qualities of this Sign. Straightforward, manly ambition, success through hard work and application, are typical of Mars in Capricorn.

Once again, Mars functions less easily in the opposite sign, Cancer (where Jupiter was so happy). Energy, aggressiveness, decisiveness, do not manifest happily through this feminine, motherly Sign, except perhaps in the home. The correspondence in human behaviour is excess of fuss or in over-possessiveness. Emotion and intuition gain force.

These, I would add, are only instances of the different workings of a principle in different models. Other factors are also at work helping to balance or adding to imbalance in any direction.

One of the most difficult things to explain to a non-astrologer is the significance of Signs or Planets or Aspects as they affect the human being. (I have touched on the possible mystical reason for this significance elsewhere.) I would ask the reader to think of them all as ingredients, the combination of which forms the total picture of any one person.

Popular astrology in magazines increases confusion, as the general public has it rammed down its throat that by reason of being born between certain dates a given individual is Libran, Taurean, or whatever it may be, whereas nobody in fact is undiluted anything. Each Sign, Planet, Quality or Element has its own characteristics, and like the ingredients of a cake before mixing can be seen and described separately. But, as any cook knows, separate ingredients when treated and mixed produce totally different results. So with the chart. Each chart is a

Table 3

Signs	(Positive or Negative)	Quality	Element	Numerical Combination	Ruler
Aries	(Pos.)	Cardinal 1	Fire 1	1 and 1	Mars
Taurus	(Neg.)	Fixed 2	Earth 2	2 and 2	Venus
Gemini	(Pos.)	Mutable 3	Air 3	3 and 3	Mercury
Cancer	(Neg.)	Cardinal 1	Water 4	1 and 4	Moon
Leo	(Pos.)	Fixed 2	Fire 1	2 and 1	Sun
Virgo	(Neg.)	Mutable 3	Earth 2	3 and 2	Mercury
Libra	(Pos.)	Cardinal 1	Air 3	1 and 3	Venus
Scorpio	(Neg.)	Fixed 2	Water 4	2 and 4	Mars
Sagittarius	(Pos.)	Mutable 3	Fire 1	3 and 1	Jupiter
Capricorn	(Neg.)	Cardinal 1	Earth 2	1 and 2	Saturn
Aquarius	(Pos.)	Fixed 2	Air 3	2 and 3	Saturn (or Uranus)
Pisces	(Neg.)	Mutable 3	Water 4	3 and 4	Jupiter (or Neptune)

Note: There is similarity of meaning in Cardinality and Fire, Fixity and Earth and Mutability and Air. It can be seen therefore that only the first three Signs, Aries, Taurus and Gemini are uncomplicated by conflicting mixtures of Quality and Element.

different end-result of a most intricate mix-up of ingredients, and attempts at short-cuts or simplification only lead to inaccuracy.

In the following notes on Signs and Planets I am NOT describing people whose Sun is in a particular sign, or those whose Sun is 'ruled' by a particular planet: what I *am* doing is to describe important basic ingredients which play their part in the total chart.

Before describing each Sign, it is necessary to explain the qualities and elements under which it is classified. There are three Qualities, namely Cardinal, Fixed and Mutable, and four Elements, Fire, Earth, Air and Water. As can be seen from Table 3, each sign is made up of a different combination of these Qualities and Elements and further modified by the ruling Planet and the fact of being either positive or negative. So, just as we suggested that when it comes to interpretation of the whole person the relevant Sun-sign was but an ingredient of the whole chart, so each Sign is also made up of ingredients, and varying characteristics are found in the subtle mingling of Quality, Element and so on.

It will be seen that Cardinal qualities have much in common with the Fire element. Fixed qualities approximate largely to the Earth element and Mutable to the Air Element. This is why in Table 3 I have numbered them 1, 2 and 3, and in the combination of numbers in the right-hand column it can be clearly seen that the first three Signs alone are clear cut and primitive. All the succeeding ones are composed of contrasting or conflicting ingredients.

In the following brief interpretations I will try to show how the traditional Sign meanings of characteristics derive from the sometimes contradictory Quality/Element/Ruler combination.

3. THE SIGNS AND THEIR CORRESPONDENCES IN HUMAN CHARACTER

It cannot be said too often or too strongly that *no one* is solely and wholly Libra, Taurus, Aries or whatever Sign it may be that corresponds to the birth-month. The Sun-Sign doesn't even necessarily give the best description of how you feel yourself to be. Indeed if you read through the following Sign descriptions, you may well recognise qualities possessed by some friend whose Sun-Sign is in fact nowhere near the Sign in question. For instance, you may detect strong Aries qualities in six people of whom only one has Sun in Aries. As the same applies to any of the twelve Signs, let us call the Sign 'X'. The following explains why you can recognise 'X' characteristics where, for all you know, Sign 'X' is definitely NOT the sign of the birth month.

Friend A proves on calculation of chart to have 'X' rising.
Friend B's chart shows his ruling planet to be in 'X'.
Friend C has the Moon in 'X'.
Friend D proves to have a group of planets in 'X'.

For 'X' substitute any Sign which, as you read through all twelve Signs, reminds you of some person you know whose Sun-Sign is *not* the Sign containing the recognisable trait.

Aries
Ingredients which go to make up Aries characteristics are:

> Quality or Quadruplicity* – Cardinal
> Element or Triplicity* – Fire
> Ruling planet – Mars

Cardinality in all its fours signs, Aries, Libra, Cancer and Capricorn, manifests in a need for action. In Aries this is very evident, and, heated up by the Fire element, the native of Aries will be decisive, quick to the

* See Glossary.

point of impatience, and self-assertive. There is something primitive and simple about Aries, whose attitude is somewhat that of the cave-man who knows he depends on his own courage and initiative and does not 'disrelish' the struggle for survival: he responds well in moments of danger and is at his best in an emergency. Aries cuts his way through, often literally, for he is at home with weapons, offensive or surgical, and if there is red tape about, this, too, will succumb to the shears. 'Deeds, not words' is his motto, but when the heroic deed is done, he is by no means shy of adulation. At home he needs a wife who responds warmly but not clingingly to his endearments and appreciates him for his cleverness and resource – but if she talks too much, she will get silenced by a blow from his club.

Anyone with an overdose of Aries is more at home in a male than a female body. But of course there are Aries women! These are frank, warm-hearted, decisive and capable of rising to the occasion. What they derive from Aries is their more masculine side, so if you know a very feminine Aries woman, her calculated chart will show gentler Signs prominent in Rising Sign, Moon-Sign or planetary groupings. A strongly Aries woman comes out with home-truths and is not the 'little woman' type.

Aries can be brusque and aggressive, but does not shrink from the same qualities in others. A wire-haired terrier has a lot of Aries in his personality: enjoying a good fight and bearing no malice when it is over.

An instance of Aries mixed with a less decisive Sign emerges in a question I received from an Aries girl. She wrote, "I have read that Aries are decisive, forceful types, but *I* can rarely stick to my decisions. Has my full chart a reason for this indecisiveness?" As she told me when she was born, it was easy to answer this. Born at sunset, she had the opposite Sign to Aries, namely Libra as her Ascendant. Libra is the most vacillating and indecisive of all the Signs. Her Aries Sun made her keenly aware of her failing, as a strong side of her nature longed to be decisive. I explained that to be aware of her failing was a great help, and I suggested that, to begin with she should try in little everyday matters to be more decisive and gradually build up to more important decisions. In fact, in time, people grow more like their Sun-Signs, so this girl was probably still reacting overmuch to Libra, her Ascendant, and will find her Aries traits easier to employ in later years.

It is a fact that some Signs are more easily described in masculine terms and others in feminine. This girl was probably fortunate to be more Libran in youth. Aries qualities, when overdone, can seem aggressive. But in some jobs, such as medicine and especially surgery, one needs Aries attack to make the incision, along with, say, Pisces to give the anaesthetic and Virgo or Scorpio in analysis or pathology.

Aries works well at speed, and gets things done before he has time to get bored. Initiative is his or her strong point. If you employ an Aries to do a piece of work, he will get it going with skill and energy and then suggest that someone else carries it on when it reaches the stage of duller, routine follow-up work.

Aries is the Ram, but one must remember there are also sheep in the herd. When unmoved by some urgent need, your Aries can browse calmly and seem no more energetic than the next man.

Basically extravert, there are Aries folk who dash confidently through life, scarcely realising that they offend the sensitive. They get away with frank remarks, because these are spontaneous. Impatient? Yes. 'At once, if not sooner!' is their motto. They have scant sympathy with more complex, emotional people. When annoyed, they come straight out with some pungent remark and quite enjoy the occasional battle. Brooding, sulking and self-pity they consider a waste of time.

Are you employed by Aries? A secretary perhaps? Then you will have to go along with his frankness. Be ready to tone down his correspondence. He can be brusque, but he is straightforward and warmhearted and it takes very little to cheer him up. You will like his masculinity and air of command. At least he (or she) doesn't niggle over details.

Arien Qualities	*Arien Faults*
Courage	Aggressiveness
Initiative	Egoism
Decisiveness	Bullying
Frankness	Rudeness
Quickness	Violent temper
Warmth	Lust
Daring	Accident prone
Good in a crisis	Inability to tolerate boredom

TAURUS

Ingredients which go to make up Taurus characteristics are:

Quality or Quadruplicity – Fixity
Element – Earth
Ruling Planet – Venus

Fixity in all its four Signs, Taurus, Leo, Scorpio and Aquarius, manifests in powerful determination, obstinacy and rigidity. No astrologer will unfailingly guess a person's Sun-Sign, but a very easily recognised characteristic is shared by all in whose charts the 'fixed Signs' are strongly represented. There is a bulldozer quality, a relentlessness or, at worst, remorselessness or toughness that makes the Fixed among our citizens the types to be reckoned with.

A neighbour of mine had an old aunt, a nonagenarian, who seemed to be taking her time to relax her hold on Earth. I remarked to my daughter, "Auntie must have a lot of 'fixity'." We enquired the birth date. It was in autumn 1875. This must have been a vintage year for toughies, for Pluto and Neptune were in Fixed Taurus, Uranus in Fixed Leo, Saturn and Mars in Fixed Aquarius, and in Auntie's case Jupiter, Mercury and the Moon in Fixed Scorpio. In short, eight out of ten.

I imagine that this type of determined longevity is a concomitant of strength in Fixity.

It could be said of most of the Signs that to have too much of them is a bad thing. Too much Taurus, for instance, gives a stolid, immovable, stick-in-the-mud quality. Nevertheless it is like the flour in the cake: without it there would be no cake.

Possessiveness and conservatism are Taurus key-words, and if Aries can be likened to a primitive cave-man, Taurus is the one who finds a piece of land and enters into the joys of ownership. When he settles down in his home, he finds time to beautify it. In common with the other Earth Signs, Virgo and Capricorn, he loves his garden and has patience with the slow rhythms of earth. While Aries rushes about, Taurus sits back and enjoys the fruits of his labours, with leisure and quiet to discover the music in nature, which he echoes in song. He is a man of peace and likes all the creature comforts he has created for himself. Taurus will not pick a quarrel; but if finally aroused, his anger is quite terrifying in its intensity. Like the bull, he goes in for heavy, blind rages.

Taurus women are good-looking and have solid, well-made bodies, with a good notion of what such bodies can produce in the way of agreeable sensation. If Aries is 'cave-man', there is certainly a good deal of 'cave-woman' about the Taurus female, for she has all the primary qualities necessary to sustain and comfort the male: an honest recognition of sex impulses, a talent for producing comfort in the home by all sorts of practical gadgets. She will not make a fuss when her man comes home late, hungry, and accompanied by thirsty friends. When she falls in love, something really fundamental is touched off, and overnight she changes from a light-hearted girl into a woman for whom love means everything. Without realising it, she gears herself for the full cycle of love with its logical conclusion of childbearing and responsibility. If her emotions are reciprocated and she can swing into productivity and fulfilment, she is radiant.

The world of ideas is not enough for Taurus. The world of sound *is*, and Taureans abound in the world of music.

As for the Taurus attitude to money, Mr. Taurus is the financier. The need for comfort is strong in him and he likes to know that his life rests on the solid foundation of a fat bank balance. He has a natural feeling for money, together with the steady qualities needed to acquire it. He may be over-conscious of possessions, but he can be relied on to spend wisely when it comes to home comforts.

Ms. Taurus is much the same. She, too, likes to have a good balance on the credit side and may sometimes seem mean, in a miserly sense, as she dislikes spending on ephemeral pleasures. A round of drinks in a club seems a waste of money when she thinks of the sum spent on drinks brought home. She prefers to buy useful things and is seldom out of pocket.

One has to be very careful in writing of the signs. However many times it is repeated that a sign is only an ingredient of the whole person, people are indoctrinated by the popular Press to believe that 'he is Virgo, or she is Taurus', and they scarcely read anything about the signs which they think, often wrongly, have nothing to do with them.

Taurus is a musical sign and many people with Taurus accentuated have good voices. But if you are musical and 'know' you aren't a Taurus, your calculated chart may disclose the fact that your energy (Mars) or capacity for serious work (Saturn) is in Taurus, to account for the fact that you are a keen choir singer or member of an orchestra.

Taurus is associated with the throat. Many singers have the Sun in Taurus or Taurus rising, and their throats are particularly strong, while other, less well-aspected Taurus folk suffer from throat troubles.

Tempo of living is something to watch throughout the zodiac. I recall telling a Taurus Ascendant friend that she could do some task quicker if she did it another way. "But I like doing it slowly," was her – to me – revealing reply. The quickness I was so proud of appeared to her as a disadvantage.

The odd thing here was that I am a Sun-Taurus, with speed-loving Sagittarius rising and she was Sun-Capricorn, but had Taurus rising. This illustrates the point I make elsewhere that the Rising Sign is more indicative of personal characteristics than the Sun-Sign, which one grows more like as life proceeds.

Taurus likes to prove theories by experience. To my own Taurus Sun and Mercury, the seed of an idea has to be seen to *grow*.

Taurus Qualities	*Taurus Faults*
Thrift	Miserliness
Reliability	Dullness
Love of beauty	Sensuality
Affection	Possessiveness
Appreciation of good food	Greed
Deliberation	Sloth
Sense of humour	Silliness

GEMINI

Ingredients which go to make up Gemini Characteristics are:

41

Quality or Quadruplicity – Mutable
Element – Air
Ruling Planet – Mercury

Mutability manifests in four signs (Gemini, Virgo, Sagittarius and Pisces) in the ability to change and adapt. This shows itself in Gemini in the urge to be perpetually in the know.

Following our trail through the signs, in a basic sense one could say that by the time Man reaches Gemini, he has progressed through the primitive, initiatory phase of Aries, has settled down in Taurus, and now in Gemini discovers he has a mind. This is indeed an enormous discovery; and he goes to extremes of rationality. He cuts himself off from the intuitive, heart-qualities, abandons what he will call childish things, and decides that what is important is to *know*.

People with an overdose of this sign can only appreciate, and will only accept, what has been ratiocinated and 'proved'. Everything must be talked over, indeed almost argued away; for Gemini will sit up all night; if he can find another Geminian, splitting hairs. Aries, we may say, is primeval Fire, Taurus primeval Earth, Gemini primeval Air, in which element man gets his feet off the ground and experiments with the freedom and expansiveness of thought.

With the average man or woman, where Gemini is found to be strong in the chart, need for communication is the keynote. They have an urge to impart by speech or writing whatever they learn, and the necessity is to feel 'with it'. The symbol for Gemini is the Twins, which pictures the deep need for communication, if only with the 'other half' of the personality. Duality is also seen in many-sidedness, versatility, and the ability to live a double life, not necessarily in the domestic sense.

A parent wrote to me that her Gemini child showed lack of perseverance and wondered if it would be possible to remedy this deficiency.

Well, of course all qualities have corresponding faults. The Gemini temperament needs constantly changing interests. I would not advise forcing anyone to try to be other than they are. The line to take is to develop the advantages of the same trait, which are quickness and adaptability. A child will only suffer, or develop, some protest problem, as the child mentioned above, if he is forced into monotony. There are plenty of jobs which call for his temperament – journalism, reporting, agency or travel work. The true academic type often seems to lack perseverance or concentration, except on his one, chosen subject. So-called faults in people are often valuable pointers to the work they are best fitted to do.

Don't expect a Gemini type to stop talking and asking questions. People with Gemini strong have the urge to communicate. They are not necessarily clever. Intellectual ability depends on many more factors than the urge to write, talk or learn, which, with a lively curiosity and talkativeness, typifies the Geminian. Acute wit and the gift of repartee are not the result of education. The lightning, mercurial (or Gemini) note of Cockney wit can be heard daily in London streets. Gemini is alert and on the spot. He knows things, from what play is on television to the private lives of the actors. These people are not necessarily well informed, but they have the potential to acquire information.

If you have a Geminian child, it is important to educate him fully. He will talk, argue, split hairs, whether he knows what he is talking about or not. Gemini talks as easily as he breathes. You cannot be dull with him, but you may be baffled by his elusive, mercurial mind.

Obviously not all Gemini women are intellectuals. Many are found in agencies, where a fluent tongue and quick mind are needed to cope with a constant flow of enquiries. Clever at running her household, Ms. Gemini knows where to find bargains and will plan her chores so as to leave time to keep abreast of all that is going on.

Gemini on its own is not musical, yet many are in fact musicians due to other facets of the chart. The Gemini quickness and urge to communicate will further any talent by giving it means of expression. It is not much use to have ideas if you can't express them fluently, or a love of singing if you can't actually 'put over' the song. Gemini helps by acting as the communicator for many more people than are born between dates in May and June.

Gemini Qualities	*Gemini Faults*
Versatility	Superficiality
Variety of interest	Curiosity and gossip
Understanding (in the sense of a quick grasp)	Cunning, slickness
Expressiveness	Verbosity; talking for the sake of hearing their own voices
Brilliance	Slickness

CANCER

Ingredients which go to make up Cancer characteristics are:

Quality or Quadruplicity – Cardinal
Element – Water
Ruling Planet – the Moon

Whereas the first three signs, Aries, Taurus and Gemini, are straightforward and in a sense uncomplicated, with Cancer there is inner conflict owing to the busy, active, cardinal quality being part of an otherwise emotional and intuitive nature. Signs are alternately termed 'positive' and 'negative'. Taurus has many negative or feminine characteristics and this is true also of Cancer, but let me reassure readers that this 'feminine' or 'negative' business is not to be taken too literally. To carry on the picture of gradual growth from primitivity, woman has now fulfilled herself in motherhood. Whereas in Taurus her man came first, her priorities now are her child and her home; and her energy is expressed in the effort to protect and preserve these. The 'caring' potential in any person, male or female, can be traced in the chart to some emphasis of Cancer.

Thus, in all whose charts show strength in Cancer, there is a love of home or family, and great loyalty to these. Just as a mother instinctively knows the need of her child and senses the approach of danger, so the Cancer type is intuitive and aware of the surrounding atmosphere and public feeling. During the period of gestation any woman increases in sensitivity; she protects the child in her womb and has a natural feeling of self-importance in this act of creation. Cancer women seem to have such feelings as a normal part of their emotional make-up. It might be taken amiss if I suggest that all Cancer folk, male and female, are like permanently pregnant women; but indeed it is true that the hypersensitivity and tendency to take things personally, so typical of pregnancy, is typical of this sign.

The ability to learn of the Cancer person is enhanced by a retentive memory. So when Cancer chooses the academic field he can be very clever indeed, with the added something of what could be seen as 'mother wit'.

It will be apparent by now that certain signs, notably Taurus and Cancer, are easier to describe in feminine terms, just as the Aries and Capricorn adjectives tend to be masculine. This is where it is important to stress yet again that in *every* chart, or horoscope, *all twelve signs figure*, and to have the Sun in a sign, or a particular sign rising or heavily tenanted by planets, while it gives important emphasis is not to be thought of as the whole picture. We are all mixtures, and it is best to think of all twelve signs as representing different modes of behaviour. I see individuals as a sort of cocktail of two, three or more signs. We grow more like our Sun-Signs as life goes on, and it is our Rising-Sign and our Moon-Sign that are more typical of us in early life.

The Cancer ingredient contributes sensitivity. Indeed, so thin-skinned are some Cancer folk that one has to be more than ordinarily careful not to offend them. They are intensely aware of atmosphere and as they enter a room, they seem to know what other people are thinking, sometimes to a most disconcerting extent.

Imaginative, romantic and partisan, they make idols of public figures and identify themselves with their interests. They can be good actors or mimics because of their ease in imagining other people's feelings. This ability also helps Cancer doctors and nurses, some of whom even feel their patients' conditions too keenly.

Cancer is a negative sign, and it is easy to think of qualities that the sign's natives have *not*. They are not aggressive, but neither are they spineless. They are not natural leaders, but many show good organising ability . . . like the true matriarch, who is proudly aware of her femininity but does not envy or compete with the male.

It may seem odd that the thin-skinned Cancerian has the hard-shelled crab as his symbol. But it is because the inner body is so sensitive that the shell is necessary. Cancer children need plenty to do. They are both active and imaginative and identify with the sufferings or joys of others, so that stories or plays on television make a deep impression on them.

Sensitive or shy children of all the Water types (Cancer, Scorpio and Pisces), sometimes need encouragement to show off their talents. What may seem quite a trivial triumph, like turning the best cartwheels, may be enough to spark off an important urge to establish supremacy. "Let's play standing on heads!" may be the *cri de coeur* of some shy child who excels at this strange pastime.

Cancer women may look very demure, but just watch them take command in their own sphere, or turn on the feminine charm when in the mood. When they retreat into their shell you may be sure it is well provisioned. They are not greedy, but 'the children might be hungry'.

The combination in this sign of alert activity with sensitivity and emotionalism is hard to describe. The 'caring' professions are appropriate.

Cancer men love sensation, big ball games, political meetings, etc. They take a very personal interest in their particular hero. 'Good old Al!' as he scores the point is personal property. Cancer's pride is as keen as if Al were a blood brother.

Cancer people 'feel' and 'live' the books they read or the plays they watch. They can be shy, but they warm up in their own surroundings. They have a sense of value and of property. They are good 'family' people.

Cancer Qualities	*Cancer Faults*
Sympathy	Possessiveness
Domestic competence	Fussiness
Sensitivity	Touchiness
Thrift	Hoarding
Romanticism and imagination	Sensationalism
Ability to memorise	Inability to forget a slight

LEO

Ingredients which go to make up Leo characteristics are:

Quality or Quadruplicity – Fixity
Element – Fire
Ruling Planet – the Sun

45

The conflict or contradiction here is surely in the thought of Fixed Fire. The answer in terms of Leo characteristics is in molten gold. Where Aries, the primitive Fire-Sign, rushes round in restless activity, Leo is content to glow in one place, preferably a palace. We can imagine that the primitive community has grown and the population has increased through the willing cooperation of Aries, Taurus and Cancer (Gemini doing his part between journeys and debate), and now a leader has to be elected. Leo fills the bill. His natural self-confidence and upright bearing, combined with his ability to command as if by right and without aggressiveness, ensures his unanimous election. He takes his place on the throne with no false humility. Like the king in fairy tales, he is noble, just and kind; his palace glitters with gold, and crowns are worn rather than kept for special occasions, for he is only too happy to give the commoner a treat by his gorgeous appearance. He has a proper sense of hospitality, and at his banquets food, drink and dancing girls arrive in sumptuous succession.

How do such glittering and regal qualities fit into the charts of everyday men and women? Upstanding young men with big, well-shaped heads who captain teams or lead their schools are often found to have Leo rising or somewhere prominent in the chart. There is a big, sunny, warm-hearted quality and an infectious power of enjoyment that is very endearing when this sign manifests without too much opposition. What is sad is to find Leo strong in an otherwise unhappy chart. In this case there is a thwarted urge to greatness, resulting in ineffectual swank and bombast.

Leo is a positive, masculine sign, and women Leos have to be careful not to be over-dominating. It is essential that they should find some position where they can usefully take the lead – but they must learn to keep the brakes on in social circumstances where they will not be so popular if they throw their weight about. Leo children can be controlled best by appealing to their sense of dignity and magnanimity.

In case you recognise these qualities in a child of yours born, say, in Libra or some sign other than Leo, may I remind you that to have Leo characteristics you don't need to be born at a particular time of year. Every day of every year a child is born with Leo rising (or any of the twelve signs of the zodiac, for that matter), and personality is judged even more by the Rising-sign that by the Sun-sign. Rising-signs can only be known by calculation from the birth time, but Leo characteristics, wherever they occur, are very recognisable. There is a big-hearted warmth which springs from the love of doing things in the grand manner. It is easy to think of Leo faults. They stick out a mile, in swagger and showiness. It takes a really noble character to handle kingly qualities without a touch of swank. But even badly behaved Leos have a lovable side, as there is nothing calculating about their showiness, which springs from natural exuberance. Leo men will entertain you, because it is natural for them to shine and take the limelight – literally, on the stage, or as hosts.

But the Leo urge to command, so useful in a career, is less appreciated in the home. Leo children need guidance to handle their natural urge for authority. They respond well if smaller or weaker children are entrusted to their leadership. Please note that I say leadership rather than care or protection, both of which are more Cancer qualities.

The Leo ingredient contributes something happy and attractive to the personal chart. Leos like prominence, yet never seem to make great efforts to attain it. They naturally gravitate to the top where they feel they belong. Of course not all Leos can take the lead, and it is sad to see the dejection of one who is snubbed or kept under. Leos hate the apprentice stage. They are impatient to shine, and as they have often achieved some measure of authority at school or college, they don't like starting at the bottom again.

If you have a Leo child, try to provide him with some means of creative self-expression. Don't force him to take a back seat because you think it would be good for him to be taken down a peg or two. It is natural for him to lead a group or even a gang. If thwarted, he will become demanding and difficult. As a child and again as an apprentice, his urge for prominence will be ahead of his means to achieve it.

Leo is a Fire-sign, but the temperament is not easily inflamed into anger. Leos manage without getting undignifiedly fierce. They dominate by their imposing appearance and take success for granted.

Leos are uncomplicated and unsubtle. But they are often so attractive in youth that they become dangerously conditioned to adulation. In the bringing up of this type of child (whether you realise that he has Leo characteristics or not), it is wise gently to inculcate the habit of taking second place *sometimes*.

If you are a typical Leo, it is no use thinking that you will be popular with introverts whose ideal is the modest violet. How sorry one feels in retrospect for the Victorian 'Miss' with Leo urges. But nowadays, even if you are a woman, you can seek your place in public life with few hindrances. Co-operation is not Leo's strong suit, so best aim high and negotiate or even by-pass the apprentice stages if this proves possible. You may be a charming character, but humility is not your middle name.

Leo Qualities	Leo Faults
Warm-hearted generosity	Bombast
Leadership	Overbearing manner
Honour	Boastfulness; showing off
Affection	Don Juan type sensuality
Strength of personality	Boring egoism
Ability to organise	Bossing everybody and everything

VIRGO

Ingredients which go to make up Virgo characteristics are:

Quality or Quadruplicity – Mutable
Element – Earth
Ruling Planet – Mercury

In Virgo we come to a sign made up of what would seem to be thoroughly uncongenial factors. How can Earth be mutable and mercurial? This combination involves a struggle, certainly; a struggle to confine the mercurial, mental quickness within the earthy vehicle; and this induces a tendency to worry in the Virgo native. Everything has to be right. What is thought of has to be brought to fruition through Earth, perfect in every detail.

If we follow the feminine sign-sequence, it may seem odd at first sight that the mother (Cancer) precedes the Virgo virgin, although, perhaps, when considered mystically, the Virgin could be said to be beyond or above average womanhood. But when considering the qualities of Virgo, it will be seen that woman has progressed through primitive femininity and motherhood to a more thinking and evaluative state. It is almost as if she has discovered that she has a mind and can do without men, if she so inclines. The virginity can be assumed deliberately as evidence of her own fastidiousness.

The main characteristic of both men and women with this sign strong is discrimination. They are thinking types with a practical, down-to-earth streak. The 'virgin' quality must not be taken literally, and in practice it manifests in high ideals of perfection, accompanied by marked critical gifts. In search for perfection, Virgo will endlessly develop techniques or pick on weak spots in the techniques of others. A weak Virgo type is prone to dissatisfaction or to giving up in despair if things are difficult; but those who are strong representatives of the sign can go very far in mental achievement or the perfecting of a technique or talent.

Basically, the bent for precision, order and tabulation is strong in those who are strongly Virgo. Don't forget, though, that if you are not born a Sun-Virgo, you can still have this sign rising or your Moon may be in Virgo, or your ruling planet. Virgo strength can be traced in the following characteristics: reserve, the habit of criticism, analysis, and the need to communicate. Virgo may be shy, but ask him a question and he's off! He likes facts and takes the trouble to find out about things. In fact, Virgo *when efficient* has no equal. He directs his instinct for perfection to maintaining his own standards. If, however, this is not matched by ability or energy, we meet the less attractive type for whom just nothing is right. The power of analysis turns to introspection and self-pity, and the ability to discriminate degenerates into grumbling and fault-finding. The Virgo type can be quick, clever and alert, thorough and gentle, but the other side of the same coin can make him or her irritatingly know-all, highly strung, mournfully painstaking; and what can be a charming reserve or shyness can manifest as over-diffidence.

The earthiness of Virgo is the ingredient that produces the good gardener or the good cook. All 'earthy' people like to see results, or taste or even hear them, if they apply their skills to the musical fields. Domestic Virgos have immaculate homes, while Virgo intellectuals make splendid teachers, lecturers or college dons, because they like to see their ideas bearing fruit in others.

Many successful people in all walks of life are Virgos, but the extraverts among these probably have very different signs also prominent to enlarge and back up the thorough, reserved, perfectionism of the basic Virgo. Given other more out-going qualities in the chart, Virgos can be brilliant, and their mental working capacity is considerable.

It is important to educate a Virgo child to the full, as he or she will be a natural critic, and this is a quality which, if not applied intelligently, can degenerate into discontent or carping at life in general.

Whatever Virgo does, he does thoroughly, positively or negatively. No sign of the zodiac is better at fussing over details. It is essential, then, for Virgo children to fulfil themselves through some skill or the perfection of a talent. A shy child may prove to be an excellent dancer or musician.

Virgos are worth their weight in gold in banking and accountancy firms and as treasurers; and you find them too in laboratories and research departments the world over. I believe it to be true to say that to have Virgo prominent somewhere in the chart, not necessarily as the Sun-sign, is extremely valuable. It seems to be the factor that pulls the rest of the chart together into orderly productivity. And yet Virgo, in a weak chart, with no talents to pull into shape, can be a dismal carping failure. The self-pity of such characters is largely due to the sense of un-fulfilled potential.

Virgo Qualities	*Virgo Faults*
Steady application	Drudgery
Accuracy with figures	Penny-pinching
Discrimination and analytical ability	Fault-finding and cunning
Quiet dignity and reserve	Dreary martyrdom
Lecturing skill	Incessant talk
Shrewdness	Shrewishness

LIBRA

Ingredients which go to make up Libra characteristics are:

> Quality or quadruplicity – Cardinal
> Element – Air
> Ruling Planet – Venus

This may be the second of the Air-signs, but it by no means echoes the

uncomplicated Gemini intellectuality. One has only to look at the contradictory make-up of this sign to understand why. The ruling planet is
Venus, and this at once brings a feminine softness with a feeling for
beauty, harmony and cooperation. A blend of heart and head both cools
the heart and while not exactly 'softening' the head, certainly distracts
from sheer intellectuality.

In Taurus the expression of Venusian femininity was more primitive,
centred in the man-woman relationship, while in Libra it is
sophisticated. Libra is a positive, not a negative sign; thus in following
the gradual development of man through the signs, one can see that in
Leo he had leisure to enjoy luxury and admiration, in Libra he has
learned to value refinement of intellect. Art and beauty take their place
in the scheme of things, not merely in nature or in the form of a lovely
woman, but in things of the mind. Just as woman in Virgo has learned to
be free of man through mental independence, so man in Libra finds
beauty elsewhere than in physical form. This general refinement of mind
is seen in Libra in all forms of social graces. Diplomacy is possible
through the combination of the 'cardinal' need for action with the
factors signified by Venus (harmony and co-operation) and Air (communications and intellectuality). It is easy to see why Libra is the
diplomat rather than Aries, whose combination of action, fire and initiative is undiluted by Venusian charm.

Men and women with Libra strongly in their chart will reflect all this
in their appearance, in good looks of the Grecian type, a ready smile and
a suave, conciliatory manner. It is typical of Venus to find points of
agreement (Mars will find differences); and it is a kind of active
gentleness that is part of Libra's charm.

Libra at best is perfect. But in fact it is not always easy to have a basic
ideal of beauty and peace, as, when unfulfilled, there will be dissatisfaction and criticism. Criticism often enough, of the partner. Libra tends to
expect the 'other person' in whatever the partnership or combine, to
take the initiative and make decisions. He or she does not seek to
quarrel, but he makes his displeasure felt. Unconsciously he demands
justice, which is a noble aim if the 'eye for an eye' attitude is not overdone. Libra likes to sail through life effortlessly and elegantly, unruffled
by excessive emotion. But let no one underrate his ability. A Libran who
wants his or her own way will get it by charm and not by aggression.

But owing to the probability that quite another sign will be rising, a
Libran may, for example, have Pisces on his Ascendant, accounting for
untypical qualities of secrecy, shyness and romanticism. Again, an un-
typically forceful Libra may have battling Aries ascending. Both,
however, have the ready Libra smile and are diplomatic and socially
competent with a sense of beauty and harmony, although the Aries one
would be more ready to fight to preserve the peace, and the Pisces one
would be yielding and self-sacrificing.

Typical Libra faults are gentle ones such as laziness, indolence, vacillation and indecision. The feeling for love and beauty can degenerate into making a person think only of love-affairs or outward appearance. It is not typical of Libra to be actively cruel to children, but in the home, the results of neglect through laziness and sluttishness can be as disastrous.

No one can be more charming and successful than the best type of Libra, who combines beauty with brains and social graces.

The Libra ingredient, however it occurs in your chart, possibly through the Moon or the ruling planet being in this sign, gives the capacity for intelligent appraisal. The Libran scales are no fancy symbol – Librans really do weigh things up and balance and harmonise. A sense of order and symmetry emerges in their creative work. They see both sides of a question, and although problems in human relationships seem to crowd in on them, they are essentially peace-loving.

Libra men make good military leaders. Not because they love fighting, but because they actively wish to promote peace. Libra needs companionship but is not deeply emotional or intense.

What really suits these people is to sit back comfortably while someone else does the spade-work. They are rewarding to spoil, as they seem so at home in languor and luxury. I don't mean that they are useless. Far from it. They have many talents and are pleasant to deal with.

A weakness lies in their tendency to agree with everyone. This can lead to their being vacillating and indecisive. Most of us accept that an omelette can't be made without breaking eggs, but Libra will have a good try.

Many Libra women are beautiful and get away with an easy-going attitude to money. Why waste money on dull things when one needs a new outfit or expensive make-up? What is a partner for if not to find more money? But beneath the frivolity and artless charm can lie capability, brains and balance.

Libra men need a partner and rely on her to do her share and a bit over. If they are passionate, you may be sure that the full birth chart will disclose some other ingredient that is responsible. But they are satisfying to be with, and unfailingly courteous so long as things go well. With his capacity for mental brilliance and judgement, the Libra man or woman can reach high places. Once at the top he or she spends graciously and takes pride in well-chosen possessions. They are clever at delegating work.

I was asked once why it is that the sign Virgo shows strong characteristics of Libra. I answered that it is not the sign that does this but the person, and if we studied that person's chart, we should probably find that Libra featured strongly. Adjoining signs to the Sun-sign commonly contain both Venus and Mercury, as these are never far

from the Sun. This accounts for apparent similarity between any
adjoining signs.

Libra Qualities	*Libra Faults*
Refinement of intellect	Over-nicety
Diplomacy and tact	Degeneracy. Can't say no
Artistry, sense of beauty	Liking for the pretty-pretty
Talent for partnership	Over-reliance on others
Gentleness	Laziness
Ability to see both sides	Inability to decide
True love and affection	Venality

SCORPIO

Ingredients which go to make up Scorpio characteristics are:

> Quality – Fixed
> Element – Water
> Ruling Planet – Mars

Here we really do reach complications. No wonder that those with this
sign strong are deep and unfathomable personalities, with plenty to
cope with in their own nature; for what could be less compatible than
the assortment of ingredients above? Fixity combined with water is hard
to imagine, and when we add fiery Mars as ruler, it is a puzzle to envisage
the whole.

The difficulty may diminish if we work backwards from what we know
as Scorpio traits to the warring components.

Intensity of feeling and emotion is typical. Emotion comes from the
water element and gains passion from Mars and tenacity from fixity.
Scorpios have none of the pioneering dash of Aries, the other Mars-
ruled sign. The force of Scorpio is indeed not the quick, decisive flash of
Fire, but more like the terrifying weight of Water in a sweeping, inexorable tide. If Cancer was a gentle, moonlit stream (it is the Water-sign
ruled by the Moon), Scorpio is the tidal wave or the thundering weight of
Niagara.

Martian passion and desire are never easy to control. In Aries where
all is simple, primitive masculinity, the sex force is quickly roused,
expressed and forgotten. In Scorpio it is harnessed to emotion and fixity
of temperament, and runs deeper, with a potential for complications
and sorrow.

But if he can sink to the depths, the Scorpio can also rise to corresponding heights of pleasure, ecstasy or spirituality. It is illuminating to find
that the second symbol for this sign is the Eagle.

Men and women Scorpios make a powerful impact on those around
them. The strength of their feelings and of their needs and desires makes
them selfish. They really appear to suffer more keenly than the average

person and need comforting demonstrations of love or sympathy. They can be wonderful lovers, but are not the type to pick for a passing love affair. If the affair is to end, this must be of their choosing. They can be ruthless, the flood of passion sweeping away all obstacles – and they can outlast anyone in feats of physical endurance. It is not that they are so strong, but intensity combined with fixity of purpose make them oblivious to anything but the aims of the moment.

The best type of Scorpio makes a charming companion, for the enjoyment he feels is infectious. He enjoys life to the full, from carnal pleasures to the highest poetical or mystical adventures.

Unhappy Scorpios of both sexes (and this applies particularly to those who are found to have Scorpio rising) are the most unhappy and degenerate of people. Dangerous, too, for passion running riot at flood tide is not readily controlled. The feelings of these and of Sun-Scorpios, are not to be trifled with. Their fierce pride can be alarming.

As a boss, Scorpio is demanding and stands no nonsense. He neither forgives nor forgets an error and you cannot pass anything off as a joke. Not that he lacks humour – on the contrary – but it is wise to let *him* dictate the mood of the day. Scorpios are not easy-going, and are either loved or hated.

Happily nobody can be entirely Scorpio, with no modifying factors. This is astrologically impossible. It could not happen for the very good reason that all the planets can never be grouped in a single sign.

When trouble arrives, Scorpios suffer with the same intensity that goes into everything they do, and they seem to invite trouble with their exaggerated emotional reactions. Complications persist, because they cannot forget and forgive and take things lightly. You may get on very well with a Scorpio friend, only to discover that he or she still remembers some slighting remark you made fifteen years ago.

All power can be used for good or evil, so the intense, emotional force of Scorpio when directed to crime or sex tends to hit the headlines. But the higher symbol of Scorpio, the Eagle, soars on powerful wings to higher planes of consciousness. There is no finer character than the spiritually evolved Scorpio.

Hyper-sensitivity is a disadvantage. These people cannot bear a pin-prick, yet can be brave in enduring major wounds. They enjoy to the full. They suffer to the full. Feeling becomes an almost tangible thing and they create lasting emotional structures in their minds. This is why I warn against playing with the affections of one with this sign prominent in the chart, for where a light-hearted type will throw off an infidelity with a shrug, a true Scorpio will undergo torment, and, in certain cases, will react violently. This is due to their natural pride which, when in proper control, gives them dignity. And when, as is often the case, they reach the top of the tree, they command respect. The power they wield is like a relentless tide. They move inexorably forward, not wasting strength in impetuous bursts. Usually strong and healthy, they dread illness and feel cheated when it descends on them.

The magnetism of Scorpio is such that those who fall in love with them find, if the affair comes to an end, that they have them 'under their skin' in a most distressing way. No one else will do. Thraldom such as this can be an ecstatic experience when all goes well, but when it does not, there is a sense of tragedy and star-crossed love impossible to throw off maybe for years. I associate an afflicted Moon or Venus in Scorpio with such cases of thraldom or projection.

Scorpio Qualities	*Scorpio Faults*
Staying power	Rigid obstinacy
High libido	Debauchery
Ability for poetical or satirical writing	Sarcasm and mental cruelty
Dignity	Pride
Magnetism	Ability to corrupt others
Discretion	Over-secrecy
Fidelity	Tendency to cling

SAGITTARIUS

Ingredients which go to make up Sagittarius characteristics are:

Quality – Mutable
Element – Fire
Ruling Planet – Jupiter

In earlier signs, and indeed until I came to Scorpio, I wrote of the gradual progress or development through the signs, and how the first three signs were straightforward and gained in complexity until in Scorpio this reached a high level.

In Sagittarius we have a respite, and this is easy to understand when we study the ingredients. It is not hard to think of Fire as mutable, and the ruling planet, Jupiter, expands or exaggerates whatever it contacts. This gives us exaggerated fire and mutability which, in a phrase, describes Sagittarius, the mutable or adaptable expression of an ardent temperament.

Thus Sagittarius is friendly, impulsive, impatient, light-hearted and optimistic. People born with this sign prominent feel warmly in love but acknowledge the need for freedom; and where Scorpio will be bogged down in emotional thraldom, Sagittartius will detach him or herself, an eye cocked for the next adventure. At a high level of consciousness or development here is the philosopher who has learned the value of non-attachment and the futility of fear and emotional suffering. Even if he has not advanced as far as this consciously, he knows instinctively the value of *laisser-aller* . . . the art of letting go.

It will be remembered that the first five signs all have different ruling planets, and that each sign is strongly of the nature of that ruling planet. Then came Virgo, Libra and Scorpio, all with ruling planets in conflict with either their quality or their element. In Sagittarius we once again have a ruling planet in complete accord with the sign, and what is written here about Sagittarius applies to the planet Jupiter, as was the case with the first five signs of the zodiac and their rulers.

But Sagittarius is in no sense a primitive sign. Its diverse ingredients combine harmoniously, giving the power of relaxed enjoyment, and Jupiter, the biggest of the planets, seems to give the 'big' quality that enables Sagittarius to see things from a distance. Intuition is stronger than intellect, but there is no weakness here: it is more that the mind ranges beyond the confines of reasoning or book-knowledge.

Sagittarius is often thought to be too casual or careless, yet this is an advantage when it comes to trouble, as it seems to slide easily off his back.

Sagittarius children say eagerly, "I know," where another child will look blank. As often as not neither have understood, but the Sagittarius child has probably intuitively got the sense of what is being talked about. This feeling for broad outline is characteristic.

Sag. doesn't like niggling over details which offend his sense of freedom and he will not be tied down by them. He likes loose, comfortable clothing, too.

Sagittarius is happiest leading a varied life, changing location or jobs when they become restricting.

If you stay with a Sagittarian household, you may find it casually run, but this has its advantages if you are late for a meal or bring friends at the last moment for dinner. If there is a shortage of food, drink or even crockery, your host will suffer no embarrassment. Friendship means more to Sagittarius than domestic perfection.

Jupiter 'rules' Sagittarius, and Jupiter is said to be a lucky planet. This doesn't mean that all Sagittarians are lucky. How could it? And if it did, how unfair to other signs.

Sagittarius provides a kindly, tolerant attitude. Because he loves freedom himself, he respects that of others. He reads widely, but his learning is not confined to books and extends to the wider ranges of intuitive thought and direct inspiration. Optimism is strong, and in spite of set-backs he is confident, like Mr. Micawber, that something will turn up. Unless factors in his chart introduce order and method, he is untidy. This trait stems from impatience to be doing the next thing rather than a tolerance of disorder. Rather like Libra, he is delighted for someone else to tidy up.

The symbol of Sagittarius is the centaur, half man, half horse; and in his nature he seems to be torn between animal instincts and the higher mind. Warm and affectionate, Sagittarians of both sexes dash into love affairs. There is a love of sport, too, particularly horses and horse-racing or racing of any kind. They like speed.

Sagittarius is generous to the point of giving himself away! For this reason he is not always a safe recipient of secrets, although his loyalty may make him more discreet with other people's than with his own.

Don't be surprised if young Sagittarius delights his teacher with an instant grasp of essentials. But don't be fooled, either. This seeming mastery of a subject may be superficial. Grounding must be sound if he is to make real progress. A ready answer with not much to back it up is typical. At all ages he excels as a conversationalist, as he has a ready wit, and his sense of fair play ensures that he does not hog the scene.

His attitude to money is generous and unpredictable. Bursts of economy are often an unconscious effort to save up for a burst of extravagance. Money is not valued for itself.

Sagittarian Qualities	*Sagittarian Faults*
Justice	Taking the law in his own hands
Friendliness	Over-heartiness; toadying
Tolerance	Slackness; untidiness
Optimism	Trusting to luck
Quickness	Irritability; impatience
Philosophy	Hypocrisy
Respect of freedom	Lack of discipline
Ability for counselling	Over-frankness
Sense of comedy	Coarseness of speech

CAPRICORN

Ingredients which go to make up Capricorn characteristics are:

> Quality or quadruplicity – Cardinal
> Element – Earth
> Ruling Planet – Saturn

Capricorn is a straightforward sign in that it is all of a piece. It is at one in character with its ruling planet, Saturn.

It will be remembered that Aries, first of the Cardinal signs, combines action with fire and passion through its ruler, Mars. Cancer is action through the Moon, in emotion and sensitivity. Libra, the third Cardinal sign, is action in airy, mental concepts, in art and co-operation through its ruler, Venus.

In Capricorn the same active cardinality combines with Earth, and we see action allied with caution and common sense. The ruler, Saturn, has a chilling effect, so there is no heat in Capricorn activity; no hurry, no impatience. Earth signs (Taurus and Virgo are the other two) know and understand the rhythms of nature, and Capricorn knows that the seed must be given time to grow and bear fruit. Steady, driving ambition and one-pointedness will bring the Capricorn person slowly but surely to the top. He can be a hard worker and hard taskmaster, for he will exact from others just the amount of work he feels it is their duty to perform. Sentiment, compassion do not enter into the bargain. An eye for an eye . . .

No one, fortunately perhaps, is all Capricorn, any more than any one person can embody or exclusively manifest any one of the signs; but for the man or woman who wants to suceed in the world, the chart can hold no better ingredient than Capricorn. To have even one planet in Capricorn can give ambition in matters to do with the planet, sign or house involved. Regarding Taurus, the first Earth-sign, I wrote that it was like the flour in the cake. Capricorn is like reinforced concrete in the building, giving human character the core of toughness, the quality of endurance, so necessary if one is to cope with the difficulties of human life. Seriousness is perhaps the most outstanding quality of Capricorn. Whatever the profession, Capricorn gives the ambition, cool and deliberate, to ensure success. A successful actress who combines Capricorn with one of the Venus-ruled signs will put her beauty to effective use. A politician or orator who combines it with mercurial communications will do the same thing with his gifts. The general balance of the chart may indicate a talent or aptitude – but strength in Capricorn gives ambition or the will to succeed.

I have heard it said, "Capricorn men are described as being cold, self-contained, calculating and selfish. How does one reconcile this with the fact that Jesus was born under this sign?"

I reminded the speaker that the birth of Jesus is celebrated at the time of the age-old festival of the winter solstice (winter in northern climates, that is to say), rather as in England the sovereign's birthday is honoured in June, regardless of the actual date of birth of the reigning monarch. But supposing Jesus had been a Sun-Capricorn; saints and sinners can easily share a birthday. Identical energies can be put to good or bad use, and Capricorn is a most valuable sign with its cool common sense and down-to-earth realism. A Capricorn knows that steady application and patience will win in the end and he doesn't rush impulsively from one interest to another. He produces results.

For one's Capricorn friends and relations, however, one likes to find gentler or more tender qualities elsewhere in the chart, in Rising-sign or Moon-sign, to modify the seriousness, pessimism or sense of insecurity of Capricorn at its bleakest.

Capricorn undiluted would be formidable, but as an ingredient among others I, personally, value it highly. In fact, when interpreting the chart of someone with no obvious Capricorn strength, I look to see if the planet Saturn, the ruler of Capricorn, shows some compensating seriousness and application to duty.

If Capricorn is the Sun-sign or Rising-sign, much depends on whether the planetary pattern as a whole makes it easy to use or misuse this potentially stern and resolute sign.

Capricorn children can be appealing. One is reminded of the beauty and innocence of the baby antelope leaping on the mountain-side, and sometimes in their look there is a touchingly mature dignity. One does not feel one should take liberties with Capricorn, young or old.

Capricorn Qualities	*Capricorn Faults*
Ambition	Ruthlessness; social climbing
One-pointedness	Using any means to an end
Coolness	Callousness
Method and steadiness	Irritating deliberation
Order and precision	Bureaucracy; sternness
Realism	Pessimism
Business acumen	Meanness (in the miserly sense)

AQUARIUS

Ingredients that go to make up Aquarius characteristics are:

Quality or quadruplicity – Fixed
Element – Air
Ruling Planet – Saturn and/or Uranus

As the world enters the Aquarian Age with all its inventions and Uranian technology, we don't all have to be born under this sign to respond to the new inventions.

Uranus could be called the New Age ruler of Aquarius, but before mankind had all this technology, it probably responded more to Saturn as ruler.

It seems to me that the combination of Air (communications and intellectuality) with Fixity gives the key to the Aquarian personality.

Aquarius types are determined, independent people who can be obstinate, headstrong and perverse. They show qualities that are typical of both rulers, Saturn and Uranus. There is cold detachment (Saturn) and also the Uranus urge to disrupt. These people can be the reformers or visionaries, or, if they go wrong, the fanatics and perverts. Here is the type who goes against law and order through an instinctive revolt against restraint. But, and I cannot repeat this too often, no person is wholly of one sign; and in character interpretation it is found that the way a sign is expressed through the individual depends on the general shaping of the planetary pattern within the twelve signs. Aquarian characteristics could manifest through you, perhaps, who think of yourself as belonging to quite another sign. We talk, then, of the Aquarius ingredient, and this manifests in independence, detachment and a wide interest in humanity. Nobody with this sign strong likes being pinned down to intimate personal relationships for longer than such links are felt as a personal need. Aquarius is a horse that must be ridden on a loose rein. If he feels that he is making the decisions and working in his own way, all is well, but at a hint of coercion he rebels. He cannot act a lie and is thus often considered unconventional.

Aquarius may carry the 'Watering pot' as the rhyme says, but this is not a Water-sign. Watering the earth or bringing water to his fellow man benefits humanity, and Aquarius is certainly humanitarian. Not, however, in a domestic way, and for all his lofty ideals he is still capable of forgetting wife and family while busying himself on behalf of more distant sufferers. Both sexes can be bafflingly detached in a basically kindly way. They are a law unto themselves. They don't care for other people's new ideas or reforms and unfailingly come up with alternative suggestions. It may be that they feel it to be a weakness on their part to follow another's lead in what or how to do things.

"Mistress Mary, quite contrary" was certainly an Aquarian. "I don't think so," "I don't agree," or just plain "No!" is often on the lips of Aquarius. They genuinely seek to improve conditions and are ingenious in their ideas. Instead of arguing at every turn, they get on better when they use their originality to invent or to plan. But it is wise not to expect co-operation from Aquarius unless you plan to delegate the job to him. He won't do it *your* way. If he is the boss, he knows what he wants and sees that you do it his way. He gives orders brusquely, but would be sad to think that you considered him rude.

This all sounds very male and bossy, and indeed there is this side to Aquarius, but women with this sign strong can be very attractive. It is a good-looking sign; striking rather than pretty. In love, Aquarians feel strongly but dislike any public demonstration of affection.

My own Aquarius daughter, when small, would walk deliberately as far behind me as would give the impression that she was on her own. In London one day I saw a small child behaving in exactly this way, and as the mother waited for her near me to cross a busy street, I couldn't help myself saying, "Your little girl must have been born in February, was she not?" She was! And on the same day as my daughter. This independence is a useful trait in later life but needs careful handling if it is not to turn to aggressive wilfulness or rebellion. A difficulty lies in the fact that Aquarians are positive they are in the right, and if a mistake is glaringly obvious, the attitude is an impatient. "Well, it can't be helped *now*!"

Evolved types are among the finest in the human race; loyal, discreet and as true as steel.

Aquarian Qualities	*Aquarian Faults*
Idealism	Fanaticism
Independence	Lack of co-operation
Resourcefulness, invention	Doing it the other way
Faithfulness, loyalty	Rigidity; obstinacy
Originality	Perversity
Detached, disinterested	Isolation

PISCES

Ingredients that go to make up Pisces characteristics are:

> Quality or Quadruplicity – Mutable
> Element – Water
> Ruling Planet – Jupiter and/or Neptune

As with Aquarius, Pisces has double rulership. There is no doubt that Neptune has much in common with Pisces, but, for my part, I find that Jupiter fits in far too well to be discarded. There is a kindly warmth and a generous, philanthropic quality about Pisceans that I cannot associate solely with a planet as nebulous as Neptune.

In Pisces we come to the last of the three Water-signs. There is none of the complexity that we find in Scorpio, where emotions are ruled by Mars (passion), and where fixity of temperament adds to the difficulties. In Pisces, water combines easily and naturally with mutability, for it is the nature of water to conform to the shape that contains it; and Pisceans are the most adaptable of people. They like to be with someone stronger (a vessel, as it were, that contains them) and they give in to others' wishes, not from servility but because they are naturally generous and amenable. Pisces is the 'actor' sign because of the ease with which Pisceans assume another personality. Where Aquarius has the positive urge to help humanity at large, in a detached spirit, Pisces, impressionable and emotional, has kindly sympathy for individuals and readily sacrifices self-interest.

The evolved type of Piscean is patient, sympathetic and broad-minded; but it is obvious that such qualities can either be put to good use, or degenerate into sloppy sentiment or spineless dissipation. All signs have their qualities and their corresponding faults. If gentle Pisces predominates and nothing in the individual chart pattern introduces, for example, a Mars streak of aggression, then we can be sure that the individual's reactions will fall largely within the limits of this sign (with, as always, an admixture of whatever sign is rising or otherwise prominent). We will suppose for the moment that this mixture is not a highly contradictory one. When Pisces is angry, his Jupiter dignity is aroused, but the reaction is not in the urge to hit out or wound, as would be the case with a strong Mars.

Many Pisces folk are psychic. Aquarius can be 'aware' in flashes of thought, but Pisces is emotionally intuitive. There is a sense of humour and a love of laughter. Pisces doesn't make heavy weather of things, but he is capable of going to the other extreme into escapism. He needs partners who are practical, and must take care not to drift into relationships out of sympathy.

Pisces will yield, not just with good grace, but because he or she really prefers to give in when the companion feels strongly about something.

Stronger characters would call it 'living a lie', but it is more that the Piscean finds much of life too unreal to make an issue of anything so trivial as a difference of opinion.

People of all signs can be mystics, but if their individual charts were studied, it would probably be found that Pisces played a part, as Rising-sign or Moon-sign or by containing the ruling planet – or even what seem like Piscean characteristics could come from accentuation of the 12th 'house' of the chart, which is the part of the chart associated with Pisces which is the twelfth sign.

Both the Jupiter-ruled signs, Sagittarius and Pisces, need a faith. Joan Rogers in her excellent study of the signs and planets, *The Art of Astrology*,* points out so rightly that without a faith Pisces can degenerate into a greedy sensualist, an unhappy person who doesn't know what he wants. A chronic grumbler, nothing is right for him because material things can never fill the need of one who is, even unconsciously, in search of higher things.

This sense of 'searching' is a problem which can arise for many who do not realise that they have a Piscean lack. To be a 'whole' person, we need knowledge and understanding of each factor of the 'whole' of which we are a part. Only a calculated chart can show just how each of the twelve signs figures for the individual.

You may feel that you don't really know your Pisces associate. Don't worry. He most likely doesn't understand himself, either.

Some Pisces people are a bit of a menace in their attitude to money. People and their needs and comforts come first, and 'It sounds so decorative to be in the red, doesn't it?!' A charming attitude and one that goes a long way with the biblical injunction to 'take no thought for the morrow', but it leads to trouble in a harsh world.

There is something chrysalis-like about Pisces, typical of it being the last sign of the zodiac before the circle restarts in Aries in a fresh cycle of experience. Pisces is nothing if not well-disposed and philanthropic – but he always seems ready either to disguise himself or to disappear into some other realm of experience. He is the least down-to-earth and the most romantic of the twelve signs.

The native of Pisces does well, then, to associate himself with some slightly unreal occupation. The stage or entertainment world, the magazine world, romantic fiction, film-making, playwriting or photography. Or something that suits the Piscean affinity with water – something to do with the sea, liquids, drink or drugs; or any of the level-shifting pursuits which can include religious activity or anaesthesia. Secret work also suits Pisces, or work behind the scenes. A Piscean with her ready sympathy makes a good nurse, sensing the needs and moods of the patients.

A danger can be the ability to 'let go' in so many ways that these

* Herbert Jenkins, 1960.

61

people are vague to the point of carelessness. But they know the meaning of give and take, with the accent on the 'give'. This is a characteristic likely to promote harmony in any partnership.

All this doesn't sound very male or manly, but in fact Pisceans are good sportsmen. Skiing, swimming, ball games suit them as well as boating, sailing and travel.

Piscean Qualities	*Piscean Faults*
Sensitivity; gentleness	Weakness; sentimentality
Adaptability; acting talent	Deceit
Dignity	Hypocrisy
Tolerance	Dissipation
Self-sacrifice; generosity	Playing the martyr
Patience	Peevishness
Broadmindedness; humour	Spineless tolerance, even of evil

4. PERSONAL APPEARANCE THROUGH THE SIGNS

I greatly regret the death of the astrologer Hilda Jaffa in this connection, as she had not only made a study but had considerable flair for this subject. I think she would agree that the individual's appearance is very much a blend of the main signs and planets prominent in the birth chart. It is very obvious that all people born with the Sun in a particular sign do not look alike, even though once the astrologer knows what this sign is, he will spot something in looks or behaviour that is typical of the sign governing the date of birth. Many astrologers find they can recognise the Ascendant or Rising-sign more easily than the Sun-sign. Others see a strong indication of a sign or planet, which proves on calculation of the chart to be typical of the planet (or sign containing it) which is the ruler of the native's Sun or Rising-sign.

So it is truest to say that each ingredient of any chart has its recognisable characteristics, and very occasionally someone seems to the astrologer to be the walking embodiment of, say, Leo, yet calculation of the chart discloses that he or she has the Moon in that sign, and most probable of all, that Leo is on the Ascendant.

I have known people, not all of them astrologers, with such a flair for spotting birth-signs that I wouldn't try to compete. These people usually have some psychic ability and they evidently recognise a subtle quality, rather than strict appearance.

Some astrologers ask for a photograph before working on the chart. This is probably because the time of birth is so often uncertain, and the clue given by the photograph can help to establish an uncertain Rising-sign. Some signs have marked facial characteristics – e.g. the Scorpio nose and penetrating eagle eye – and if such a feature is seen in the photograph and unaccounted for by the Sun- or Moon-sign, the astrologer might guess at the Rising-sign. But a chart arrived at in this way should be marked 'speculative'.

Many signs, if undiluted, would not make for good looks. Happily we are all such a mixture that the admixture of what are traditionally 'plains' signs can add an interesting quirk to a face. There is often an attraction and piquancy in an irregularity of feature. Standard books on astrology sold in our Western markets are designed for the white races, or so it would seem in their descriptions of astrological types. But astrology applies to all races and while hair and complexion are less varied there are infinite and subtle variations. One finds no difficulty in recognising Sign characteristics in the facial proportions. A reader once wrote saying that all orientals and all Africans looked alike to her. I cannot agree. Their hair and complexion may seem similar to our eyes but in fact there is as great a range of beauty of feature or of physique as exists in Europeans or Westerners. And the astrological Signs are as easily recognisable in character and disposition in one race as in another.

Character and looks go hand in hand. Temperament and mood, reflected in the expression and habitual emotions, modify features sooner or later. The birth chart certainly gives a living picture and reflects even the physical appearance: only the other day I was fascinated to meet a hitherto unseen client, a girl whose features and build bore out astrological tradition. A well aspected Venus gave beauty and charm; but with Scorpio rising, it was a Scorpio type of beauty and I would never have guessed a Cancer Sun, although it was this that contributed womanly attraction. She had deep-set, piercing eyes, an aquiline nose and a slight, not very tall figure. It is quite commonplace to find the Sun-sign playing a minor part in appearance and this bears out what I am always having to repeat, which is that trying to assess anything – character, looks or future trends – from the Sun-sign alone is impossible. In her case, leaving Signs out of it, Venus played a strong part and Venus is kind to women in regard to looks, giving a softly rounded body and good features. Men with a lot of Venus tend to plumpness and are definitely not the rugged type.

I am often asked to guess what Sign people are born under. I find I nearly always spot a prominent Sign, but not necessarily the Sun-sign. This was borne out at a meeting of astrologers where we all tried to guess one another's signs. Frankly none of us shone. It is easy to spot the characteristics of a Sign or planet but impossible to guess where it will manifest in the individual's chart. I see someone in the street and think to myself, 'round, feminine Moon-face. Typical Cancerian.' I know what I mean when I say 'typical Gemini' or 'typical Leo' just as we all know what we mean when we see a family likeness and say "Young so-and-so is a typical member of his family."

It has taken me years to recognise Sign characteristics. Leos often have attractive cat-like faces and a proud bearing. Taurus and Libra are both Venus signs, but each has its brand of good looks. Taurus is more solid and neck and shoulders are well rounded; Librans have a more delicate brand of beauty. I look for marked eyebrows in Ariens. Scorpios are two distinct types, eagles or bullet-headed, but they share an intense look and ability to project themselves. I will try to write about each Sign before the end of this chapter, but I don't want you to think spotting Signs is easy. The more you try it the more you are likely to be wrong. No two persons sharing a birth month need look alike but they can easily share some characteristic that will disclose their kinship to the observant eye.

I think it is reasonably true to state that the Sun-sign is the more basic so that we grow to be more typical of it both in behaviour and looks as life goes on. I often guess a Sun-Leo by the way he or she accepts an invitation in a lordly way as if conferring a favour on the host or hostess. And a Sun-Libran's ready smile demonstrates a basic urge to please. But these characteristics may just as well correspond to the Rising-sign. Bearing all this in mind, how would I describe each sign in terms of appearance? . . .

ARIES is not easy to recognise. Often the whole head is narrow and delicately formed, but delicate is not usually the right adjective as Aries folk have an air of determination and decision. It is not a specially tall Sign, neither is it a fat one. Bony structure is strong, chin often pointed, eyebrows delicately arched or otherwise noticeable. Arien women have an attractive, athletic look and seldom go in for frill or decoration. They are not the fluffy type. Aries men give you the feeling they would be good in a crisis with their flair for taking the initiative. This shows in their faces.

TAURUS in women can give considerable beauty; well-formed, if sometimes rather pronounced, features and appealing eyes with a direct candid look. Taurus men, while handsome, can be podgy, and a tendency to fat is more often found when Taurus is rising than when it is the Sun-sign. Legs and feet look well able to support the weight. Taureans of either sex have a sweet expression and love to laugh. When the Sun is in Taurus and a taller, slimmer sign rises, such as Gemini, Leo or Sagittarius, there is no heaviness and often considerable good looks.

GEMINI is a youthful sign, and Geminians (by Sun or Ascendant) retain their looks and figures to a remarkable extent. I have found that the Northern Hemisphere 'Summer' signs, Gemini, Cancer and Leo, tend to have small noses and pleasant, roundish faces and frankly I often muddle them and think 'there goes a Cancer' only to find it is in fact a Geminian or a Leo. But the Geminian has alert, quick-darting eyes and a quick wit which shows in the expression. The brainy, academic type of Geminian as opposed to the alert kind have high foreheads and a dome-like top to the head, to house the brains. Some Geminian women have a hopetty, skipetty bird-like appearance and are small and slight. But on the whole Gemini is one of the 'tall' signs.

CANCER seems to have two distinct types, as indeed do all three Water-signs. One is the round, friendly, moon-faced type with the slightly short or snub-nose; not very tall, comfortably built with feminine, rounded knees. The eyes brim with vicarious suffering for the ills of the world. The second type is also attractive, but the nose can be large in an aquiline way: it is a distinctive feature, but not straight in the classical style. Cancer men are well made but not craggy. Often they have anxious eyes, as though appealing for sympathy.

LEO is a handsome sign for both sexes. Often tall, but when short the back is straight and there is an air of command and confidence. Leos wear their clothes regally, regardless of their vital statistics (which may exceed model measurements). They enjoy dressing up and creating an effect. The head is often large and well-shaped and the gaze sunny and benign. The nose often has a rounded-off catlike look and the turned-up corners of the mouth add to the feline appearance and frank sex appeal. The body is attractive, supple and well made – again rather like a relaxed member of the cat family. Leos exude confidence unless other features of the chart are strongly inhibiting.

VIRGO looks are unobtrusive, which is perhaps why many film beauties are under this Sign. The superimposed personality transforms the basic features and perfectionist skill in make-up and general grooming is ideal for an actress. Virgo men are usually hard to describe as often they have no outstanding feature. I read that there is a Virgo nose with curved nostrils, but I can't say I've noticed it. I *have* noticed a look about the mouth, rather as if it has been ironed out. Virgos are rather slight and delicate with an air of reserve or shyness. Studious, deep-set eyes are a recognisable feature in the brainier type of Virgo.

LIBRA is quite the most powerful Sign ingredient for beauty. Of course it depends on what other Signs dilute it, but given a chance, Libra has a beautiful body, taller than Taurus, the other Venusian Sign, and slimmer; well proportioned, with delicate features. Sweetness of temperament shows in a ready smile. Libra hates to say 'no' to any agreeable proposition, so unless he or she is strong-minded, the result inevitably shows in increased weight in middle age. The Libran nose is well shaped, on the long side and ending in a point. One Libran friend of mine told me her small grandson remarked, "You've got a nose like a witch's hat!"

SCORPIO has two types. There is the striking, hook-nosed, vital type with piercing eyes and there is a rounder, bullet-headed type with a slightly crooked, humorous mouth. The Scorpio ingredient adds vigour and character to a face, but not until after the sex life has got going. Before this the Scorpio young man can seem watery and gangling and the Scorpio girl willowy and shy. A Scorpio beauty is memorably lovely, with magnetism as well as good features. Unlovely Scorpios can be equally striking. In fact, the distinctive thing about Scorpio is the strength of impact. Like or dislike, you don't forget meeting a Scorpio.

SAGITTARIUS shows his dislike of restraint in his dress. Both sexes look wonderful in casual sports clothes, tailor-mades and riding kit. This can be so much their natural garb that if you meet a Sagittarian girl at some function where she is all got up in conventional gear you will hardly recognise her. Sagittarius is a handsome Sign with a longish, narrow nose and friendly eyes. At home on a horse or in the wide open spaces – contemptuous of all the fuss some people make about appearance they can still manage to look as elegant as anyone. Their friendly manner makes them easy to distinguish from some of the more indrawn and reserved Signs.

CAPRICORN along with Virgo is not considered a beautiful Sign, and yet there have been famous beauties born with this Sun-sign such as Madame de Pompadour and in the thirties the actress Diana Wynyard, who combined Capricorn with Taurus rising. Capricorn adds dignity and a sense of purpose, so that Capricorn women know how to make the most of themselves and, as with Scorpio, there is a depth and seriousness of personality that makes itself felt. The bony structure is often marked, and the craggy type of male often owes his attraction to this. In women it is rare that the looks are conventional or Grecian. An attractively turned-up nose or other irregularity of feature can in fact enhance attraction.

AQUARIUS, unlike many of the Signs, has certain characteristics that are easy to spot. If you were drawing the profile you would find that nose and chin were prominent, the jawline pronounced and the mouth set back. In exaggerated cases even the teeth have an inward slope. In short the face is the opposite to the kind with prominent teeth and mouth. Unlike many of the Signs, these features seem to go more with people who are born with the Sun in Aquarius (the February folk) than those with Aquarius rising. But in case you think this sounds unattractive may I assure you that Aquarians are often extremely good-looking in rather a Grecian way and have slim legs and well-shaped ankles.

PISCES. And having said that all the Water-signs have two distinct types, I don't think this applies to Pisces! This very adaptable Sign in true actor fashion can seem to change his face. Pisceans give the impression of having a rather large face with prominent sleepy-looking eyes which water easily. The ready tear is quite a characteristic. The build is fleshy rather than athletic, although riding and water sports keep them fit in early life. There *are* tall Pisceans, but Signs other than Pisces contribute to their height. The expression is kindly and humorous and they seldom look fierce or impatient.

Apart from Signs having characteristics, the Signs group into other categories through their associated Elements and Qualities. For this reason, too, there is as much variety and contradiction in astrology over appearance as there is in real life. "Little Johnnie *is* like his father!" "Nonsense, he's the image of his mother's brother!" In other words where one astrologer will detect, and rightly, a Cardinal Sign, another with equal justification will spot the main Element. I can identify the strong face of the Fixed-signs and am getting quite good at recognising Water-signs. But after years of practise, I admit I am often wrong.

5. THE SIGNS IN THE CONTEXT OF LOVE, MONEY AND AUTHORITY

In psychological analysis the reactions of the individual under varying stimuli are noted. People behave in their own way when courting or making love; they have different reactions to money and possessions; some take more easily to a position of authority than others.

Astrologically all these variations in reaction are traceable in the map or chart of the individual, although the weighing up and balancing of conflicting qualities is no straightforward matter. It has to be borne in mind that the circle of the zodiac represents total experience, which, while following a recognisable sequence, can be interpreted at *any* level from the cosmic to the individual.

In personal charts the main Sign-accent is provided by the zodiacal position of the Ascendant degree, the Sun, the Moon and the planets which rule the Ascendant or Sun-sign. If therefore we wish to assess the reactions of an individual in a given situation it is necessary to make a mental picture of him in very broad outline. The personal cocktail of two Sun-Cancer people will be of very different flavour if the one has Taurus rising and the other Aries rising; and it would be wrong to suppose that their reactions to any situation would be the same. Nevertheless there is such a thing as a 'Cancerian' or 'Aquarian' or any other sign-reaction to a given situation even though the reaction is modified by other characteristics.

In the following attempt to give typical reactions I ask the reader to bear in mind that work done on the basis of the Sun-sign alone is bound to fall well short of complete accuracy.

In relation to love, the Sun-sign would play a part, so would Rising-sign and so would the Sign containing Venus (which is never more than two Signs away from the Sun-sign). To give an example: for an individual with Sagittarius rising, Sun in Taurus, Venus in Pisces and Moon in Scorpio one could expect a Sagittarian respect for freedom and a dislike of being tied, combined with intense feeling when roused from both Taurus and Scorpio and high potential of jealousy. Such a person would have a lot to learn in the field of emotions. When 'in love' the

Piscean Venus might make it very hard not to give way out of sympathy, egged on by the strong sexual feelings of the Taurus Sun and Scorpio Moon. Exactly how the individual would cope with this dynamic and impulsive emotional set-up would depend on the chart as a whole. If as a whole the chart were well aspected and strong, the Sagittarian sense of justice, Piscean self-sacrifice and Taurean common sense would triumph. If the chart were weak, Sagittarian impulse, Piscean weakness and Scorpio and Taurus sensuality could bring downfall.

I hope this gives some idea of the difficulty of judging reactions. The study of aspects and total chart-picture is necessary. The following word-pictures describe only one ingredient of an individual reaction.

The Zodiac in Love

Aries in Love is ardent, passionate and impatient. when satisfied he will kick his heels and canter off. The graph of his self-control is in inverse ratio to that of his desire. He can be jealous in the heat of the moment, but having clubbed the other man over the head and taken what he wanted he bears no grudge. Aries men and women take the initiative in making advances in love or friendship.

Taurus in Love feels strongly and sensuously. He or she needs to give and receive love and they appreciate beauty, comfort and slow, luxurious fulfilment of their needs and appetites. There is a matter-of-fact, animal need for the full cycle of experience and the Taurean woman when in love is geared for the whole process of child-bearing and caring for husband and family. Don't expect a Taurean to be light-hearted. For him love is a deep and fundamental necessity. A fault is jealousy or possessiveness.

Gemini in Love . . . very often he isn't! Geminians can be so cool that it is quite possible to imagine their not wanting love at all. When they do (according to other factors in the chart) they can be verbally very persuasive and charming and say all the same things to someone else the next day. They can be relied on to talk and analyse their feelings, a characteristic in men that appeals to women who enjoy chatting about their reactions. In this way they seem to be cosier than they really are and often have success out of proportion to the sincerity of their emotions.

Cancer in Love is tender, protective and loyal. These people hang on to what they've got and are quite capable of having ardent love affairs while keeping a solid home front. Generally the home is sacrosanct. Cancerian men have a subconscious respect for the mother-principle and their ideal woman is a fertile, full-breasted figure of comfort. Cancerians have a need for someone who gives a steady, background source of affection and they remain faithful in their fashion to those they are fond of. Emotion is easily roused.

Leo in Love has all the attraction of confidence and ardour combined. Warmth and sensuality combine in a rich enjoyment of love that can be irresistible. Leos always have to be master of the situation, and if they feel their authority slipping they move to fresh fields. Noble, kindly and generous as they are, one has the impression that the 'dancing girls' are round the corner awaiting their summons.

Virgo in Love seems a contradiction; but in fact the choosy, virgin attitude springs from a feeling for perfection and Virgos can be perfectionists in this field as in any other if they turn their minds to it. They tend, however, to go to extremes: if a Virgo is modest he is just about untouchable. In women this gives the attraction of the inviolate. Virgos do not rush into experience, as everything has to be 'just right'. They are often disappointed.

Libra in Love is in his element. This sign seeks co-operation, harmony and a partner; so that Librans at their best are the perfect lovers, seeking to give pleasure and provide the complement to their companion. It can be a weakness in them to be dependent on partnership and they can be parasitical, leaning on the other person and expecting their burdens to be carried. But in the art of love and understanding and in attractiveness they are most satisfying to be with and very often beautiful into the bargain.

Scorpio in Love takes himself very seriously. This is the most strongly sexed of all the signs. Emotional intensity and depth of feeling are backed by vigour and staying-power. There is no trifling with these people when they are roused and they are not easily thwarted. 'Hell hath no fury like a woman scorned' was surely written with a Scorpio woman in mind, for pride plays a big part in Scorpionic reaction to love. A Scorpio man or woman is magnetically attractive and also egotistical; a dynamic and dangerous combination unless self-control is well developed. Unleashed Scorpio passion is a *sine qua non* among other ingredients in any *crime passionel*.

Sagittarius in Love rushes into action with impulse and enthusiasm. An individual with this sign strong will often spoil his or her chances by announcing his or her feelings prematurely. Warm-hearted, they are always in love; but if you have not seen them for some time it is best to ask the name of the present favourite, as you may be out of date. Unlike Scorpio, they forgive and forget and respect the other person's freedom. Not only do they feel there are 'as good fish in the sea', but most likely they already have their eye on one or two for future requirements.

Capricorn in Love sets about getting what he wants with determination. He is not rash and there is often a soundly practical basis to his choice. Capricornus is the goat, and like the other animal signs (Taurus the Bull, Aries the Ram and Leo the Lion) he does not shrink from the fundamentals of sex. There is a strong sense of possession and value. Capricorn men or women are unlikely to throw themselves away, but although they keep their heads there is nothing half-hearted in their approach.

Aquarius in Love is careful not to display his feelings in public.

Exaggeratedly detached and casual, he is also highly intuitive and is rarely deceived about the other person. Sagittarius seems detached because he is freedom-loving and hates to be taken for granted, but Aquarius carries this to extremes. It is dangerous to assume that you have 'hooked' an Aquarian as if all the initiative does not come from his side he will quietly evaporate from the scene. Those who are in love with an Aquarian may well find it a fascinating exercise to penetrate the cool exterior and find out what is going on.

Pices in Love makes no bones about it. Like Sagittarius, who broadcasts his intentions, Pisces is just frankly loving and emotional. Not blatantly so, as there is a hidden, shy quality, but there is powerful need to give out sympathy, tenderness and often even to sacrifice himself. At its best it is the highest manifestation of human affection. At its worst it can be overdone and sloppy. Piscean women make good wives as self-adaptation is second nature.

The Zodiac and Money

Once again reminding the reader that the personal chart will show a variety of reactions to any subject, let us look at what may be termed the undiluted sign reactions to money or possessions.

Aries is not keen on possessions except perhaps in theory. He is the pioneer who, fired by ambition, will set out for the gold fields; but it is the excitement, the promise of future extravagances, or the dangers involved in his adventure, that stir him more than any lust for possessions.

Taurus, on the other hand, is the financier *par excellence*. The need for comfort is strong in him and he likes to know that his life rests on the solid foundation of a fat balance in the bank. He has a natural feeling for money and the steady qualities needed to acquire it. He may be over-conscious of possessions, but he can be relied on to spend wisely when it comes to home comforts.

Gemini will have theories about how to make money and as he reads everything anyway will surely know the condition of the stock-markets. But the fact that he succeeds in his career is due to his intelligence and his efforts towards success come from interest in his subject rather than from any fundamental urge to acquire possessions. The riches of a Geminian lie in breadth of knowledge. The world of thought is his oyster.

Cancer has a sense of thrift rather than an interest in money for its own sake. He likes to collect and he holds on to what he has. The instinct to protect others is strong and he will see therefore that he has enough to ensure that his family or dependants are nurtured. He can spend generously but would be careful to replenish the funds. There is a strong feeling for conservation.

Leo is too lordly to bother about petty cash. Kings do not handle money. His attitude, then, is a mixture of disregard as to where it comes from and indifference as to where it goes. His generosity is quite un-calculated and he does not spend to make an impression or to buy pop-ularity; he simply finds it natural to provide for his entourage and dis-tribute largesse. His big ideas may land him in trouble, but no amount of punishment will induce a humble attitude.

Virgo is careful and makes little lists and tots up the items. It matters to him if the milkman cheats him out of a halfpenny, not so much because he grudges the halfpenny, but inaccuracies offend him. He probably invented the saying about taking care of the pence. He is very good in banks or solicitors' offices, explaining to less careful types just how wrong they are in their ideas. He makes his way in the world through attention to detail and accuracy. Like Taurus he has a liking for solid results, and he has the brain-power to help in their achievement.

Libra prefers to ignore money except when it can be acquired pleasantly and used in increasing the beauty and comfort of the world. Libran women like to dress well and be surrounded by expensive things, but as they are often beautiful and attractive they are apt to marry well and have their needs supplied. A Libran man gets on in the world because he is charming and tactful. His attitude to money would be light-hearted but intelligent. He is not likely to get into financial difficulties except through indolence.

Scorpio feels intensely about everything that concerns himself. He likes power and will devote himself untiringly to any task that will increase his own prestige. But money in itself is not important except as something that can give him the creature comforts he so enjoys; and of course his appetites are considerable so that he needs a lot. Scorpio likes the best and plenty of it. He can be selfish.

Sagittarius is casual, generous and optimistic; but he hates to feel he is being imposed on. His essential love of freedom asserts itself if he thinks that others are making demands on him that threaten to constitute a permanent bond or tie. He would rather give away a large sum than be tied down to some small regular contribution. Money and possessions are unimportant to him and he is undismayed if circumstances force him to part with his belongings. Even such a mishap makes a change and Sagittarius welcomes anything new.

Capricorn is down-to-earth and practical about money, as about everything else. He is ambitious and likes to see solid results for his labour; and money is a very satisfactory foundation for the kind of result he is looking for. Capricorn is not much interested in money for its own sake, but he wants to get somewhere in the world and money will help him to do this. He can be careful to the point of meanness on the way up the ladder, but he will spend what is needed to further his ambitions.

Aquarius is impersonal and detached. He will spend generously for any cause he feels to be worthwhile, even if he himself goes without a new overcoat. The mental concept is more important to him than close or personal facts and if he carries this to extremes life with him can be chaotic. He will reform the finances of the entire globe in theory while his wife goes out to earn his keep.

Pisces is sympathetic and generous. He can adapt himself cheerfully to circumstances and will cope with poverty or riches as needs be. Money in itself is not so important and he can be a bit vague or muddled in his attitude. Big schemes and South Sea Bubbles attract him and he is apt to trust to luck. He will lend money or take a chance without so much as a glance at his bank balance if his sympathies or enthusiasm are aroused.

The Zodiac in Authority

Aries takes authority in his stride, but does not seek it specially. The Arien is the pioneer and therefore expects to be followed; but although he likes to be in the forefront this does not derive from any power complex or wish to dominate. He will assume quick command because he likes to take the initiative and is capable of quick action and decision; but there is no wish to assemble a group of disciples around him and if this happened he would be rather casual with them.

Taurus can organise very well, but is happier dealing with practical problems than in bossing people around. He is content to get on with the job and will encourage others to do the same; but he could not be relied on to drive them should this become necessary.

Gemini can lead in the realm of thought and ideas, through writing and oratory. His influence can be widespread through the Press or by means of books and teaching; but when faced with a class of unruly boys his power in the exercise of authority is not necessarily on a level with his power to impart knowledge.

Cancer is competent and active, but tends to be too self-effacing to enjoy authority outside the home circle or his familiar sphere. Nevertheless, Cancer is the 'mother' Sign and quiet guiding or the protection of others comes naturally to this Sign. Tact and ability to sense the feelings of others would help the Cancerian to bring out the best in those working under him; but this same sensitivity might make it hard for him to put up with rebellion or criticism, which he would sense even before it was manifest.

Leo is happy in command. He assumes it naturally. People obey him because it seems the obvious thing to do. He is warm-hearted and humane and expects the best of others, which draws more from them than would sternness or mistrust. His authority is of the kingly variety. He takes a following for granted and does not care to share his command. There cannot be two kings.

When it comes to *Virgo* (and this applies to all the gentler Signs) I must remind the reader that I am *not* saying that a person with this, that or the other Sun-sign would not make a good ruler. What I am getting at is that it would not be the qualities of their Sun-sign that supplied the urge or ability for rulership and, if in fact they were competent leaders, such characteristics would be shown elsewhere in the chart.

Virgo, then, if undiluted, would not be a popular person in authority. His tendency would be to criticise and find fault, which is not the best way of getting good work from others. In a purely scholastic or literary field or in work demanding attention to detail and analytical faculties the good Virgo brain might take the lead and enjoy respect; but this is a very different thing from the confident assumption of leadership which is typical of Leo.

Libra is much the same as Virgo, in that unsupported by more martial qualities the Libran would rather let things slide than risk unpopularity by action or self-assertion. But, diplomatic as Libra likes to be, it is a fact that Librans are often associated with battles. The 'other person', the partner, is of prime importance, and if this manifests in the life as a need to achieve harmony through learning how to work in double harness there will be much treading on toes in the early stages. Paradoxically, then, the 'peaceful' Libran is often to be observed learning this quality in active battle and Librans make good soldiers of the kind who fight in order to promote peace. In authority, the Libran uses persuasion or tact rather than bulldozing methods.

Scorpio has an urge for power and an ambition to command which has little in common with the natural assumption of leadership shown by Leo or Aries. The force is there and the staying power, but instead of pushing to the front or assuming the lead, Scorpio has a quiet and even secret determination that carries him gradually forward on the relentless tide of his ambition. Make no mistake, Scorpio can be dangerous; but the power that can work for evil can be turned to good and the regenerate Scorpio can soar like the Eagle (which, appropriately, is another symbol for this sign). In authority Scorpio is demanding. Capable of driving himself to the limit of endurance, he may not be aware that other people reach their limit much sooner than he does. His inability to forget an injury or slight makes him a bad enemy and woe betide the junior hoping for promotion if at some time he has blotted his copybook. Scorpio in command, then, is powerful, efficient, unmoving and often unpopular.

Sagittarius is best as leader of some flexible, light-hearted mission where intuition and dash is needed. He assumes command readily, but his love of popularity and being thought a good fellow is apt to hinder him when important issues are at stake. Just as Scorpio would ride roughshod over anyone's feelings and scorn public opinion, Sagittarius likes to please everyone. This is a charming quality, but not one that gives strength to a commander. Fortunately there are many fields where leadership is needed and in the world of philosophy, religion and adventure, Sagittarius comes into his own. Courage is not in question and Sagittarius would rather risk his own skin than send another to fight for him.

Capricorn can be rather frightening as a leader because of his lack of warmth. He gets to the top because he is one-pointed. Steady work has got him where he is and this is the quality he looks for in others. Essentially practical, no sentiment will sway his decisions. He is steely and unimaginative and not to be trifled with. Business is business.

(When other factors in the chart supply warmer qualities, Capricorn is perhaps one of the *most* valuable Signs that contribute to success in leadership or otherwise.)

Aquarius is a wilful, determined character who when he assumes leadership admits no argument. Impersonality, contrariness, are keynotes; the Aquarian is really happiest when organising some movement 'agin the government'. Leader of the Opposition, in fact.

Pisces is not a leader, and if anyone with Pisces strongly in the chart is in fact a good leader the reason for this will be found elsewhere than in the Piscean element. This gives him adaptability and the capacity to see another's point of view, which is of great value to a leader; but in isolation these are not leadership qualities.

6. THE PLANETS

My object in this section is to describe the principles of the planets, best thought of as energy factors, as they display themselves in the chart, where they will appear modified or emphasised in accordance with the individual configurations.

Working at astrology as a consultant from the personal or psychological rather than the mundane or political angle, I have found that I regard some of the planets at least as having distinct personalities. The Sun and Moon embody the principles of male and female, somewhat impersonally perhaps, and Mercury is often too elusive to capture in human form. But Venus, Mars, Jupiter and Saturn all seem to be strongly individual types whom one recognises in the moods, desires and acts of a friend, acquaintance or public figure. It is perhaps not too far-fetched to suggest that in some sense we can see ourselves or each other as ventriloquists with puppets which we animate with conviction or otherwise in as far as we are or are not at home with the character. Thus, decisive people act Mars with confidence and enthusiasm, displaying the hero, while in those who are not at home and cannot control him he becomes the bully. Even the part of Venus can be interpreted as slut or wanton by those whose affinity with her is not complete. But each one of us is called on to animate all of the characters, since all the planets are in every chart or sky picture. In a balanced performance all of them would be playing in harmony with their true nature. If our Jupiter is weak he must be rehearsed until he no longer spoils the part with ill-timed buffoonery.

A chart (see Fig. 1) gives a complete picture of planetary strengths and inter-relationships. A planet is not powerful merely by virtue of being the ruler of your Sun or Rising-sign. True, it gains prominence from this position – but if it is otherwise ill-aspected the native will feel an impulse to act in the character of the planet concerned, yet will do it without ease or confidence. Frustrations and 'complexes' arise from this situation.

What makes a planet prominent in your chart? Briefly,

(a) if it is in one of its own signs (e.g. Mars in Aries) or in a sign sympathetic to it where its energy functions easily;

77

(b) if it is rising, or near the Midheaven, or opposite either of these points;

(c) if it is the ruling planet of either the Sun-sign or the sign rising at birth;

(d) if it is strongly aspected by other planets.

Strong or weak, *all* the planets figure in *some way for each one of us.* Knowledge of their strengths and inter-relationships can give insight into our own tendencies and abilities and make us usefully aware of our impact on other people.

The following descriptions do not attempt to be comprehensive, nor do they include any reference to mundane or political astrology. Each planet represents a different energy principle which operates in modified form through the various signs, so that in practice John's Venus in Capricorn will be acted by him as quite a different character from Mary's Venus in Pisces. The following descriptions are of the unmodified ingredients.

SUN

The Sun is undoubtedly the most powerful energy factor in a chart: not surprisingly, since without the Sun life would cease so far as the Earth and the planets are concerned. This does not mean that the characteristics of the Sun-sign are the most obvious features in every horoscope. The Sun corresponds to the deeper individuality that rides through life, as it were, in the vehicle of the Ascendant sign, which very often has more to do with the appearance and physical energy expression of the person under study.

This accounts for many complexities, as can be imagined, if the deeper self of a strongly extraverted Sun seeks expression through the vehicle of a shy and introverted Ascendant sign. Indeed, it is rather as if a person who loves large, flashy motor-cars is forced to drive round in a Mini.

No single feature of the chart should be isolated from the whole, and this is especially true of the Sun. It is always important as heart and life-giver, and even if unaspected or in its so-called 'fall' (for the Sun this is Libra, opposite the Sun's 'exaltation' in Aries) or in its 'detriment' (that is, in the sign opposite the planet's own sign, which for the Sun is Aquarius – opposite Leo). This in no way implies that the native is weak or vitiated. Indeed, an over-prominent Sun with its bombast and egoism may do more to wreck a life than a so-called weak one. For if the chart as a whole is weak, the mere fact of the Sun's being in Leo will not pull it together. If the chart is strong, to have the Sun in Libra or Aquarius will not weaken it. The Sun, rather like Jupiter, emphasises. The question to ask oneself is, "What is being emphasised?" If a man is a fool, the Sun rising or overhead could make him a bigger or more prominent fool.

Many prominent figures in public life have virtually unaspected Suns. Her Majesty Queen Elizabeth II is one. Similarly many stage notabilities. These people lack neither vitality nor prominence. All of which goes to show that the Sun is not always easy to interpret. It varies, of course, with the individual, but it appears to me that many people grow more typical of their Sun-signs in maturity. In youth we are too preoccupied with our new vehicle (our Rising-sign). We hardly realise that there exists a deeper, controlling self. A soul-self, if you like.

Mystically, the Sun represents our link with this more permanent reality of the soul. It is our lifeline to higher things. At this level there is no discrimination between signs. Man is no less a part of universal life if his Sun is here or there in the Zodiac, or is well or badly aspected. All of us incarnate at different levels of evolution or soul progress, but each and every one is of importance as part of the 'whole'. The realisation of this link with totality is important as a reminder that there is no such thing as an outside, arbitrary influence that mysteriously affects humanity. Sun, Moon and planets constitute one whole; the Sun being the heart and centre, giving light and heat and *being* to the rest. Any chart that we study is not only your chart, or Mr. So-and-So's chart, it is also the chart of a moment in time. Like a photograph that records a scene for posterity, the chart crystallises the planetary pattern at birth. Such a chart may look static, but it remains forever in sensitive contact with the changing cosmic pattern, and it is the Sun, by progression throughout the life, which vitalises in turn the various planetary energies or urges, providing us with the opportunity to exercise our natal forces for good or ill.

The strength of the Sun is very evident to the astrologer in its 'bringing to life' of significant natal potentialities by progressed aspect. And it is important in this connection to remember that progressed aspects and positions of planets can never wholly be interpreted by means of a text-book, because the Sun will stimulate an *existing* trait which is not the same for one person as for another. In short, to have the progressed Sun squaring your good natal Saturn is *not* the same thing as Mr. X having the identical aspect to his 'villainous' natal Saturn. All depends on what in the basic natal chart is being activated.

Because the Sun moves at the rate of a degree a day, plus or minus a minute or so, its effect by transit is often forgotten, but it is by no means negligible and can account for the fact that certain times of the year seem to bring deaths or illness, other months seem to mark times of added energy or creative ability. It is not by chance that one's birthday is often a happy, social time when the Sun is in the degree of one's natal Sun. Social life is equally stimulated when the Sun goes over the degree of the natal Ascendant, and there is a pleasant glow of well-being. This at least, is my own experience. If one had a negatively aspected Sun or Ascendant, it could be otherwise.

Consideration of the Sun in a chart is not unlike consideration of the heart in the body. We may not have a heart strong enough to allow us to attempt climbing Everest, but it is still the most vital organ in our body. And if its possibly faulty ticking were to stop, we would cease to use our present physical vehicle. So I find it unwise and inaccurate to talk glibly of faults and failings due to the Sun being 'weak'. I cannot subscribe to the theory that the whole time the Sun is in Aquarius or Libra it is, as it were, up to no good. This is tantamount to saying that these signs are fundamentally deficient; whereas the truth is that they have their good and bad, positive and negative sides like any other sign. More – they are the poles of the signs most in accord with the Sun itself.

The poles of the signs do not work out, astrologically, in any sense of 'opposites'. The second six signs operate in a broader and less personal field than the first six, and the truer simile in terms of opposites in this connexion is 'inner and outer'. For instance, Aries is a very primary, personal sign; Libra, opposite, concerned with the partner or the 'other person'. This also applies to 'house' meanings. The first sign relates to the 1st 'house'. This is detailed in the Keywords on p. 265 in the Appendix.

A person with an overdose of Sun aspects can be overwhelmng in his impact or enthusiasm. The right amount of Sun emphasis, on the other hand, ennobles the nature. Sun-aspects, even when difficult, are action provoking, and without action there can be no results. Where fields of activity or 'houses' are concerned, it is the Sun which constitutes the most important point of emphasis.

MOON

Whenever I am asked questions about the Moon, I always take care to explain that, having the Moon in Scorpio, I am not the best person to be approached about lunar attitudes. It is a fact that most writers on astrology are pretty unflattering about this placing of the Moon.

I tend to think of the Moon in its deeper, more fundamental sense. It only shines because it reflects the light of the Sun. During its total eclipse, the Moon looks like a tired old, rotten potato hovering precariously in the sky, if you happen to see it at the right moment.

Because it has no light of its own, the Moon in the individual chart represents what we get by imitation and reflection of the moods and behaviour of those in our close environment. This is especially so in babyhood, when we are totally dependent on our mother or others for protection and sustenance.

Whereas the Sun represents our higher, soul-self, our long-term reality from before birth, during life and in our life after death, the Moon on the other hand represents the temporary expression of life on earth in the present incarnation. In its waxing and waning it can also be thought of as symbolising birth and death into and out of successive phases or incarnations.

Sun positivity and Moon negativity or *receptivity* are equally important, just as male and female are both needed to bring forth new life-forms.

It is important to remember that while we associate negativity and receptivity with femininity, there must be both positive and negative, male and female, animus and anima, in any perfect whole. A man totally lacking in caring, tender qualities is no more a perfectly integrated human being than is the woman who has no ability to cope with a crisis and deal with life's battles.

Can an experienced astrologer guess a person's Moon-sign? Not specifically, I would think. But I have in fact often guessed a person's Moon-sign by mistake when trying to guess their Sun or Ascendant signs. The Moon can stand out as a characteristic, although not necessarily the main one. Someone with the Moon in clever Gemini may not be an intellectual, yet be capable of finishing a difficult crossword puzzle in a matter of minutes.

Something in the individual's manner can indicate either the Moon-sign or a close aspect to the Moon, such as the belligerence of a close square of Mars to the Moon, or the exaggerated manner of Jupiter or the defeatism of Saturn in the same aspect.

The Moon, when not playing its feminine, tender, motherly role, has much to do with the public, as M. Gauquelin* found in his valuable research projects.

To have the Moon near the Midheaven tends to bring one to public notice, and it is a useful placing for politicians, actors, and all others who seek public recognition.

It could be said that all through life it is the Moon energy that helps us to learn by example or imitation. Notable mimics have been found to have Cancer (ruled by the Moon) rising or a strongly aspected and well-placed Moon. But for everyone, the Moon shows the interaction between us and our environment. What we get or make from school, work, people around us.

In some charts, where the Moon represents the public and is placed in the 7th 'house', the 'house' of marriage and partnership, it has been noticed that the public has taken the place of a more usual partner; being, in fact, the 'other person', i.e. not husband or wife but the audience, partner or opponent, with or against whom the person plays.

Moon-signs

Many people may not even realise that they have a Moon-sign to consider as well as a Sun-sign and Rising-sign. The reason that popular

* M. Gauquelin, *Les Hommes et les Astres* (Paris: Denoël, 1960)

astrology does not deal with Moon-signs is that it is necessary to consult the Ephemeris for the year of birth for each person. The Moon changes sign roughly every two days and is one of the many factors that account for the fact that people born within a few hours of each other have such different characteristics.

The planetary pattern for a day is almost unchanged in 24 hours. Only the Moon moves as much as 11°–14° in 24 hours; other planets cover 1° or less. (The Earth's revolution means that the Ascendant and Midheaven degrees move right round the circle every day, which is why these are the most personal degrees in the calculated chart.)

I recall a case where a client wrote of a sense of emotional restriction. This was a case where Saturnian limitation wellnigh imprisoned the Moon. I wrote that her emotions seemed to be set in concrete. (This case is also mentioned more fully in the section on Dreams, etc., Pt. III, Ch. 5, but in so far as it concerns an afflicted Moon it belongs in this section, too.) I told her, "If you can progress consciously into the mature you, seen in your Mars energy, it is evident that in time you should enjoy the physical satisfactions of sex that such a normal Mars seeks. In my view it is a question of integrating this courageous force into the rest of you and not allowing your fearful, inhibited, control-ridden Moon (which was in the same degree as Saturn) to dominate the scene. This will not be easy. No question of integration is easy when there are no lines of communication between members of a disintegrated team of energies. But the thing to remember (and this applies to all whose charts contain weak or inhibited members) is that the whole chart is YOU. Don't disown any part of yourself. Love and cherish and gradually build up any weak member as you would re-educate a weak muscle."

It is perhaps because the Moon is a relatively fast-moving factor that little happens, astrologically, without its 'permission'. It is, as it were, the mistress of the appropriate *moment* that triggers off what the more general forces manifest.

I find that the late Vernon Clark wrote to me in a letter about the Moon that "it's placement in the chart will usually indicate a point of concern to the native; or a point of itching, anxious irritation". This fits in with what I have found over many years, namely that the Moon-sign in some way portrays a main lesson of the life. To come round full circle to our earlier statement that the Moon has to do with the persona of a single life or incarnation, it is evident that this being so, the lesson or the purpose of the present incarnation would logically be found somewhere in the pattern involving the sign containing the Moon. The Sun-sign indicates what our deeper, real self is like. The Moon-sign tells us of a sign in need of perfecting or acquiring knowledge. My hunch is that it may represent a sign we have not yet mastered; and added experience of it may come through having to meet, to marry or work closely with people who are strongly of our own Moon-sign.

MERCURY

Mercury, messenger of the gods, is very important in the individual chart because its aspects from other planets show how a person reacts mentally and communicatively. But, possibly because Mercury has winged feet and gets around so fast, he himself never stays anywhere long enough to leave a personal impact.

I tend to think of Venus, Mars, Jupiter and Saturn as recognisable characters in their own right. Mercury far less so, if at all. For it is he who, by aspect, is coloured by the other energy forces. When it comes to what he says and how he says it, we can soon guess if Venus is adding charm and agreeability (by aspect to Mercury), Mars punch and pungency, Jupiter humour or exaggeration, Saturn pessimism or seriousness, Uranus brilliance or perversity, Neptune vagueness or artistry or Pluto some sudden reorientation of thought.

It is the positive planets which colour neutral-toned Mercury.

A seriously distorted Mercury can be found in the charts of handicapped children whose speech or general mobility is defective. And presumably also in the charts of criminals whose mentality is warped, although (as I discuss under Evil, pt. II, Ch. 3), a complete distortion of the Venus sense of values and lack of love can also warp the nature.

Medically, Mercury has to do with the nervous system and all the communication lines throughout the body.

A person with a strong Mercury may appear very similar to a Gemini or Virgo type (both being Mercury-ruled signs), and each of us has Mercury as the member of our team in charge of communications. If Mercury is weak or afflicted by aspect he is a rather sly member of our planetary energy group; he is quick and wants to get around, but his communications are faulty in some sense – he tells lies, or is slick or drives badly. All Mercury faults relate to the mind or communicating.

In misuse, Mercurial activation can be apparent in a sort of intellectual congestion, in psychosomatic troubles. Typical of its exaggerated expression are the kind of people who get described as being 'too clever by half'. The adjective 'mercurial' has passed into the language, so there is really no need to labour the point of what a Mercury person is like. But study of the individual Mercury in a chart will show, even for a new-born baby, if the child will grow up to acquire facility of speech, agility of mind or body, grace of expression or the reverse. Travel and knowledge both come under this planet, but it is difficult to foresee whether Mercury aspects will work out in terms of travel of mind or body or even the lines of communication within the body.

It puzzles astrologers and those who have some ability to read charts, when seemingly strong potentials and talents are unfulfilled. If it is the case that a talent remains uncommunicated – a considerable talent, possibly – this may be accountable for by a faulty Mercury. A singer needs more than musical talent; the song has to be sung. Poetical thoughts need to be written down if they are to establish the person as a poet. The rudeness and ungraciousness of a difficult Mercury can offend those who would otherwise be helpful.

So, just as Mercury can serve or hinder the talent, the planet Mercury and the 6th 'house' of the chart, which is much linked with it, has to do with service and those who work for you and your attitude to them. And here may I point out that understanding of the chart and its planetary energies must include a two-way approach, for the good or ill in any field of activity can be active or passive. Your 'rude' Mercury may mean that it is you who can be unpleasant. But it can also be that you are at the receiving end.

VENUS

Venus is the first of the planets to be considered as a personality in her own right. Why do I say this? Because the Sun and Moon are basic, and Mercury in a special sense is neutral, in that Mercury, or the mentality, is modified by another planet which is itself unchanged by contact from Mercury.

At her best I see Venus as the goddess of beauty and love. Like a lovely woman entering a room, she brings a special aura or fragrance with her and so influences or even transforms her surroundings. And so in the chart it is not fanciful to consider Venus as a personality, with a positive influence on the planets she contacts.

When assessing the natal chart, the astrologer looks to Venus to show the capacity of the native to make friends or enemies and to attract or repel others in intimate relationships. When comparing the charts of two people in love, one likes to find the true love of Venus figuring in the comparison.

A strong Venus occurs when the Sun or Ascendant are either in Taurus or in Libra, making her the ruling planet. This does not, however, guarantee a beautiful or harmonious nature. Venus can be shrewish in a quiet, insidious way, and if it is this sort of Venus, mean-spirited or afflicted, which is prominent, the astrologer can fall into considerable error if he relies on an idealised textbook description.

How then should Venus be assessed? I suggest that first of all it should be decided, on the basis of sign-placing or angularity, if the Venusian urge or potential is strong. Having decided this, pass to consideration of aspects and judge if it is an attractive Venus that is in a position to make her mark or an unattractive one. Or, indeed, is it a sluttish one? For Venus can be indolent about anything except her outward appearance. When I was describing the afflicted qualities of Venus to a Nursing Sister, she remarked, "I know the type well. In hospital we called them 'Mink coat and dirty stays!'" For stays, now obsolete, read any concealed garment.

In addition to the potential for forming relationships, and being diplomatic or artistic, Venus, as the ruler of Taurus and the 2nd 'house', has a strong bearing on the attitude to money. The 1st 'house', of the chart represents the native himself. The 2nd represents everything that he accrues or draws to himself, and the primitive possessiveness of Taurus covers a wide field. A primitive Taurus/Venus attitude, whether applied to people, to belongings or to gold, is possessive: "I love it, it's mine!" or "I love him, he's mine!"

Venus, when unafflicted, is deliciously light-hearted and charming, and I am not suggesting that Venus herself when in the 2nd 'house' of the chart, adds to possessiveness – for indeed the contrary is the case, and a well-aspected Venus here gives a generous and light-hearted attitude to finance. The native likes to aquire beautiful objects while avoiding financial considerations. Such a woman does best as the wife of a rich man.

All planets function best through signs where they feel at home. They function ill in alien surroundings. Venus is least happy in the critical signs. After all, as the hymn says, "Love is meek and sees no wrong". Working through the hypercritical signs of Virgo and Scorpio, Venus sees plenty wrong in those she loves, and artistically this blend is the natural perfectionist.

Venus is an important facet in our nature, being the principle we summon when we wish to be agreeable, to please, to love or to beautify. How far we succeed depends on the initial strength of our personal Venus in sign or 'house', and to what extent this planetary energy is fortified, weakened, ennobled or distorted by aspect.

An easy method of checking the effect of Venus on your life (although you may need to ask the help of a friendly astrologer) is to see what happens if it is shown in the Ephemeris to be hovering exactly in the degree of the Sun, Ascendant or other sensitive point in your chart. This is called a transit of Venus. Much depends on what sort of a Venus it is natally. If you personally have a fine capacity for love or other Venusian pursuits, the transit will be agreeable. Less so if such capacities are limited. Even the quickest transit of Venus over, say, your Sun, can correspond to a pleasantly social day, or with a telephone call that makes you feel loved or appreciated. Or you may buy yourself a treat. Beauty or affection will figure; or money. A sense of feeling loved is typical of a Venus transit at its best. "Everyone loves me and I'm beautiful," as a friend of mine put it.

But even a good Venus cannot compensate entirely for basic coldness and inadequacy. And it must be remembered that everyone has Venus somewhere, just as everyone has all the planets and all the signs, in different emphasis.

The basic sense of values has to do with Venus; so has the emotional life and therefore if there are difficult aspects to this planet in the natal chart, it is certain that when such aspects are activated in future years there will arrive some test in the emotional life. It doesn't at all mean that such a person will suffer emotionally all the time.

It is difficult to write of Venus attributes except as feminine. In a man's chart it has to do with his very necessary feminine side (not in the sense of effeminacy). The strength or weakness of his 'anima' in the Jungian sense is shown in the chart as a whole. If Venus and the Moon are in masculine signs and the gentler Water-signs have few occupants, a man will be in danger of lacking tenderness and understanding of women. A woman with the same lack could have an over-active animus or masculine attributes.

Venus exactly rising adds sweetness or charm, even through a cold or detached sign. Venus likes to agree and to please people; although not, perhaps, to the extent of taking life over-seriously.

MARS

When it comes to Mars, it is easy to see why the planets have been deified as distinct personalities. In order to understand astrology, it is highly necessary to recognise each planetary energy; and to do this one should think about each in isolation. Mars in this sense is a vivid, battling, courageous personality. While remembering that each person is born with a team of all the planets somewhere in the chart, and, like the manipulator of a puppet show, has to learn to display each one to advantage in its own role, it will be found that an over-strong Mars is liable to steal the scene. He may be the strong-armed hero or the villain, dagger in hand – but in one role or another he will push his way to the front.

Mars is especially strong working through his own sign of Aries or Scorpio, or when he is placed on an angle (near to or opposite the Ascendant or Midheaven), or if he is the ruler of the chart, which happens if Aries or Scorpio is the Rising-sign, or if the Sun is in one of these two signs.

A strong Mars is a force for good or evil. All planets are best thought of as energy factors, but Mars indicates the main energy potential; the ability to take the initiative or to react well in a crisis. But sheer strength is not all, and it depends on the remainder of the chart where or how the energy is directed.

In a material world, the power to accomplish a task is of value; so is the battling Mars spirit that copes joyously with opposition. I would stress, therefore, that while an excess of Martian aggression is unattractive, a complete lack of it may be as bad. Thus in assessing the ability of the individual to fulfil a potential or talent, we may go astray if we assess ability by other indications, such as musicality or artistry, and fail to note that the Mars driving force is too weak to allow of sustained effort.

Mars traits are in many respects the counterpart of Venus ones. Where Venus placates, Mars enjoys a fight. In conversation Mars finds the points of difference where Venus sees similarity. Venus equates with the abiding love of the heart; Mars symbolises transient, carnal love. Mars is physical, and while afflicted Venus types lack true affection or don't want it, an afflicted Mars misuses (or lacks) sexual potency.

It is a fairly straightforward matter to assess potential strength. It is less easy to assess the actual ability to make the most of a basic urge. For example, a person with Mars powerful in Aries is potentially a fighter, but an aspect from Saturn may so limit strength or health that in actual fact the fighting urge is thwarted. In this case there is more complexity and inner struggle than if the inhibited Mars were in gentler Virgo, when the native might be happy in a sedentary occupation, felt by Aries to be frustrating.

Martian faults spring from misapplication of energy or from impatience. An inadequate Mars, however, shows in lack of guts and initiative.

Mars is termed a malefic. It is a potentially violent energy which is dangerous when allied with the energy of other planets. Jupiter in aspect with Mars blends exaggeration with Martian heat; the result is uncommon strength, exaggerated enthusiasm or temper. Uranus, at best sudden and explosive, only needs the fire of Mars to produce the bang. Neptune, mystical but sensational, can be energised by Mars to good work, or be degraded into sordidness or active escapism. Saturn's one-pointedness can be turned by Mars into calculated cruelty, although this combination *can* also lead to a constructive use of channelled energy.

Without enough Mars there is too little fight in the nature. No ability to cope. A good Mars adds that little bite: humour, satire or salt. A bad Mars can be just violent.

Mars energy is easily recognisable in the person who always has to 'do something about it'. He can't let things be. He or she will never concede a point. "I can't *not* argue when I *know* I'm right". Multiplied, it is this sentiment that prolongs war. Mars was the god of war, and it is when the Mars counterpart in man is stimulated that wars break out.

Regardless of the femininity of the Rising-sign, a person with Mars rising has courage and initiative. There is no squeamishness, no prudery. Mars has a broadening effect. Indeed, when Mars rises, the impression may be of Aries or Scorpio being strong in the chart. I have a small Cairn terrier who has Mars rising in independent, contrary Aquarius. What does he do? He barks and nearly bites when people *leave* the house.

While Mars rising can increase the impact, regardless of sign, the impact is diminished if Mars (especially when the ruling planet) is in a gentle sign. Mars in Pisces can put its energy into matters such as hospitals, healing or anaesthetics. In any Water-sign, the same energy may be expressed in one of the water-sports, ski-ing or skating. Mars in

Gemini or Virgo puts energy or even fighting ability into communications. In these signs the battles of life, via Mars, will be verbal.

The small boys with violent cutting urges will be found to have an excess of Mars energy. This should be educated rather than repressed. Such a boy may be a potential carpenter or surgeon. In the charts of two doctor friends of mine born on the same day in the same year but at different times of day, the surgeon had Mars rising, the psychologist, Venus.

But do not imagine that if you were not born in a Mars-ruled sign, i.e. Aries or Scorpio, Mars had quietly disappeared from the sky at your birth moment. All planets have significance for all people. Strength or weakness is equally informative to the astrologer. I hear people say, "I'm a Libran, so Venus is *my* planet," rather hinting that they can't possibly have any of those rude Mars urges or aggressions. How wrong they are. The main emphasis of the chart may be right away from what is thought of as 'their' sign or planet.

An average Mars, when activated by progression, will show in increased initiative or energy. In a young person it may mark the beginning of the active sex life. In later life it may give the energy to tackle a project that has lain fallow.

In a vicious person, it may be found that a combination of calculating coolness with cutting Mars is behind his purposeful and deliberate cruelty.

I have already told you about an unaspected Mercury. The following remark was made to me by a client with an unaspected Mars. "I don't like the world. Indeed I have been accused of going through life with one eye closed: to man's inhumanity to man; violence; injustice; corruption; cynicism. How *can* one successfully compromise one's ideal world with the one around us?"

The psychologist astrologer would be interested. To have one eye closed to life is surely indicative of a lack of integration, and corresponds to a failure to co-ordinate one of the planetary energies with the rest of the team.

JUPITER

The picture we form of Jupiter is of someone a bit larger than life. A jovial, kindly person, but one whose friendly slap on the back nearly knocks us over. Jupiter belongs among the gods, and when he descends too far into matter, he is apt to perpetrate jokes that are not in the best of good taste. Think of Leda and Europa. Jupiter should stick to the heights. His expansion in religion, philosophy or philanthropy is admirable. At lower levels he becomes the buffoon.

Jupiter is strong in a chart if he is to be found near the Ascendant or Midheaven or in one of his own signs, i.e. Sagittarius or Pisces, or if he is in close aspect to the Sun or Moon or ruling planet.

Unlike Mars or Saturn, a strong Jupiter is never a force for evil. But it is a great mistake to think that because he is termed 'the greater benefic', he can be relied on to produce prosperity, good luck or benevolence. What he *can* be relied on to do is to expand or exaggerate an existing situation. In the individual chart, therefore, if Jupiter is rising, the personality is magnified; but (as is also the case when the Sun is rising) it is necessary to study the complete chart to see what kind of a personality is to function with this increased impact. If the chart shows a generous noble or talented individual, then the accentuation of the rising Jupiter will help him to shine forth beneficently or to demonstrate some talent. If the chart shows mediocrity and insensitivity, then Jupiter will descend to his lowest as a loud-voiced outsize bore; possibly kindly and well-meaning, but a bore none the less. It is like looking at something under a magnifying glass. Unless it is worthy of study, it doesn't improve by being enlarged.

In his researches, Michel Gauquelin (see page 91) found that Jupiter angular (near the Ascendant or Midheaven) is found in the charts of people who enjoy the limelight. Actors, comedians, or just the ebullient types in many a profession; extraverts, 'good sports' and so forth.

It does not happen to everyone, even in the progressed chart, that any outstanding activation of Jupiter occurs during a lifetime. But if your natal Jupiter is well placed or prominent in some way, it is certain that when the Sun progresses to a strong aspect of its natal degree, that period in the life will be a time of maximum expansion or exaggeration. Exactly what form the expansion will take depends on the natal chart. Jupiter natally in the sociable sign of Libra, in the part of the chart to do with friends or groups, when activated by the Sun, could being a time of increased friendship or joining clubs or groups and/or meeting important and helpful people. If natally in another part of the chart, in another sign, the expansion would vary accordingly. If the natal Jupiter is badly aspected or excessive, activation of it will also be excessive or extravagant.

Humour is a Jovian quality. In excess it may manifest in a loud or irritating laugh. Over-generosity is an admirable trait, you might say, but less so if it leads to domestic chaos, as in the case of a man who is broke through standing treat to all and sundry. Jupiter at his worst spends his money to no profit. The buffoon, the playboy, the back-slapping hearty, the unfulfilled comedian belong to that category.

It is difficult to live up to the best of Jupiter, because the best is so very good. Nobility, justice, kindness, truth – he represents all the qualities that should be aspired to in maturity. And in fact, maturity is the period in life governed by Jupiter, when the active Martian phase has borne fruit.

Jupiter's tremendous energy was found by Professor Thomaschek to contribute to dangerous energy imbalance at times of earthquakes, so forget the idea that Jupiter unfailingly brings luck or happiness. If you are a reckless type, a Jupiter transit may spur you on to some excess which will not be fortunate at all. On the other hand, a good Jupiter is associated with benefit and protection or preservation. In short, it is intrinsically far from evil, but if there is danger around, Jupiter can provide the extra energy that triggers off or exaggerates what is going on.

Jupiter is the greatest of all the planets – a huge energy; and all energies are complex and all are subject to misuse. Jupiter in misuse can account for the social wreck, simply because at best Jupiter is sociable and friendly, the other side of the coin being the person who eats and drinks excessively and persuades others to do the same. An unfulfilled Jupiter can give rise to a guilt complex born of disharmony in group relationships, whereas a good Jupiter helps the preservation of human activities through friendship.

Jove and Jupiter are two names for the same god and there is no need to underline the word 'joviality'. The man who cannot make use of his Jupiter-side will be dull, morose, pessimistic and lacking in humour and tolerance. Thus of all the planets this is one that it is most desirable to have in good balance.

SATURN

Saturn is thought of too often as the bringer of trouble, delay, restriction and frustration, yet to be lacking in Saturnian energy would be to lack control . . . a car without an adequate braking system . . . a balloon with no ballast . . . a house with no utility room. These are different ways of expressing the lack of a very necessary member of our planetary team.

Troubles and complexities in the individual life often spring from an inability to say no or to apply the brakes.

Saturn is very much connected with solid achievements; with materiality and the productive work that goes to build the restraining walls and the mountains of concrete that present-day mankind chooses to build. The very descent of the soul into material life is a descent into Saturnian restrictions and limitations. But while some people resent limitations and duties, others, the naturally Saturnian types, and/or those with good aspects to this planet, are conscientious. They welcome law and order and productivity.

The astrologer when studying progressions for a client, will find that a helpfully Saturnian patch will coincide with finishing a job or perhaps bringing out the book or selling the picture that has been inspired during a less solid but more imaginative Neptunian period. He can suggest to the client that he make use of productive times to suit a prevailing energy factor, in order to go with the tide rather than struggle obstinately against it.

Personally I achieved no public standing until my fifties when the progressed Sun reached a degree exactly sextile (a good aspect), both the natal degree of my Saturn and Midheaven. Saturn has to do with old age and the Midheaven is often known as the career point. Very appropriate. A good natal aspect from Saturn to this career point suggests achievement latish in life.

Saturn has to do with hard work and with basics. Digging, putting down roots, spadework, all that sort of thing. Nothing easy about Saturn. And so its placing in the chart shows in what field of activity work will be taken on, inhibitions or phobias met with. According to the tone of the chart as a whole, Saturn indicates the lessons of the life, whether these are met with positively in productive, responsible work or negatively in sorrows, burdens, disabilities and restrictions.

Saturnian energy can manifest in controlled usefulness or in cold, calculated cruelty or harsh severity. But no two people feel serious or even severe or cautious about the same things, and only the complete analysis of the whole chart will throw light.

At this point I considered going right through the 'houses' and describing how Saturn might manifest through the different fields of activity. But as I looked through hundreds of charts of people well known to me, I found that, as always, generalisation would be misleading and possibly alarming. Saturn at his callous worst is so unpleasant and at his reliable best so valuable that it is truest to say that Saturn represents the *serious factor* in everyone, and therefore each person has some lesson to learn through Saturn. If your Saturn is weak, the lesson may be to find out for yourself that it is dangerous to race through life with no brakes or self-control. If Saturn is strong, you may have to cultivate tolerance and recognise that while you have an inborn sense of timing, responsibility and punctuality, the other person may be differently constituted.

Your ideas on punishment reflect your Saturn just as another person's reflect *his*. To have Saturn in the 12th 'house' (which has to do with prisons and institutions) could make the individual feel, as I quote in the section about children, that if a child is naughty, the remedy is to lock him up . . . and so on.

My search through charts shows that Saturn near the Ascendant or Midheaven is found in prominent people with a strong sense of duty or dedication to work. Michel Gauquelin in his massive researches found scientists and doctors to have this placing of Saturn.* This is very fitting. But it is the inner, psychological attitude to career or public service that really counts. And while Queen Elizabeth II is no scientist, she is certainly a dedicated holder of her high office. President John Kennedy was another such person. Sir Edmund Hilary and Yehudi Menuhin also belong to this category.

If, in your astrological work, there is some block in your client owing to the severity or cruelty (past or present) of some relative or person in

* *The Spheres of Destiny* (Dent, 1980).

authority, this would surely be discovered by a medical practitioner or psychologist. An astrologer of good standing could be of value in setting up the comparison of the client's chart with that of the person responsible for the emotional block, and considerable light would be thrown on the quality of the experience that proved so traumatic. The value to the adult still suffering from the memory of a severe parent can be considerable if he or she is shown the whole chart of the seemingly terrifying, unreasonable character; and is then able to see him or her as human after all, with faults, virtues, strengths and weaknesses. And more than this, the mutual links can show how qualities in the one triggered off bullying traits in the other.

I am sure that full chart comparisons would reveal that in certain cases recipients of violence have some quality that brings out violence in the attacker.

Saturnian faults can be mistaken for Capricorn characteristics and vice versa. The faults of both are unattractive, and a lot of gloomy things are written about them. But the truth is that successful people need ingredients which make them coolly competent, one-pointedly determined and a tower of strength to their colleagues. It is only in misuse or negativity that these same energies can prove ruthless, calculating, pessimistic and as hard as nails. There are two sides to every coin.

A slow moving transit or 'Station' of Saturn (see Glossary), when the planet appears to hover for days or weeks in a single degree will hit off, shall we say, my own, or maybe your, obstinate and determined Taurean Sun. This means that at the same time it will hit off the obstinate trait in humanity's millions of tough Taurus types, not to mention that when in this position it will also be opposite Scorpio and square to the other tough 'fixed' types – Leo and Aquarius. And who can be more difficult and tough than the 'fixed' sign people when they so determine? Admittedly they can determine to be useful or good, sometimes. But at times of strikes and unrest one can imagine that many leaders must be 'fixed' sign people whom the passage of cold-hearted Saturn makes doubly cold, doubly determined to get their own way.

What can the astrologer say when he sees something heavily Saturnian looming up for a client?

I can only tell you what *I* say if I see heaviness and frustration ahead. If I think the particular individual could take a whimsical idea, I tell him to think of himself as a knight in armour going out to meet a dragon. He is not bound to be killed by the dragon, but it is a time of extreme opportunity. Even so, the dragon *will be there* in some form. I think it ethically wrong to think up some specific trouble, even if circumstances point to one, as in long years of consultancy I have learned that for the most part the expected doesn't happen. Saturn delays and hinders, or quite simply burdens, by hard work. The best thing to do is to be prepared for this and not expect everything to go ahead at full speed. Just exactly what will constitute the hindrance is best not guessed at. But I would advise the young astrologer against suggesting that difficulties ahead can be avoided. Suggest rather to prepare for a slower tempo.

In a natal chart, in the case of twins or those born a few minutes apart, if Saturn is exactly on an angle for one and not for the other, the former will be the more serious in personality or in choice of career. Should the other have Venus or Jupiter angular, the difference in temperament can be heightened, in spite of other identical factors in the chart, and identical home background in the case of twins.

Troubles come in patches. I often get asked how best to overcome such periods. My answer sounds like preaching, but the way to come through times of difficulty is to meet each successive blow with acceptance and without resentment and use your battling spirit to keep courageous and cheerful. I know this is easier for some temperaments than others, but in the long run it is *not what happens to us that matters, but how we react to events.*

It is a moot point how far astrological advice should be followed, if at all. I try *not* to advise. But much depends on the seriousness of the situation on which advice is requested. I like to think it is comfort rather than advice that is sought. To talk over a problem with an unbiased listener can be of value.

At one time I had clients abroad who travelled to Europe every few years, and at their request I picked what looked like the most trouble-free month for the holiday. Who wants a holiday with delays, set-backs, missed connections, lost luggage, hi-jackings? There is something to be said for planning times of enjoyment during relatively trouble-free periods. But, in general, life has to be coped with during times of frustration, and we cannot avoid bother just because we know it is in the offing. The astrologer would have to be very clairvoyant to say precisely what form the trouble will take. Strong forces can affect people actively or passively, Saturnian limitation can manifest in a broken leg (physical) or a deep depression (emotional). Or again, your sorrow may be concern for another person.

It is the fashion nowadays to protect people from shocks, and astrological textbooks follow the fashion. I have a book by one Sepharial, published in 1833, which has no such inhibitions. It tells me that afflictions involving Saturn under certain circumstances bring accidents by being crushed or buried alive, while the same aspect from Mars brings violent diseases and pestilential complaints. There is plenty about evil, violence and sudden death! These days more common sense is used. Saturn *is* the limiting factor, but even in bad aspect it is unlikely to cause wholesale death by crushing. That might happen in earthquakes or in one extreme instance, but life is not only experienced in physical events. We talk of circumstances weighing like a 'ton of bricks'. When the difficulty passes we say 'a weight has lifted'. One reason why it is impossible to generalise about Saturn is that its energy can operate so differently in extreme cases. In your own chart or in any chart Saturn could be described in several ways. It could be –

1. Strongly beneficial, by placing and aspect
2. Strongly adverse, by placing and aspect
3. Functioning weakly, by placing and aspect

For example (any planetary energy can be over-emphasised or under-emphasised):

1. A 'good' Saturn working through its own sign or one congenial to it, and rendered less alarmingly cold and efficient by being in a chart that has warmth and geniality . . .

This person has a well-developed sense of duty or civic sense. He or she is reliable and thorough. Punctuality is a strong point. He doesn't waste his time and has consideration for that of others. He does his best at any task and expects others to do the same. For him, life is important, because it gives a chance to achieve something of value, and he doesn't grumble if the struggle is uphill, as he feels that effort makes a job all the more worth while. He is careful and considerate; sensible with money, and has dignity. He or she can say 'No' with firmness.

2. A 'bad' Saturn strongly placed and with no redeeming aspects . . .

The person (male or female) with such a Saturn could well be cold and stern, or worse still, callous. There is a streak of the Victorian parent in him. He is not merely punctual, he is tyrannised by the clock, and woe betide latecomers to his table as meals are prepared and served on the dot. Latecomers get it cold or not at all. Enjoyment is suspect, and he pours cold water on young people who in his eyes 'live for pleasure'. To such a person morality is something that follows strictly defined rules. He has no pity for sinners, but if he himself inflicts excessive punishment (mental or physical) he finds moral justification for his conduct. Here we have a ruthless Saturn.

I have in front of me the chart of a murderer which has the dangerous combination of a strong need for sex and sensation, but these exaggerated impulses go unchecked by Saturn. The Saturnian brakes are not lacking, but are applied to what should be energies for good: those which enrich relationships and humanitarian instincts. Furthermore, difficulties involving the pliable, easily led Mutable signs weaken his ability to resist temptation and bad advice.

This murderer's Saturn puts the brakes on only where they should not be applied. He has no trouble in switching off kindness, true love, generosity, but has no means of controlling his wildest impulses, which include eccentric and perverse sexual violence.

He does not quite fall into any of my three categories, which are intended for more normal types, but he is nearest to the following one . . .

94

3. This type lacks all ability to put on the brakes and is swung in all directions with no powers of self-control to protect him. He (or, of course, she) cannot say 'no' and is his own worst enemy, as well as a menace to those who are only too ready to follow the lead of one who preaches that 'nothing matters'. Being without brakes, he only too often comes to a stop against a brick wall or in a ditch. He complains bitterly that life is against him, but the truth is that he lacks direction and invites trouble in his aimless drifting from one thing to another.

People talk of being born under an unlucky star, but no planet or constellation is lucky or unlucky in itself. The first represents an energy, and the second the modifying channel through which the energy operates. Obviously some combinations are happier than others.

The chronically unfortunate person will, on study of the natal chart, be found to have some highly tense or restrictive arrangement of planets. It is the placing and grouping of different energies that are informative. A weak or badly aspected Saturn exactly rising (and so conjunct the precisely calculated Ascendant) certainly limits or inhibits the personality. It can only be in this position for a very few minutes, which explains why one twin may be afflicted and the other live a useful life. If Saturn is in closely difficult aspect to, say, the Sun, Moon or Ascendant at birth, the native will be put through it one way or another. He may as well accept that he must work hard and condition himself to set-backs. But this very process can make a finer man or woman than uninterrupted good fortune. Saturnian lessons are not to be shirked. Those for whom reincarnation is an accepted fact will see in the Saturn picture the indication of what has to be taken seriously. A heavy Saturn may correspond to a phobia. Why a phobia? Because there is an unconsious memory of a past event in early life or even a former life when he (in different guise) created this pattern. For all of us it may be that in this present life we endure troubles passively or through circumstances engendered by others. But until we have in some way adjusted the scales and paid the debt, there will the painful pattern remain, a part of us.

We hate or fear faults in others that we recognise unconsciously as something we personally need to overcome. Our own critical or irritable reactions may be a useful signal that a quality *in us* is manifesting in response to a particular stimulus. So it can be said that the Saturnian guilt/fear makes us alive to certain signals, and we can, if we will, make progress in overcoming the tendency in ourself that is, as it were, triggered off by particular annoyances.

Suspicion is a very Saturnian fault and is an indication that we are still capable of what we suspect; or at least have been so in a life which resonates to the present one, and that we are in the process of adjusting, characterwise.

The Extra-Saturnians – new age energies, Uranus, Neptune and Pluto, are known as the Extra-Saturnian planets because until the year 1781, when

Uranus was discovered by the astronomer Herschel, the planet Saturn was the outermost planet in the Solar System known to man. Neptune, still further out, was discovered by Adams and Verrier in 1846 and Pluto, even more distant, was discovered by the Lowell Observatory in Arizona in 1930.

Before writing of each of these three in turn, there is something to be said about them, along with any more that may shortly be discovered, as a group on their own. In thinking of the various planetary energies as furnishing the 'rooms of the mind', I used to think of these Extra-Saturnian planets as too remote and impersonal to come under this 'room' concept. Latterly, however, I have come to think of the Extra-Saturnian energies too in this way, as important 'rooms' which must be furnished; partly by the mind and in part by the Higher Mind. No rooms of the mind should be untended or empty. Nature abhors a vacuum and it is highly dangerous to allow haphazard occupation of the Uranus, Neptune or Pluto spaces of our individual dwelling.

The Neptunian room is particularly open to chaos and occupation by undesirable entities if we have not, by long habit of light-producing meditation, filled it with nobler denizens. (Here I would draw an analogy with what the late Tudor Pole called the seven facets of the mind. In his valuable book, *The Silent Road*,* he talked of Facets A to G: ABC being wholly the brain of man, D a connecting link, and E, F and G unrecognised factors except in rare souls. I am suggesting that Uranus, Neptune and Pluto can be thought of as corresponding to Tudor Pole's E, F and G.)

In the present New Age, and since the discovery of Uranus, certain pioneering souls – souls in the vanguard of the human race, the mystics and leaders of thought – have incarnated with these rooms already furnished. This must always have been the case with leaders of thought. At present it is noticeable in certain children as a heightened awareness or sensitivity.

This 'room' concept is only partially valid. We need a strong team of the more basic planetary energies to control what goes on in the upper rooms of the mind. An individual with too little Saturnian control or ballast, and too much Neptune, will be in danger of floating along on waves of psychic bliss or in fogs of psychic illusion.

Before the discovery of the Extra-Saturnian planets, Saturn was the most distant of the known planets. It represented the containing box of materialism into which mankind incarnated. Its fall from precedence as the ultimate authority is reflected in the permissive age and the diminished respect shown to 'establishment' rule. Uranus, Neptune and Pluto take humanity out of the confines of Saturnian discipline into disciplines that are less personal and less obvious. Established authority, as of the Church, the Army and the State, is superseded at best by those

* Neville Spearman, 1960.

who develop a higher awareness and inner knowledge, at worst by rebels and mindless drop-outs. Uranus can span the octave from brilliant awareness down to destructive anarchy. Neptune's octave is from spiritual heights down into mindless escapism, into the drink, drug or sensation scene. Pluto contains all the wonders of technology together with the frightening capacity to destroy the planet.

All three Extra-Saturnians help man to transcend the lower self, the ego, and to emerge from the safe, familiar box. Once we rope in our higher faculties, the Uranus, Neptune and Pluto energies, we can fly; we are 'winged'. While Saturn dominates, there is imprisonment in orthodoxy. Neptune is the dissolver, the universal solvent of the alchemists. And yet to rush into using these more way-out faculties without enough Saturnian common sense will lead to chaos. We all know of the inventions of the last hundred years. But as well as these outward and visible evidences of Uranian thought, there has to be an awakening in the consciousness of man.

Before planets are actually discovered by astronomers, they would seem to represent an unawakened potential, unawakened, that is, except in the rare, pioneering soul. A Pythagoras, a Leonardo, or Paracelsus. One of the qualities of Uranus is the capacity for being different, sudden, rebellious, avant-garde . . . able, in short, to stand out against general, stick-in-the-mud opinions and say – "I have invented a steam engine; an iron ship – a submarine – anaesthetics – or a way of going to the Moon."

That such inventions and thousands more are virtually commonplace feats of the modern mind is a demonstration of the enhanced brilliance and consciousness of the Extra-Saturnian energies which have lifted such a proportion of mankind into the New Age.

URANUS *in the individual chart*

Uranus is the planet of sudden disruption, unorthodoxy and eccentricity. The person with Uranus strongly placed, and especially when close to the Ascendant or Midheaven degree, likes to be unusual. This may take the form of exceptional talent and awareness. But at worst there will be an urge to shock and disrupt. Uranus is an unpredictable force.

Being unpredictable, the astrologer cannot be other than uncertain as to what form the disruption will take if it is in the offing. But it is a fact that Uranus is most obligingly punctual in its effects. Uranus stays for seven years in a sign so its leisurely passage over a sensitive degree of a chart makes itself felt. Try asking someone, "What happened to you on such and such a date, when Uranus was in X degrees Scorpio, right on your Sun?" Being a cagey and secretive Scorpio you may not be told much, but with franker signs activated you will get a positive statement in most cases.

A favourite elderly professor client of mine, who comes regularly to chat about his chart, jotted in his notebook what I had mentioned, that Uranus would be right on his Sun during his holiday in August. "What will that mean?" "I haven't the slightest idea. Uranus is highly unpredictable, but he is punctual and tends to be disruptive. So sit loosely in the saddle because what you think is going to happen probably won't." "Can't you tell me a bit more?" "No, absolutely not. I'm just sticking to keywords. Disruption and/or surprise." I got a letter from him at the end of August. "Dear Ingrid, You couldn't have been more right. We were in our car on our way to the North of Scotland and at our night's stop – where I had arranged to pick up messages – there was a telegram saying my brother had died in Iran. We had to turn smartly round and cope with business in London before attending the funeral."

The professor stressed that it was in fact a disruption rather than a tragedy because he had been on pretty distant terms with this brother.

This is just a single instance of how Uranus by transit over a sensitive degree in your chart is always interesting. Why? Largely because it takes eighty-four years to complete the circle, and in these days this is roughly a lifetime. At any rate, what is certain is that few would experience a second time round of its attentions. Uranus has been called the 'Awakener', and I have observed that its passage through a sign or 'house' galvanises the activities or emotions to do with the relevant parts of the chart under consideration.

The action of Uranus has been shown to be surprising, sudden and unexpected. Alan Leo, the Theosophist astrologer, wrote that Uranus "as the great Regenerator, tries every soul who is aspiring to rise above the senses, and may be said to be the greatest enemy of feelings when they are made too personal or purely selfish".

I am sure that this is true, but it is certainly not necessary to be working or thinking at a high level of consciousness to feel the effects of a Uranus transit. Disruption or shock can be felt at any level, and as Uranus has quite a lot to do with sex, it is surely having a high old time in this permissive age. A transit of this planet over any sensitive point in your chart will be felt as in some way involving change. Change of the whole life-style, maybe, a feeling of high tension, financial changes, mental reorientation, sexual activation, there is no set answer.

The late Charles E. O. Carter, whose books on astrology are known to all serious students, used to say he could 'feel' Uranus around if it was on any of his planetary degrees. So can I – and it is the oddest feeling. If it is in the degree of my Mercury or Venus (and possibly on other planets) I feel tensed up as if I've said the wrong thing to someone. Most uncomfortable! As I have Uranus squaring my Sun natally, albeit widely, this planet has a bearing on the less admirable, impulsive or eccentric sides of my own nature. So, by my own theories, the more I can transmute and *use* my Uranus energy as it is meant to be used, in New Age thought and constructive work, helping others towards increased awareness, the more I shall make it possible to experience a transit of Uranus that makes me feel blissful . . . or at least constructively highly charged and not tense. I am old enough to have proved the validity of Uranus transists round three-quarters of my chart along with a major activation of my planetary energies, and I can assure you that if you are looking for a reliable indicator of seven-year phases, you should check the passage of Uranus through your own signs and 'houses'. What you find will depend, of course, on the position at the same time of other factors, such as the progressed Moon, for example, which also accentuates matters related to the sign and 'house' through which it is passing, and many other possibilities arising through general progressions and transits. But I can assure you that in broad outline, this Uranian stimulation as it travels just once round your chart, can be observed to do its work as Awakener or, at its lowest, as disrupter. If you aware of its passage and co-operate, you will find that much will happen to stimulate your inner life and awareness, possibly at the same time that disruptions happen over which you have no control, as was the case with my friend the professor.

The student should check especially for its passage over the Sun, Moon, the angles, and important planetary groupings; also Trines, T-squares, etc.: wherever it touches off more than one planet at a time owing to their being in the same degree of different signs. When this happens, a high tension state may be experienced and it can be helpful to know the time factor involved, when it intensifies trouble or emotions.

It is obvious to any trained astrologer that the effect of Uranus or indeed the activation of any planetary energy will depend on how it is placed and aspected natally. Ask yourself, when Uranus is activating the Sun or whatever it may be, "Is this Uranus a rebellious, off-at-a-tangent energy or is it a valuable, aware, New Age factor that is about to stimulate this individual?" Because according to what Uranus is *in the pattern under consideration*, so will it operate in the particular life, until the owner of the chart takes his Uranus energy in hand. If the individual encourages it to be disruptive, compulsively sexy, overcharged with high tension or whatever the habit pattern dictates – so will it continue.

Can the average human being use his Uranus energies? At a controlled level it takes a rational, thinking person to channel the brilliance and magnetism of Uranus, and the danger is that a strong Uranus energy will be expressed in rebellion and going off at a tangent. I find that good aspects between Uranus and Mercury occur in the charts of clever people, and that in otherwise well-aspected charts even a so-called 'bad' aspect can add to brilliance . . . but tension is heightened, and children with Mercury square Uranus tend to whine.

I would say, then, that Uranus, unless good mental foundations are laid, is subject to misuse and eccentricity. At best the power works in raising the consciousness and awareness. At worst it seems to correspond to an incapacity to relate harmoniously.

NEPTUNE *in the individual chart*

The Neptune energy is that force in man which seeks escape, either upwards or downwards. Escape can be through the upliftment which is found in music, art, religion, worship and mysticism: Neptune seeks the 'Way', and the 'Way' is heavenward and the path is one of exaltation of spirit. The 'escape' represents a form of liberation.

It takes a strong soul to cope with a powerful Neptune, however, for escape can also be sought in the depths of depravity and sensation. Sixth sense experiences which come easily to those with an over-active Neptune may only be experienced by the average person in hallucinatory states or under hypnotism or LSD, which are not to be played with by anyone who prefers to stay reasonably sane.

The client should realise that the individual astrologer analysing the Neptune force in him cannot but conduct his research within the scope of his own chart and his personal Neptune. No two astrologers are likely to agree totally on either the full ranges of a 'good' Neptune or on what Neptune problems consist of and their best handling.

Neptune is a fascinating but mysterious energy force. If you have wondered why your son took to the drug scene in his teens, or why your uncle died of drink or your friend ended up in a mental home or why any of the way-out escapist types of trouble occurred, the astrologer will look for the answer in the Neptune energy pattern in the chart of the individual so afflicted. Any escapism is Neptunian. It can be in search of kicks, as when a kid turns to smoking, drinking or misuse of drugs. It can manifest as an over-preoccupation with romantic imaginings and daydreaming. Or it can find a legitimate outlet through beauty and the arts which provide right, true and needful escapes. Man *should* rise above the purely physical level of material life. Neptune can be seen as a higher and more spiritual octave of the love life, but misused in sex it can be very terrible.

If Neptune is energised and coarsened by Mars while receiving no purifying or beneficent beams from other planets, the sensation-seeking can be of a very low order, and one finds such aspects in the charts of criminals, confidence tricksters, those who trade in depravity or perversity or employ their energies or talents in secret goings-on. Advanced souls with adverse Mars-Neptune aspects find, if a reliable seer keys their former lives, that there is some hangover of misuse of magical power in black magic or corrupt practices.

But every one of us has Neptune in our chart somewhere and there is by no means always any mysterious or magical connection. I did a chart the other day for a girl born in the fifties. She had some difficult aspects pointing to sex complications. Mars and Neptune were in the 5th 'house'. I felt she was young enough and sensible enough to take the odd warning. I said, "Do be careful, my dear, because while lots of your age group can plunge into all kinds of fun and games and get away with it, you will not be so fortunate." Indeed I even said, "If anyone in your crowd gets landed with an abortion, it will be you. They can be careless and get away with it. You can't!" All her difficulties had to do with love, sex and amusement (the 5th 'house' concerns) but in her case the potential for sensationalism to turn sour on her was very great. The Neptune capacity for muddle and chaos energised by Mars needed very prudent handling.

The warning came too late and she told me that at the worst moment she had even tried to commit suicide. This ultimate escapism is typical of a violent Mars activation of Neptune.

Not many of those with difficult Neptunes take action of this kind. Some may be innocent victims of mistakes or accidents. This kind of tragedy can only be understood by those who accept the workings of the law of Cause and Effect from former lives, the afflicted Neptune pattern corresponding to the misuse of Neptunian forces in the far past. Obviously, however, when clients tell you of some such disaster you can't exactly say, "You, perhaps, were one of the Borgias or some other poison-happy Roman." Not many people give way to such urges nowadays, although some might like to, and under provocation there may be latent Lady Macbeth urges in many of us.

All tendency to misuse of energy has to be faced and worked through at some stage, and the astrologer should point out to the client who is tormented by feelings of hate or rage how *any* force *can* be used constructively rather than destructively. Think of the valuable yet macabre work of the pathologist.

A prominent Neptune is hard to handle, largely because it is not a down-to-earth, tangible energy. In fact the urge is to operate at a different level of consciousness. The Neptune in you or in me is our means to comprehend other planes of being. This may throw light on why transits of Neptune often correspond to painful events and emotions.

All three Extra-Saturnians are a bit this way, for it is only at the level where a man transcends his down-here ego that these three (Uranus, Neptune and Pluto) energies work happily in what could be termed legitimate outlets.

Valuable seership and genuine priestly activity or certain branches of healing work, including hypnotism at a psychological level, and anaesthesia come to mind as ways of working off a difficult Neptune energised by Mars. Mars energises what it aspects very thoroughly, in fact it coarsens and introduces an aggressive or battling urge.

In the fifties when so many young people chose to 'drop out', as they called it, this was a very Neptunian opting out of material life, and increasingly young people seem to be born with an intense awareness which gives dissatisfaction with solely material aims.

What about the placing of Neptune in the individual chart?

It is unwise to be too specific. Neptune is undoubtedly at its best working through what are called the 'occult' houses, the 4th 8th and 12th, for when this intangible force seeks outlet through too material fields of activity there is the tendency for there to be some sort of let-down or muddle. Certainly, to have Neptune in the 2nd House (money and attitude to possessions) encourages a 'super-colossal' approach to spending. I noticed this particularly for the generation that was born when Neptune passed through Virgo, i.e. between 1929 and 1942. I did the charts for many who proved to have lavish and lordly Leo rising, for whom Virgo would have dominated the 2nd House. Some of these had a very exalted idea of what is reasonable to spend.

The expression 'super-colossal' reminds me that the film-world, television and all photographic work are constructive Neptunian activities. Consider the unreality of a photo. There is the person, but in fact he may be dead or in the next continent and certainly not physically in your drawing-room talking at you from the Box. Unreality is a Neptune characteristic, as is illusion or deceit. So is anything liquid, anything non-solid: water, ice, snow – oil – gas, ether, the etheric . . . In astrological charts, the 12th House is particularly akin to Neptune, as Neptune 'rules' Pisces, the 12th sign. Enforced removals (or escapes) from life, imprisonment, or deliberate escape from materialism into religious orders: all these are 12th House concerns.

Sensitives of all times and ages have used Neptunian faculties such as telepathy, astral travel and suchlike. The man of today can only 'fly' in machines – Uranian inventions. A forthcoming stage in consciousness may be that New Age man will travel without machines, communicate without telephones or other technical aids, see without television, and communicate with other planes of existence. The imminent dawn of a new Cosmic Day is foretold by prophets.

Neptunian sensitivity and sense of rhythm and colour are found to figure in the charts of musicians and artists. Taurus is one of the musical signs. But Neptune stays in a sign for around fourteen years, so to say that Neptune in Taurus accounts for the musical genius of an individual would be tantamount to saying that every child born the world over during a fourteen-year period will be a musical prodigy. And yet, as it emerged from a small piece of research on a bunch of musicians, the background fact of Neptune in Taurus provided the setting for an influx of musicians when other quicker-moving or energising factors strengthened the individual picture. The rare occurrence of Mars being in Taurus for a period of twelve months on end provided exaggerated energy to the basic Neptune in Taurus potential. Anyone can verify this by looking in the Ephemeris for 1879 and 1880. This was brought to my attention by the late Arthur Alexander, a professor at the Royal College of Music and himself a brilliant concert pianist and notable for having performed a newly composed concerto at sight. Like so many musicians he could entertain with his humour as well as with his musical genius. This is a particularly Neptunian quality. It was Arthur who asked me if there was any astrological explanation of the fact that so many musicians and composers were born around 1879/80. He gave me the following list: Frank Bridge, Joseph Haas, Cyril Scott, Hamilton Harty, Grovlez, Thomas Beecham, Respighi, John Ireland, Medtner and possibly many more.

Another year worthy of research is 1680. Handel was born in February, Bach in March and Scarlatti in November.

In the days when I wrote articles in magazines (although *not* the prediction snippets, which I find fun to read, but don't really approve of), I was quite often asked if there was some special astrological ingredient needed for spiritual development.

To develop spiritually and to develop as a medium or psychic are two different things. The first is desirable for everyone, while the second is not. It is dangerous in my opinion to develop merely psychic faculties without deeper knowledge of the many planes of life – 'In my Father's house are many mansions' (St. John xiv.2).

Those who play with Ouija boards or table-turning have been known to tune in to the wrong programme! There are jokers on the lower astral planes who delight in pretending they are famous characters or high authorities from outer space. I would agree that communications are possible but to 'try the spirits, that they be of God' was sound advice given by St. Paul.

Neptune is the planet of escape into higher realities or into sensation and if played with is a dangerous and illusory force. It is seen at work in religious or mystical experience as well as at a material level in self-indulgent sensationalism.

The effects of Neptune by aspect or transit are not easy to assess. This is because one cannot know the spiritual attainment or true stage of evolution of the client. Charles Carter often said from the platform that he didn't trust Neptune, even in good aspect. I am sure this is because the hopes, wishes and aims of so many people are materialistic. Operating in that context it tends to promote confusion, illusion and chaos. Of course, the potential of Neptune in close trine aspect to the Sun in a natal chart is considerable. But if, as I have seen, that same Neptune is squared by Mars, it can happen that it is a dangerously sensitive and vulnerable Neptune that is afflicted. An awareness of both good and evil is heightened, as is an openness to help from either the forces of good or evil.

More than with any other planetary force, the action of Neptune varies with each and every individual case. It is as though it keeps its secrets – its illusions. It manifests strictly within the confines of the spiritual capacities of the individual concerned.

If your spiritual ceiling is high, the number of levels at which Neptune will operate are increased. If your spiritual ceiling is low, if you are frankly 'boxed in', this Neptunian energy *can* only function at a physical level. Man is a trinity of body, soul and spirit, and while Neptune is the member of his team with which he can contact the highest, it can work vividly in body sensations and imaginative evil-doing. At soul level it may seek vital experience and outlet in the emotional life. Painful conflicts and renunciations are Neptunian experiences, with concomitant spiritual gain or loss.

The dark night of the soul is surely a Neptunian deprivation of a light that has been experienced and is temporarily hidden behind a cloud of unknowing. We cannot mourn for what we have not known.

Renunciation is very much a Neptune word. Spiritual gain is usually accompanied by physical loss. It is typical of Neptune that I am finding it appropriate to quote the Bible so much. In the renunciation context here is another quote (Matthew xiii.32): 'What is a man profited, if he shall gain the whole world, and lose his own soul?'

PLUTO *in the individual chart, and in general*

I have not set out in this book to write all that can be said or quoted, textbook fashion, about the subject matter. I am sticking to what I have found out empirically. In this context a random thought is that perhaps Pluto, King of the Underworld, represents planetarily the corresponding depth to Neptune's height.

Jeff Mayo in his book *The Planets and Human Behaviour* (L. N. Fowler, 1972), has gone deep into Plutonian research and produced a good keyword for Pluto, namely 'Transformation'. He means this in the sense of something new forming, following the elimination of an earlier condition.

Pluto was discovered only as recently as 1930 by the Lowell University in Arizona, and so it has been in my working lifetime that astrologers have arrived at its characteristics. We have all been on our toes watching for recognisable correspondences. How did we all go about it? Well – when you know your own chart, the obvious thing is to wait and see what happens in your life when Pluto reaches sensitive degrees or makes aspects to these. I remember waiting with interest and apprehension when in the late fifties, Pluto reached the end of Leo. 27° Leo is my Midheaven degree. The Midheaven is often called the 'career point' of the chart, and it has to do with status or one's position in the world as seen by others. Astrologers by then had come to the conclusion that Pluto brings changes or disruption of a rather eruptive kind, with an element of shock. I wondered what would change in my life. Pluto would be in 27° three times during 1956 and 1957.

The first transit, accurate to the week, brought a letter from the owners of my flat, doubling the rent. This meant finding another home, so here was the element of shock as well as change. I have noticed since, in respect of clients, that the action of Pluto is like a door slamming in one's face, forcing one to look for another opening. It is salutary in a way, teaching one to trust that when one thing stops, another starts. The new flat was in fact an improvement on the old one.

The second transit concerned work. I lost my job, suddenly. But once again the shock forced me to look elsewhere, and again the new work was an improvement on the former contract.

The third and last transit . . . I should explain that when a planet slows to 'stationary' it appears to hover and can pass a sensitive degree in your chart three times. Of course it can do this hovering act out of harm's way to anything in your individual pattern. In my case, the third time produced no recognisable event in my outer life; at least so I thought at the time. Later on I realised that something had been going on in my inner, emotional life that had a profound effect and left me with a sense of having found a satisfactory new path.

From my personal experience and by dint of asking questions of clients with interesting or dramatic Pluto aspects I have come to the conclusion that Pluto is the planet most involved in what I have come to call 'karmic sex' links. Karmic sex being involvement with a person with whom you feel inexplicably close. Whether by bonds of love or hate depend on other factors. What is common to the experience is the sense of compulsion or recognition.

I also connect a prominent Pluto – for instance, Pluto close to the Sun or Ascendant – with a marked 'sense of destiny'. Such a person will feel, "This is *not* my right path – partner – environment" – and will make a change.

When Pluto makes a strong link with another planetary energy, I suggest that it is worth asking if there has been a strong sense of destiny to do some job or career of the nature of this second energy. To give an example, I found an exact conjunction of Pluto with Jupiter in Cancer prominently placed on an angle of the chart (Jupiter in Cancer increases the 'caring' qualities), and the man in question was an internationally known healer.

Important aspects between the slowest moving bodies have bearing on the behaviour pattern of a whole generation. Outstanding individuals in a given generation will be found to have fast-moving indicators which, like the second hand on a watch, emphasise their ability to 'clock in' with some individual talent to a wider 'generational' indication, which the average person, although born in the same framework, cannot resonate to.

Dr. Baldur Ebertin, distinguished German astrologer and founder of Cosmobiology, has much to say about the effects of Pluto in the psychoanalytical field. Two paragraphs back I mentioned the internationally known healer who has Pluto conjunct Jupiter prominent in Cancer. Baldur Ebertin says that Pluto emphasised by Jupiter gives a striving for recognition and the pursuit of outstanding success.

I myself have Pluto conjunct Mars in 25° Gemini and would wholly agree with Baldur's comment in so far as it concerns my life. He writes, "Pluto – Mars . . . the ability to work to the point of collapse, to place high demands on one's own self and on others . . ." Both remarks are only too true.

I gather from what he writes that the effect of Pluto on another planet is to emphasise its characteristics to the point of exaggeration. It apparently intensifies the sensuality of Venus. He doesn't say, except by implication, that it increases Mars' potency, but then Mars is potent anyway. The ego and self-assertion are increased whatever the area highlighted by Pluto. Just as Mars coarsens Venus, it seems that Pluto, too, renders her less attractive – more possessive and demanding.

In my professional work I have found that an important solar aspect such as 'progressed Sun square radical Pluto', can disrupt and disorient the sex-life over a period of several years. Details in each case are very different, but the general underlying experiences in many cases bear the emphatic Pluto trademark. As with any aspect the intensity of the experience depends on the strength or weakness of the individual Pluto.

What then have I come to expect in the case of solar testing of a strong natal Pluto?

I am prepared to be told by the client of experiences which have involved shock, disruption and new starts in relationships. The relationships that form at a particularly Pluto period are felt as strangely compulsive. The pleasure/pain content of such bonds will be linked with diverse factors, for individual charts reflect widely different destinies; so the actual content of the experience cannot be enlarged on here. It is the Pluto part of the experience we are interested in for the moment. "There was this curious feeling of having known each other before," one hears it said. A deep knowing, or inexplicable affection and instant recognition. Not the same, by the way, as Uranus magnetism. Pluto is more deep-acting. More volcanic in its rumbling to a final eruption.

Seers who can 'key' past lives confirm that these meetings are such as to re-unite souls who have been related or closely involved with each other previously.

Such links are likely to be complex and can involve love or hate, for both emotions are equally binding, as those caught up in a powerful love-hate relationship can testify. The astrologer whose mind works along these lines can throw light on complexities of the Pluto experience for the individual. Those who disapprove of or resent this karmic theory wherever it crops up will be scornful. "Where did you get that from? What a load of rubbish!" And to him it will *be* rubbish. Astrology above all teaches one how useless it is to try to convert this type of thinker to views which are alien to him. Your truth may not be a truth for him. It is best to accept this. Argument will lead nowhere.

But not all Pluto theories are controversial. If there is a lesson to learn from Pluto, it is this: if life appears to come to a stop, the best course is to accept the fact and wait for what is around the corner. Life does not stop at every check-point and one *must* adjust. This is the challenge.

7. ASPECTS

Aspects occur in every chart of a planetary pattern, and any interpretation of your own chart will mention the fact of planets being in good or bad aspect to each other.

But what are aspects?

One planet is said to be 'in aspect' to another according to the degree of separation in the curve of the zodiac as shown in the chart.

It is perhaps desirable to remind the reader that the astrologer, like the navigator, views Sun, Moon and planets from a geocentric standpoint (from the Earth's centre, that is) in their apparent path round the Earth. The planets travel, as it were, by a prescribed road, which is known as the zodiac and this extends about 8° on each side of the Ecliptic or apparent path of the Sun. Their positions are regarded as being in a certain degree of the Ecliptic, which gives the celestial longitude, and their distances as north or south of it, which give celestial latitude. From the astrological standpoint, then, a planet overhead is 90° away from a planet rising or setting (this could only be a true statement at the Equator) and a planet rising at the Equator is 180° away from a planet setting. Planets 90° apart are said to be in square aspect one to the other and those 180° apart to be in opposition.

These and other relevant aspects are shown in the Table of Aspects on page 116 at the end of this Section.

For the layman, aspects are quite simply the angular relationships of the planets one to another. Most astrologers read them out of the Ephemeris of the planets' places for the year and date under study. But before the days of such almanacs it would have been a question of observation and an imaginary line drawn from one planet to the centre of the Earth and out again to each heavenly body, and the angle measured.

For technical explanations about aspects Charles E. O. Carter's *The Astrological Aspects* (L. N. Fowler, 1930) is still the most valuable book on the subject and one's only regret is that it was written before the discovery of Pluto.

The effect of aspects in the individual chart is to combine two energies, or indeed, in complex configurations, many energies. Just as John

Nelson discovered in respect of radio weather,* that the squares and oppositions known as the quadratic aspects work in disharmonies, while the triangular aspects, the trines and sextiles combine different energies harmoniously for both radio weather and human reactions.

Involved in these aspects for everyone of us are all twelve signs of the zodiac, the Sun and the Moon and all the planets. This is yet another reason why those interested in astrology should read about all twelve signs and not imagine that just a single one relates to each person. The same goes for all the planets.

Your Mars energy working through cool and ambitious Capricorn is a very different energy force from my Mars energy working through communicative Gemini. Yet in both our charts it represents a main energy factor, rendered more potent or less potent, more or less productive, more or less aggressive by aspect.

I notice that most astrologers find it easier to portray dramatic or horrific planetary configurations than to enlarge on harmonious arrangements. But then the daily Press exists on bad news, too.

How an aspect works depends largely on the 'houses' or fields of activity involved. Aspects between houses will combine the principles of the planets concerned – the combined urges or drives according to the field of activity of the 'houses' through which these energies operate. (See Appendix, p. 265: Keyword system of Interpretation for meanings of Houses and for what will be emphasised when particular sections of the natal chart are strongly tenanted.)

I shall be discussing aspects in various contexts in Parts III and IV of this book, and there is much about bad aspects, evil and cruelty. But one can find a potentially cruel aspect, such as Mars square Saturn between the 5th House (Children) and the 8th House (Death), occurring in the charts of women who have miscarriages or abortions or difficulties of this nature. This and other similar aspects don't at all mean that the owner of the chart is cruel, but it can very well mean that something of the nature of the aspect crops up during his or her lifetime. Aspects can work out either actively or passively, or in either way at different periods of the life. A doctor or nurse working in an abortion clinic would not fail to have some relevant planetary set-up in the natal chart.

The art of interpreting aspects is to realise that the chart is of a whole person. The astrologer can add to the person's difficulties by too much dissection. Indeed, if you are at the receiving end of negative comments on your own difficult aspects, I advise you to hang on to the thought that it is neither wise nor kind to dwell overmuch on these. It is the healthy integration of the clashing energies that should be promoted.

It is not only in relation to a natal chart that aspects are spoken of. The natal chart is the basis of all personal analysis, but a chart can also apply

* J. H. Nelson, Planetary Position Effect on Short Wave Signal Quality, *Electrical Engineering*, May 1952, Vol. 71, No. 5, pp. 421–4.

to world affairs or to businesses and to the pattern of the day in relation to these.

Then again, regardless of what chart is under consideration, the astrologer will also talk of, say, Uranus or Saturn as 'transitting' in this or that aspect to a sensitive point in the chart.

The thing to remember in all mention of aspects is that it concerns the angular relationship of one planetary energy to another and there is no cut-and-dried interpretation to be relied on from any book. A thorough understanding of how a particular planetary energy manifests for the individual is needed before pronouncements can be made. Aspect interpretation is very much a matter of common sense. For example, where the natal chart is gentle and non-violent, no amount of activation will make it aggressive. Much the same as with hypnotism. It is said, and truly, that no hypnotist could successfully suggest a line of conduct totally alien to the subject under hypnosis. And certainly no transiting planet could stimulate an individual to violence beyond his own natal capacity for it.

So let me say to the embryo astrologer who knows enough to ascertain from the Ephemeris that aggressive Mars or explosive Uranus is shortly reaching the degree of his or her Midheaven or Ascendant – don't fear that you will step right out of character and react in a manner unfamiliar to you. You are YOU. Aspects or transits can only emphasise or activate an existing facet of your own nature.

When a planet is inharmoniously aspected, it is sometimes referred to as an 'afflicted' planet. This sounds a bit like Mars with the measles; what it really means is that the Mars energy in the chart under consideration is either inhibited or exaggerated. In almost every chart one planet or another is 'afflicted' to a greater or lesser extent. Let us take Mars, which stands in all charts as the principle of initiative and courage. If Mars is manifesting through a sign where he feels at home, such as Aries, Scorpio or any of the Fire-signs, the energy principle will work strongly. Mars in a feminine or negative sign is less happy, and the individual with this weaker Mars will have to give more thought to the best use of his energy principle.

Affliction sometimes takes the form of strong aspects which over-stimulate energy and lead to violence. It can also show in lack of aspects and weak sign placing. In this case there can be inability to cope or to put up a fight.

But can we in fact overcome basic defects and potentials?

Life is lived at many different levels. We can, if we so determine, learn to rise above circumstances or emotions and tackle the same planetary clash at a higher level than the purely physical or material, or, worse still, the purely automatic.

The astrologer can help by pointing out times of maximum tension, but he would be very unwise to suggest that the worst outcome is inevitable from bad aspects. The truly self-governing man or woman can become wholly in control of reactions, although not, of course, of events.

Good Aspects

When people study their charts or those of their children they like to find, or be told of, lots of 'good' aspects. But what exactly does a good aspect mean? It is not necessary for success to have a pattern full of trines and sextiles, although an excess of inhibiting aspects may hinder progress. If you want to succeed, you need the courage to meet challenges. The charts of famous politicians and other public figures fairly bristle with the squares and oppositions which correspond to their having to tackle difficult situations. It is by no means an indication of success to have only gentle, agreeable aspects, although these can correspond to charm and sweetness or agreeability.

In a chart which has seemingly no bad aspects it must be remembered that conjunctions are very powerful. These combine different energies which may, as it were, be good or inharmonious bedfellows. They work closely by celestial longitude in the same sign, which may be harmonious to one energy and not to the other. So the interpretation of conjunctions is no easy or straightforward task. Conjunctions near the rising degree can add to power but also to egoism.

Astrologers have learned by experience that a difficult configuration – shall we say Venus in close square or opposition to Saturn – when activated helpfully, according to theory, perhaps by the Sun progressed to the degree of this natal Venus, may justify a prediction of good things for the individual. But even a Sun aspect cannot and will not transform a difficult aspect into an easy one. Such a time may prove to be the best possible period for the individual to come to grips with whatever emotional or maybe financial testing the Venus/Saturn square or opposition suggests, but to say cheerfully, "Progressed Sun conjunct your Venus, this is going to be a super time!" could be misleading.

This contradicts the textbooks which write that you can expect a happy time when the progressed Sun activates your natal Venus; you will, at such a time, learn a lot about what your natal Venus has to teach you, for better or for worse. In either case the experience may be valuable, but according to your natal Venus the scene may vary between emotional joys or sorrows when this natal relationship energy is stimulated.

Activation of aspects and transits works at all levels at once. There is no such thing as a watery Neptune aspect only corresponding to a flood. There may well be flooding in many parts of the world at times when Neptune, as it is prone to do, hovers for a long time in difficult aspect. But it will also come to expression in individual charts in manifold forms of commotion within the psyche.

In this section I am talking of *aspects* in the sense of the mingling or merging of energies. I am not attempting to teach readers the technicalities of 'progressions'. This being so, I make no apology for referring to energy combinations under the varying headings of natal charts, progressed charts, transits to natal or progressed patterns, or anything else. Aspects, however they occur, manifest energy combinations.

Transits, very briefly, in astrological language, refer to the passing of a planet in the sky at a given moment over a sensitive degree in the chart under study. These, too, operate as energy combinations, harmonious or inharmonious, and by reason of a planet in the sky being in the same degree as one of your own natal planets, you will find a noticeable effect on the energy in question. The effect of two planets in the same degree is felt as one would a conjunction, briefly, maybe, and personally, as a straightforward mingling of the forces concerned. With slow-moving planets, the effect can colour an entire year. With the fast movers, a single day can contain a dramatic illustration of the forces concerned. A transit in exact square will be inharmonious – and in exact trine or sextile it will be helpful, but as always, within the framework of the natal ingredients involved. The ingredients, unfailingly, are the signs, planets, houses and basic configurations under activation.

An Example of a Dangerous Transit

A young acquaintance, who at the time was involved in the drug scene, became highly disturbed when a Stationary Mars hovered right on the degree of his Ascendant. An ordinary transit of Mars is a hundred times worse when it does this sort of hovering act. The poor chap just couldn't handle such a violent energy stimulus of his personality, and whereas he had been nobly trying to break the drug habit, he became so galvanised that he broke his resolutions and rang me from a mental home to say sadly, "I'm in again."

This sad story illustrates a point I try to put across, which is that one can find out the true nature of a particular planet for oneself or for another individual by watching the effect as it transits a neutral yet very personal part of the chart.

The transit of any planet over another *planet* is not such a clear indication, since this brings about a blend of two different energies – whereas a planet over the degree of your Ascendant degree (if you are lucky enough to know this accurately) illustrates very precisely the effect on YOU of a particular planet. I stress this last because it will be the total 'you' of your Ascendant and whole pattern that will react to the given planetary energy as it activates this 'personality point'.

In the case quoted, the young man's Mars was in difficult aspect natally to Neptune (escapism and sensationalism), so this effect on him when his Mars hovered on his Ascendant is not something to be feared by you, when your quite differently aspected Mars crosses your quite different personality point.

What to look out for

There is no doubt in my mind that sure-fire or even dramatic results occur when planets are stationary. This is true in talking of transits or in the brief day-to-a-year span of the progressed chart.

In each year's Ephemeris in a right-hand column for each month under the heading 'Mutual Aspects' it shows the date of 'stations' marked Stat. The letters D or R in the fuller daily section give the dates when a planet changes from Stationary to Direct motion or from Stationary to Retrograde motion. At some of these times there can be quite a long period of what I term 'hovering' in a single degree when a great number of people are affected through stimulation of one or other of their sensitive points.

In the seventies, Neptune moved slowly in Sagittarius, and at times spent a whole month in a single degree. The Press of the world was full of news of strange and awful events. These involved Neptunian renunciation in countless lives – and the sorrow which follows from crimes fostered by chaotic conditions. For killer and killed are both part of the positive and negative outworkings of Neptune activation in misuse.

Good Things happen too

Hoverings of Venus or Jupiter correspond to joys and expansions for those with a corresponding natal potential. I find that to have Venus even for a day in happy aspect to my Sun or Ascendant degrees, gives me the blissful sense of everything going my way. Jupiter doing the same may or may not bring a cheque in the post, but the sense of richness makes me feel in a winning vein.

What does One say about Bad Aspects or Transits?

I was asked the other day if there is an unwritten law that prevents astrologers from being frank if they see death or disaster. Most adults know that life is not one long happy-ever-after affair, so is it right to mislead people into thinking all is well if it is not?

I can only answer for myself. I do not pretend to forsee exact events, as the same aspects differ so radically in their effects when activating individual charts. I don't hide the fact that a heavy or testing period is looming up, if this is what I see, but I most decidedly do *not* dream up some specific horror to fit the aspects. Experience has taught me that while, after the event, the astrological aspect is always found to be appropriate, an attempt at exact interpretation is often faulty because there are so many ways of analysing the same aspect, which deals only with symbols. Paradoxically, I have kept a reputation for accuracy through keeping my remarks general. As I do not set out to tell the future so much as to clarify the individual to himself, I consider it more honest and helpful to confine remarks about the future to telling anyone which basic energy factors are going to combine in which fields of activity in harmony or disharmony.

Unaspected Planets

These are a puzzle, for the simple reason that there are fewer factors to go on.

I don't think there is a quick and easy answer as to how to think of these. As always, that depends on the whole chart. How, then, did I answer this question, which was put to me some years ago: "Astrology books seem to avoid discussion of the unaspected planet. I have Mercury unaspected. Is this a disadvantage or an advantage?"

I told her that in some cases unaspected planets can provide an important key to the character. Aspects are energy combinations, and so the absence of aspects gives no helpful clue (in this instance, with Mercury unaspected) as to whether the communicative qualities of the individual are made forceful and combative by Mars, or limited and suspicious by Saturn, and so forth. So we have to look elsewhere, remembering that we are considering a whole person. Perhaps we find a strongly aspected Moon and Venus in the same chart so that the native is ruled by his emotions and reason plays a lesser role. As a palmist would say, his heart rules his head.

I recall a man with Mercury strongly placed in its own sign of Virgo. It was unaspected, yet prominent. He believed himself to be a writer but in fact had never published a word.

No general statement can be made to cover every case of unaspected planets. Try studying the whole team of energies and think of the unaspected one as an energy which is not integrated with other energies in the whole. Even then it can be a strong or weak, helpful or mischievous, active or lazy loner.

Memorable Years

In some years there are long lasting planetary configurations or groups of aspects that make the period memorable. The year 1926 was such a one, notable for a strike in Britain still known as the General Strike . . . for the birth of Marilyn Monroe along with countless others with complex lives or lives involving sacrifice of personal, domestic happiness. While there is no great similarity with Miss Monroe, Queen Elizabeth II exemplifies a notable product of 1926. No astrologer could pretend that to have Neptune opposite Mars and Jupiter, and all three squared by Saturn, is anything but a challenge. Her Majesty's dedication to duty is indicated absolutely by the conjunction, or blending, of duty-conscious Saturn with the career-point of the Midheaven. It is with such important variations that saint or sinner, actress or Bishop, Queen or sex-symbol can share the same background aspects. Certain years are vintage years. I am enjoying watching the blossoming of those born in 1964. I analysed several babies born between 21 October and 6 November, all of whom have strong aspects in the determined 'fixed' signs: Mars in Leo opposite Saturn in Aquarius making a cross with Neptune in Scorpio opposing Jupiter in Taurus. Other fast moving points can modify or intensify this cross, but *every child the world over born in that period has this interesting configuration.* I was reminded of Maeterlinck's *Blue Bird* (Oxford, 1977) with its scene of the children waiting to be born. It was a tough bunch that queued up in 1964, and they will be worth watching. I wonder what their schools thought of them? Did they wonder what had arrived to their care?

And again, those born in 1965: a whole bunch with Mars retrograding in Virgo, conjunct Uranus and Pluto and opposite Saturn. All these will experience, simultaneously, important disruptions or transformations at times when their natal cross progresses to exactness or is otherwise activated. Happily for this age group, and unlike a group born in 1922 who matured in 1939 when World War II started, I see no such generational disaster indication.

Lesser known aspects, such as Quincunxes and Semi-sextiles are not always well explained even in textbooks, as they are thought to be minor aspects. In my view their effect is felt in considerable stress and strain, when exact. A semi-sextile sounds pleasant, being half a sextile, which is indisputably a pleasant relationship between two planets, and one benefiting thought and mentality. Characterwise I would agree in regarding it as a minor aspect. Linking, as it does, by 30° two neighbouring signs, much depends on *which two signs* are so involved. But by progression or transit a semi-sextile is quite another matter. Why? Because when one of the two so divided by 30° is happily trined, the other one will be squared. And so you keep on getting the tiresome or painful situation where one side of life is going splendidly, yet at the same time there are problems.

A quincunx (which separates planets by 150°) does exactly the same thing. The more exact the aspect natally, the tenser the situation, with one set of circumstances hindering the possibilities of another. The only way to explain it is to say that there may constantly be opportunities which occur at the same time as hindrances.

Finally, may I repeat that it is not the case that something from outside is at work forcing this or that event upon us; what is activated with its 'good' or 'bad' aspects is YOU, or ME, whether we like it or not, and the only course is to do a bit of spring-cleaning on the parts we don't like. A Jungian psychologist would tell us to accept the 'shadow', and certainly the last thing to do is to glance at a 'bad' aspect and shudder and hide it away. Neither should we cherish it as if it were a savage guard-dog to be let loose on intruders.

Table of Aspects

Symbol	Name	Exactness	Orb	Implication
☌	Conjunction	0°	8°	Strength arising from the close co-operation of two principles. (According to nature of planets.)
☍	Opposition	180°	8°	Tension. Challenge. Often found in charts of successful people.
△	Trine	120°	8°	Inner harmony of unearned benefits. Talents. Easy working of combination of principles concerned.
□	Square	90°	8°	Combative. Provocative of action. Uneasy struggle to combine the principles involved.
⚹	Sextile	60°	6°	As trine but applying more to mental reactions.
∠	Semi-square	45°	2°	Difficulty. Difficulty. Strain or inner conflict.
⬠	Sesquiquadrate	135°	2°	Strain or inner conflict.
⊼	Quincunx	150°	2°	All these have a minor effect on character but work more powerfully in the progressed chart. Their effect is easy or difficult according to the relationship of the planets involved in the natal chart.
⊻	Semi-sexile	30°	2°	
Q	Quintile	72°	2°	
BQ	Bi-Quintile	144°	2°	

8. THE IMPORTANCE OF
THE BIRTH MOMENT

The birth chart is the chart of the cosmic pattern for the moment and place of a person's birth. It is as if the Creator has said, "This is your moment! Do your best with it!" Why is it that the moment of birth and the first cry are so important to the astrologer?

As I indicated in my chapter on the Natal Chart, to set up a chart (see Figs. 1 and 2,) you have to have a precise moment. A starting moment. A well-known astrologer, Mark Edmund Jones of the U.S.A., has called astrology a 'Science of Beginnings', and this is very apt because in the case of human beings, the time of the first cry marks the moment when the child becomes part of his new environment. The child is not a separate entity at the moment of conception. Similarly, if you were analysing the chart of an inanimate object, you could say, for instance, that a motor-car is wholly a motor-car the moment it leaves the assembly line ready to be driven away.

The time of birth, along with the date and place (latitude and longitude if born at sea or in the air) are the factors needed for setting up the astrological chart of the sky pattern; that is to say, the pattern from a geocentric or earth point of view of the Sun, Moon and planets against the background of the Zodiac.

In twenty-four hours the Sun, together with the sign it is in during a particular month, *appears* to circle the Earth. Of course we know that what is really happening is that the Earth itself is turning on its own axis as it travels on its yearly path around the Sun; but when you and I look at the sky, it seems to us as if the Sun does the moving along with the Moon, planets and stars, all except the Pole Star, the pivot round which they all swing, and which fittingly and most obligingly can always be found marking due North.

Solar Charts

Can a birth chart be set up if the time of birth is not known? Only within certain limits. An astrologer can erect what he calls a solar chart (with the Sun rising) which strictly speaking will be the chart of someone born at sunrise, this being the best he can do without more accurate data. Quite a lot can be read from this, but it is sadly incomplete, and what is missing may relate to important events or characteristics; points vital to interpretation, even, perhaps an important Element will just not be there. It is not reasonable to expect a complete job from incomplete data.

It is often asked if the birth chart is valid in the case of premature births or those artificially induced? To this I answer that life is what actually happens and it bears small relation to what people expect or think ought to occur. For the child concerned, regardless of what has gone before – it could even be that the obstetrician was held up in a traffic jam – the significant moment is still when the baby enters on a conscious and independent existence. So, irrespective of the above conditions, it is still the moment of the first cry that is the birth moment.

Some children take several minutes to start to breathe, which is why it is incorrect to calculate the chart for the moment of emergence.

As to how accurate the birth time must be before the astrologer can be sure he is not making fatuous generalities applicable to anyone born on that day – the first cry, ideally, should be timed with a stop-watch. When this is done, the progressed analyses for future years will be a joy for the astrologer to work with. In actual fact busy astrologers are accustomed to being asked to do their best with a vague birth time or even from the date alone. This last cannot be personal, as it applies to everyone born that day.

To one with knowledge and understanding, the accurate birth chart provides a key by which a man can know himself. The moment may be complex and inharmonious or balanced and harmonious, but whatever it is, it is for the individual to develop as best he may . . . NOT to attempt to change or disown the pattern. In a deep sense I feel it is important to accept ourselves as we are, and be tolerant of the fact that others are different and individual. It is idle to wish we were as other men, for this would be to reject the cosmic moment which is our inheritance.

Another question is about *the moment of conception*. Wouldn't this give an accurate chart?

The moment of conception? Probably, yes. But when is it? It is not the moment of coitus. It can take for upwards of 24 hours for seed and sperm to get together. So how could you determine your moment? You would get a rough 24 hour period, but that is all. The Tibetans in fact use conception charts, but whether they employ some magical or possibly dowsing* method to arrive at the moment, I haven't yet found out. But what is quite certain is that you can't say "We went to bed at such and such a time on such and such a day" and make a chart for that moment, because it wouldn't even be medically correct.

And if the birth moment is completely unknown? I can only answer for myself. Many years ago a friend of mine showed me how to use a

* *Dowsing*, by Tom Graves (Turnstone Press, 1976).

dowser's pendulum. I know from experience, therefore, that results are possible when an astrologer trained in dowsing technique checks over a letter or photograph of the subject. As always with these techniques, it is important to use them only for serious work, but I feel it is legitimate to use it for checking the accuracy of birth charts or birth times.

I do not claim unfailing accuracy. However, I had a client in the United States who had no idea of her birth time and her mother was dead. Using a photograph and her signature, I obtained the time of seven minutes past eleven in the morning. This gave the sign of Virgo-rising, and clearly she had been reading some rude things about Virgo and wrote that she was sure this was wrong. However, I saw no good reason to change the analysis, and as years went by it seemed to fit both character and circumstances very well. Years later I got a letter from her saying, "You'll be happy to learn that a diary of my mother's has been found and in it was written, 'Little Meg was born a few minutes after eleven this morning'."

Why is the exact moment so important? To arrive at the totality of the individual pattern it is vital to know the exact orientation of each planet in relation to Earth. It makes all the difference to the interpretation which planet is above or below the horizon. The turning of the Earth on its own axis means that the sky pattern for the day appears to revolve in 24 hours. Only when the exact moment is known can the all-important 'angles' of the chart be entered on the chart, and with these the fields of activity known as the 'houses' of the chart.

No two people have identical charts. In the case of twins, these are likely to arrive within minutes of each other, so it is of high importance to time each birth by the first cry. This may be needed legally in matters of inheritance apart from being popular with the astrologer. The slight difference in the two charts may only show in the degrees turned by the Earth on its axis in the short period between the two births, but this difference is vital.

The astrological chart, then, is that of a moment in time and space. As well as the individual birth, and the starting-off moment of a motor-car already mentioned there are countless other starting moments which can be analysed. The launching of a ship, the start of a business, the laying of a foundation stone. Indeed, this last could date back to a time when astrologers were consulted in order to pick the most auspicious moment for a new project.

It is rather difficult to analyse the charts of inanimate things or projects and there is an art in applying progressed aspects for these. But the main ups and downs can be foreseen. Having tried it out many times I have no doubt of this. And animals, too, can have charts. This is discussed in Part III.

Summer Time or Daylight Saving Time should be noted, especially in countries where this changes from year to year. But when ordering a chart it is safest to state the clock time of birth, otherwise an experienced calculator may allow for some adjustment of time twice over, not realising that the client has already made an adjustment. Such a mix-up could result in a calculated chart being incorrect. What I say to clients is, "Please *tell* me if some curious time change was in operation but please *don't* allow for it yourself."

We all know people born on the same day a year, or perhaps years, apart. They are totally unalike, yet the uninformed imagine that they would be given the same horoscopes. This is not the case if dealing with reputable astrologers. Their horoscopes, or birth charts, as I prefer to call them, would be quite different one from the other. For one thing, unless born at the same time of day the rising sign would be different, and this 'rising sign' or Ascendant is the most personal single indication. Indeed, with the exception of the common factor of the Sun, every planet could be in different signs and/or differently inter-related and activating quite different fields of activity.

The actual calculation made to calculate the rising-sign is somewhat similar to that used in navigation. The Sidereal or Star time for moment and place is needed. Given this, the whole planetary pattern can be entered in correct orientation.

Is it possible to find the birth time by checking on past events? Many people think that if they tell me enough past events I can tell their birth times. I tell them that I knew my husband for twenty years before I was absolutely sure that I had worked out his birth moment by such methods. This is not practicable on a large scale.

Astrological twins make a fascinating study. One of the most thorough studies of this phenomenon was made by Rupert Gleadow. In *Astrology in Everyday Life* published in 1940 by Faber and Faber he quoted many cases of astrological near twins born in the same towns and records showed that these 'twins' had, for instance, died of similar causes within a short time of each other.

My younger daughter had a cocker spaniel puppy as astrological twin. I did not imagine that the two would lead similar lives. But it is true to say that both had remarkably independent, detached Aquarian natures, and in my daughter's fifth year, when I took her to England from Africa, Jim, the dog, also changed home from Johannesburg to Lusaka, a couple of thousand miles away.

In Appendix 2 of *The Case for Astrology* John Anthony West and Jan Gerhard Toonder give cases of 'Time Twins'. A story I particularly liked was of when the movie idol Rudolf Valentino died and the moviemakers searched for someone to take his place. The one most like him proved to be born in the same region as was Valentino and on the same day.

It is undoubtedly a fact that there exists a pattern of a moment and that it can be analysed.

But where does this get us?

I am *not* suggesting that embodiment of a moment produces identical people. Not even in the event of identical twins is this the case. What is interesting is not so much the similarity resulting from the animation of an identical pattern as the difference. No two people are identical. What is the explanation? For me it has to be the incarnating soul, lodged in shells of identical energy potential, that is the individual. You are YOU, I am I, otherwise it might be possible to produce laboratory made drones as thought up by science fiction (to say nothing of 'cloning', that bad dream of science itself).

Happily it is not materialistic man who rules creation. The spirit of man is different in essence from his embodiment, and our own individuality with its spark of life force can be visualised as the animation of a moment which can be, and indeed *is* shared. Nature with its lavish provision of seed sees to that.

How wrong was Milton in his sonnet on his blindness when he wrote 'God doth not need either man's work or his own gifts'. It is quite evident that God IS man's work and gifts, not to mention Nature's work. God, in the role of creator and animator of all moments is, in a real sense, man and all life.

In this New Age which is now being entered, man has gone into outer space in his physical body while many, the world over, transcend time in meditation and in so doing glimpse the glorious freedom of life 'out of the body'.

This book, however, is concerned with the pattern of the moment for man's life *in* the body, and with the energy pattern of limitations met by the incarnating soul when, at the moment of birth, it is 'thrown into the deep end' of an Earth incarnation.

It is this whole pattern of the birth moment that astrology studies. It is like a cloak worn by man for his sojourn on earth, and discarded at death when he returns to spheres of life unlimited by anything so Saturnian as time, heaviness, gravity and density.

A real-life illustration of having exact data to work on came to me some time after I had done a film for Director Lawrence Moore for Granada: a documentary called 'Horoscope' shown in April 1968. I quote Peter Black's column printed after it was shown and headed 'Fascinating, this Astrology'. He recounted that Lawrence had given me the time, date, place of birth, the sex and married state of four persons, had filmed my analyses and cut them to the actual life stories as given by the two men and two women concerned.

"She [Ingrid] was pretty good," he allowed. "She found correctly that the first man had been in the Navy, decorated in 1945, even pinpointing July as an important month.

"She had the second man correctly tabbed as punchy and sensational." (He was in fact a showman whose speciality was promoting eccentric stunts.)

"She was right again with one of the women, describing the young wife of a Chelsea shop-owner as 'Shy, dreamy, impractical, casually dressed, imaginative, needs to get away and live her own life'; and viewers saw a charming, diaphanous creature, floating around telling of her wish to live on an ocean-going boat."

So far so good, but Peter Black and other reporters, including Nancy Banks-Smith, did not fail to point out that the astrologer's only floater concerned the other woman, described as happy and rich when in reality badly off and divorced.

I only saw the film in its entirety before the TV discussion which followed it and was too excited at its success to notice what a colleague saw when the film was repeated. He was quick enough to spot that the *date* given by the neither rich nor happy woman *was not the same* as the date picked up by a close-up of the chart I was working from. As a fellow astrologer he wanted to defend my good name.

Lawrence, however, was quite relieved that I had *not* got everything right, as he feared viewers would have thought it was rigged. Indeed he was quoted as saying that he made the film largely to prove one way or another whether astrology worked. According to this report he said, "Ingrid hadn't seen the filming and had no idea who the people were, but she was remarkably accurate. So much so, indeed, that I felt perhaps I should put in some inaccuracies to make the film credible."

Lawrence assures me that he did not in fact *do* this and that the error crept in somewhere along the line. A reliable astrologer had set out the four charts which were given me in good time before filming.

What is so eminently satisfactory to the astrological world is that the difference in the chart exactly corresponds to the resultant error.

In two days, the Moon can move 30° – a whole sign – so instead of the woman's 2nd House Sun being splendidly aspected by the Moon, it was in reality badly aspected by it. This indicated financial difficulties instead of the good fortune which was shown on the chart sent to me to interpret.

Thus, my error, or 'floater' as the Press described it, did astrology a good turn, being a perfect illustration of the fact that only an accurate birth chart can reveal a true portrait.

All sensitive astrologers will understand why, when working on the four charts, it was this faulty one that gave me a wrong 'feel'. I even asked Lawrence if he was sure the data were correct.

As the calculation would have been virtually the same, the sign containing the Sun and the Ascendant and indeed everything except the Moon was hardly changed, I could see that but for this error the chart would have fitted this fourth person too. A good, kindly creature, I called her the 'do-gooder', but I thought she was rich. I christened all four before I saw the film. My names for them were the 'Admiral', the 'Showman', the 'Dancer' and the 'Do-Gooder'. I wasn't too far out.

9. THE HOUSES
(OR FIELDS OF ACTIVITY)

I have to warn readers that this section is technical in places, but it may prove useful for anyone who has had a chart calculated and wishes to understand something of the lay-out.

When the astrologer wants to know what makes an individual tick, he has to know where the main emphasis of the pattern lies; that is to say, which field of activity is most energised. Not only does he study the working of each planetary energy through the various signs of the Zodiac, therefore – he gets further information through what are known as the 'houses' of the chart, and these can only be plotted on the chart after a calculation involving the time and place of birth. Thus we see that inside the twelvefold division of the circle into signs of the Zodiac there is yet another twelvefold division into so-called 'houses'.

The line dividing the 12th House from the 1st House is identical with the line of the rational horizon, which is drawn from the calculated rising degree (or Ascendant) to its opposite degree where it marks the boundary between the 6th and 7th houses at a point called the Descendant. (See Figs. 1 and 2, p. 000.)

The ascending degree falls in turn in all twelve signs during twenty-four hours. In fact, regardless of birth *date*, the rising degree and cusp of the 1st House can emphasise any of the twelve signs, according to the *moment* of birth. On the other hand, everybody's 1st House equates in some measure with primary 'Aries' matters, even though quite another sign may be occupying the house; the 2nd with what is basically Taurean, and so on.

However, let us suppose you have Scorpio rising. This means that for you the most primary and personally descriptive sign is Scorpio which occupies the 1st House of your chart. You protest that your Sun is in Gemini, so isn't that the most indicative of your personality? I have to tell you that this is not necessarily the fact. Although it is true that the Sun is the heart of any chart and the emphasis is therefore on both the sign and house containing the Sun, it is still a fact that your calculated rising sign is more indicative of your appearance and immediate personal reactions.

It is unfortunate that the whole scene of house interpretation is complicated by the astrologers themselves, who argue endlessly as to which house system is best. Happily there is no argument as to the quartering of the chart produced by the angles of the chart. Here we come back again to the importance of the Ascendant degree, for the cross made by the angles of the charts consists – in all the disputed house-methods – of the line of the Ascendant degree to its opposite point on the circle and (intersecting it) the line from the Midheaven (or M.C.) to its opposite point (or I.C.).

The numbered segments in Figs. 1 and 2 are known as the 'houses' of the chart. Each house stands for a different department in life. Meanings of each house are listed in the Keywords section (see Appendix). An emphasised house is one occupied by planetary energies, but if there is no planet in a house you are interested in, you don't just say, "No planet in the (say) marriage house (7th) and therefore no indication of the individual's attitude to, or prospects of, marriage and partners." You look to the sign on the cusp of the house. For example, if Leo is the Rising-sign, the opposite sign, namely Aquarius, will be on the cusp of the 7th House, and the attitude of the individual to partners will have a cool, detached, Aquarian flavour. Further light may be thrown on the same department by looking at the planet which 'rules' the sign on the cusp of the planetless house under study. In the case of Aquarius this would be both the rulers, Saturn and/or Uranus.

So far so good, but what if the dividing lines differ with different house systems?

All astrologers agree on some basic points. There is no dispute as to the broad lay-out of houses. All agree that the area close to the Ascendant is indicative of personality. This area includes most of that marked 1 in Fig. 1 and Fig. 2, but I hasten to add that research has shown that an area in the 12th House near the dividing line must als be considered vital in respect of personal interests, just as the area on either side of the Midheaven (or MC) has bearing on 'out-in-the-world' activities.

Varying House Systems

Where then to place the dividing lines, if at all? I am hoping that John Addey, with his scholarly study of the *Harmonics of Astrology** will sooner or later revolutionise this tiresomely vexed question. In the meantime students do well to test even newer systems, such as the Topocentric and the Koch systems for which Tables of Houses are available. I cannot deny that I have friends and colleagues who use these or Placidus Tables and are satisfied with their reliability.

Some charts change considerably when transposed from Equal House, which is my own favourite, to the above mentioned. My own

* L. N. Fowler & Co. Ltd., 1976.

does not, so I have not been able to use it for purposes of comparing systems.

Being for many years a busy consultant whose clients are not always sure of their precise birth moment, I have sometimes to be content to work with overlapping margins, but am aware that this easy way out can never suit those who champion a particular system.

My approach to the analysis of houses, as with the rest of the chart, is empirical. Over the years, thousands of clients have 'talked their charts', as Margaret Hone (author of the *Modern Textbook of Astrology*†) put it, during 'person to person' consultations. This has given me ample opportunity to check the validity of my own statements.

The question of the astrological houses needs continued checking of the sort Polich and Page so laboriously carried out in respect of what they finally called Topocentric houses. A danger for astrologers with too rigid ideas on a pet house system is that they amass too many sensitive degrees. A reliable, general interpretation is of more value than pages of supposedly accurate details.

The working astrologer must reach his own conclusions over what is a technical matter. All I am concerned with in these pages is for the reader to be aware of the fact that various methods of setting out a chart exist. Your own chart will not present the same appearance if it is set out by two astrologers using different house systems. The basic contents, however, should be the same if both are accurately calculated. The degrees of Ascendant, Midheaven (MC) and planets should be identical.

It is wise to check on your own chart, whoever has set it up. To do this, verify that the Sun symbol, which is the small circle with a dot in the middle, is roughly in the appropriate sky position. If you were born at sunrise the Sun must be on the Ascendant side of the map – to the left as you look at the page. If born at sunset it must be to the right of the page. If born at midday, it must be at the top and if at midnight near the foot of the chart.

A client once wrote to tell me that another astrologer had calculated his chart and made his Ascendant Scorpio whereas I had made it Taurus. I did this quick check immediately. On the client's card the clock time was given as near noon and the Sun on his birthday was in Capricorn. I saw to my relief that I had not made such a wide error, as the Sun was in its normal noon placing – overhead. I replied to him that unless on the day of his birth the Sun happened to be below the horizon at noon(!), it was not I but the other astrologer who was wrong. He saw the point of this.

I would add that for a less extreme case I would check by recalculating. Any major error would necessitate a complete re-analysis for the individual, as every field of activity would be altered and

† L. N. Fowler & Co. Ltd., 1951.

character, likes and dislikes, indeed everything would have to be re-thought.

Students' Problems regarding Houses

I am told that many of those interested in astrology, and even students in their first year, seem to come to a block when trying to understand what 'houses' are all about. Planets and signs of the zodiac are well documented and have a basis in fact. There are the planets, to be seen as an astronomical fact, and roughly the same can be said about the signs of the zodiac. But what on earth are houses? they ask. A blind acceptance of keyword meanings is not enough.

Here, then, is what I would say to anyone whose mind has boggled at 'houses'.

To start with, I would say that the 'houses' constitute one of the many circles within circles that one has to get used to in the study of astrology. The outermost circle is that of the Constellations on the rim of the ecliptic, known by the familiar names of Aries, Taurus, etc. (See also Chapter 11: 'What is the Ecliptic?', p. 135.) Inside this circle of the Constellations is that of the signs of the zodiac, which is also, rather confusingly, known as Aries, Taurus, etc., but not coinciding with the Constellations, since this second circle is the circle or 'aura' of Earth, whose starting-point of Aries very reasonably starts with the degree of the vernal equinox and is geared to the seasons of Earth.

It is inside this second circle that we enter on our charts the spokes of the wheel or twelvefold division of the circle of the 'houses', starting at the all-important Ascendant degree, which has to be ascertained for the moment and place that is being studied.

For simplicity let us choose Equal House Division (Fig. 1) and note that the spoke of the 1st House is entered at the rising degree, which in the illustration is 4° Leo. We continued round the chart entering a spoke at 4° of each sign. By the other house systems there are also twelve houses, but of varying extent.

I suggest that this entire circle or wheel of the houses is best thought of as a transparent lens through which the sky pattern of the day can be studied for the individual or for the problem under review. The twelve houses provide a means for study of the various departments of life or fields of activity. Exactly like the lens of spectacles or contact lenses, this 'houses' circle must be oriented precisely.

I have said elsewhere that the planetary pattern of any day changes very little in twenty-four hours. The Sun, Venus and Mercury move less than a degree and a half. The Moon moves quicker, but at full gallop reaches only 15°–16° and *can* slow down to under 12°.

If your personal lens (or orientation of the houses) is to be accurate, your birth time should be timed to the first cry. Only then is this lens individual to *you*. If you wear contact lenses or spectacles you will know how you feel without them or if you put on someone else's lenses. When you thankfully revert to your own, it is as if your view of life clarifies and you can once more see the world as if you are a part of it, which is indeed the case.

This simile of a lens through which the background pattern of the day is viewed is the best means I can think of for trying to clarify the question of houses to the student.

Writers of textbooks will protest that houses are well documented. This is true to some extent. There is considerable agreement about the meaning of each house, even if arguments rage over demarcation lines. What seems lacking is a more basic explanation or rationale. "Houses!" a student wrote to me. "I just don't get what they *are*! I can learn what the books say they mean. . . ." He claimed that he got a better idea from my reply, which was based on the lens idea.

Ascendant

It will have become obvious that since the starting-point of the 'houses' lens is the vital Ascendant degree, which is calculated from the moment of birth, this innermost circle of the houses relates directly to the individual. Indeed one cannot know the houses, or fields of activity, unless one is able to calculate the Ascendant. If, through insufficient birth data, the exact orientation of the chart is incorrect, then the sad truth is that the supposedly individual chart is not individual at all. Your chart or your child's chart may be not really yours or his but the chart of quite a different baby born in the town on the same day.

If the astrologer is to be expected to assist his client towards an accurate vision of himself, he must have correct data to work on. "Man, know thyself!" doesn't mean, "Man, know someone else born on your birthday whose viewpoint of the shared general pattern of the twenty-four hours is from a different angle."

Each individual views life from his particular angle or orientation to life. The importance of orientation to life may not be universally appreciated. All forms of life have their orientation. A plant, preferably a naturally oriented one, such as a healthy weed, grows at its own angle to the poles of the Earth. A dowser, or radiesthesist, skilled in the use of a pendulum, will get what he terms a positive swing over a weed which flourishes at its God-given angle. But should the dowser take a trowel and dig up this happy plant and replace it in the earth turned round 180° and again swing his pendulum over it, the swing will be found to be negative. If someone turns the plant slowly back to its original position there is no need to have recorded what this was, for when it reaches its chosen angle, the pendulum will change to a positive swing.

I am told that pot plants, too, grow more happily if checked for optimum angle, as will newly planted shrubs or roses, or any young plant.

What has this to do with birth charts? I hold that essentially the problems are identical, both being that of true orientation to life. A skilled dowser could certainly check on whether an astrological chart corresponded to its owner as to correct Ascendant degree.

10. PROGRESSIONS

I am not going into textbook style explanations of the progressed chart and how to set it up. If you want to learn astrology there is a chapter later on which tells you how to set about this. But clients of astrologers should know that if they want information about a particular year, past or present or even ahead, the astrologer will have to 'progress' the natal chart for the year in question.

In case your eye brightens at the thought of a spot of fortune-telling, I must add that unless the astrologer is some kind of psychic Nostradamus, a 'progression' will not enable him to make accurate assessments of events. Far too many people still seem to imagine that this is the main aim of astrologers.

What then *can* be seen?

It can be seen, and very clearly, which facet of a person's nature, which energy factor and which potential, is activated at a particular time. And it is this timing which can be useful. You know perhaps that you intend to move house, emigrate, marry, or start some project. The progressed chart may save you getting all steamed up about it ahead of time.

I said I wouldn't get technical, but here are a few hints to students which others may skip if they prefer.

I have already said how vital it is to look at the Ephemeris for the year of birth so as to study the life-span represented by the odd seventy day/years preceding and following birth. Look particularly for planets going Stationary during this time, and for planets changing sign. I find this a very reliable indication. According to the nature of the planetary energy involved, there will be some modification in the life, emotions or general progress of the individual. Venus moving from reticent, shy Pisces into frank, decided Aries will correspond to some brisking up of the relationship field and general attitude to love and/or art or even money, which is another Venus 'thing'. Mars working through a different sign will bring a change in the main energy outlet, in work, hobbies or in the sex-life. But, and most important of all, if, during the life-span (and of course I mean possible life-span, as there is no obvious indication, like a punctuation mark, if the life suddenly ends) a planet stays for many days in aspect to another planet, it must be remembered that by progressions *days* mean *years*, and it can happen that a happy, fulfilled period or a depressed and frustrated one is prolonged. Such a factor, which can be seen ahead, can materially affect the whole life according to when it is in operation.

A good example of this occurred for people born in 1922. Just the right time for involvement in the prolonged span of war and violence preceding and following World War II – 1939 to 1945. Mars was in Sagittarius from mid-February until mid-September of 1922. This is a phenomenally long time for a planet whose average stay in a sign is forty to forty-five days. What did this mean? It meant that in progressions for a great proportion of 1922-born people, Mars aspects figured alarmingly in long-lasting patches of potential violence.

For everyone, the natal chart shows the framework out of which the progressions 'grow' and the future develops. Put another way, the natal chart shows the potentials and the general attitude to life – *what* is likely to be experienced emotionally or physically, in the inner or outer life. The progressed chart tells us *when*.

In order to assess progressed positions, is it desirable to know a lot about the client?

It is easier if one knows something of a person's status and circumstances. And one needs to know the sex. I remember analysing a child called Evelyn which can be either a male or female name. It was curiously disconcerting to have to change my mental image of the child. In fact a pattern can be more suitable for a man than a woman or vice versa, and fortunately, in this case, the child's right sex fitted the chart more comfortably.

Analysis by person-to-person consultation is desirable at least at some point in the client–astrologer relationship. The chart can be applied to any potential problem. But no astrologer can be wholly sure, especially if he meets the client in middle age, what form the activation of a dangerous configuration has taken, although he could see that in such and such a year the client must have experienced its activation in some form. So in a written analysis the risk is that while whole pages of analysis are applicable, the astrologer may, through delicacy perhaps, have avoided the one subject which is uppermost in the mind of the client. Such a problem would almost certainly have been touched on during a personal consultation.

When looking ahead and studying a particular year, one sees which energy is most activated. Let us pretend that it is Saturn. Full details of the Saturnian energies are given in Part II, Chapter 6. The following could be said: "The present time is a Saturnian patch. You may have to tighten your belt and work extra hard or cut down on pleasures for one reason or another. The test will be one of restriction or limitation; at best a time of serious effort. Or it may be experienced in the inner life in depression or a sense of inadequacy.''

If it is a Jupiter period, it can equally be a test, but one involving Jupiter excesses, expansions or exaggeration. For example, with Jupiter activating your pattern you put on weight in a 'What does it matter?' mood, whereas with Saturn you lose weight, either through hard work, deprivation, or because you suddenly find it easy to discipline your appetites.

Any competent astrologer looks at progressions and transits automatically, since the present circumstances and mood of the client are vitally affected by these, and to talk merely about the natal potential at a time when a knock-out progressed aspect or transit is in operation gives a very wrong impression. In astrological parlance a transit is the passing of a planet in the sky at a given moment over a sensitive degree in the chart under study. (See also Chapter 7 and Glossary.)

The importance of the birth moment has been fully discussed, but it is relevant here to mention that, ideally, the highly sensitive Ascendant and Midheaven degrees should be progressed as well as all the planets, and considered vis-à-vis transits. But if this is done when working with a birth time which is even a *few minutes out*, a major crisis may appear as affecting one year when in fact it happens years later – or happened years earlier.

And this seemingly minor time error of a few minutes is even worse in the case of twins, where you may be given the right time for one twin and not the other, so you think you are doing twin A when, in fact, you are looking at B's chart.

You may now be wondering if it is ever worth while having your chart studied. Happily, great accuracy does not affect progressions involving the Sun, Moon and all the planets, so that much can be read from the progressions even when the birth time is not precisely known.

Students who know how to read an Ephemeris will find in the 'Mutual Aspects' column the years when planets which are in important but relatively wide aspect on the day of birth close to exact aspect. What do I mean exactly? Take the well-publicised chart of Her Majesty the Queen, who has a natal square between Jupiter and Saturn. If you count the number of days (which means years by progressed reckoning) until the aspect is listed as an exact square, you will find that it marks an important phase. For the Queen, this aspect closed to exact square in the year she acceded to the throne, which certainly marked the time when Saturnian duty clamped down on Jupiter enjoyment. She had to put her private life and personal enjoyments second to public duties and responsibilities.

In some cases the exact aspect occurred before the birth date. In this case you can count the years (days) *back*, and arrive at what are known as converse instead of progressed aspects. See R. C. Davison's *Technique of Prediction.** He found, as I have found myself, that if there is no correspondence for some important event in the progressed chart, it is to be found in the converse one. Obviously, if one employs enough methods one is bound to find something apt. I advise the busy astrologer to prove for himself by trial and error which of the various techniques are reliable and to stick to these. (I am well aware that in this chapter I may be treading on the corns of astrologers who are well satisfied with some technique I have not mentioned.)

An analysis can be faulty if regard is not paid to the fact that certain potentially difficult aspects *never* close to exactness. This takes the sting out of them, and is another reason why the birth chart should always be progressed (if only with this one consideration in mind) and not just studied static. In the old days, astrologers repeated parrot-fashion that Retrograde planets were unfortunate. But common sense tells me that if, by going backwards, a difficult aspect never crystallises, such a retrogradation is beneficial.

The natal pattern is unfailingly the basis of all future progression or effects of transits. This is yet another reason why textbook or computerised interpretations often seem faulty. Unless there is something in the basic, natal chart that *can be* activated. Not every chart can be dramatically affected by 'directions'. What do I mean exactly? Suppose your progressed chart shows you to have, in a given year, what is a traditionally 'bad' aspect, such as Mars square Uranus. If in your natal chart these planets are well aspected, mutually or even separately, any activations of either or both are less to be feared than if in the natal chart the two were linked in some explosive configuration. So, always and without fail, ask yourself 'what sort of a' Mars, for example, is being adversely energised by 'what sort of a' Uranus, and base your conclusions accordingly. The individual who practically needs a bomb put under him to do anything needing courage or initiative, might suddenly find the impetus to action from this sort of activation, which would manifest quite differently or even violently on a naturally aggressive type of person.

Precise-minded astrologers have been known to state that they can and do foresee exact events. But it is dangerous to assume that because certain general predictions are justified by events it is only necessary to work harder in order to foretell exactly what is going to happen – and when. Astrology cannot be an exact science. There are too many factors and too many variables. A highly evolved person will react very differently from a primitive individual who is nearer the level of automatic reactions and thus more predictable.

I think, indeed I *know*, that general trends are reliably shown in the progressed chart, not only for people, but for nations, political parties,

* L. N. Fowler & Co. Ltd., 1955.

business firms, associations and anything for which a 'beginning' or birth time can be determined. Scrutiny of trends can be used to produce a sort of weather chart. Psychologically it goes further than any weather chart, as what is seen in the progressions is a development of the natal potentials. If the natal chart shows, for instance, difficulties in the emotional life (Venus afflicted with few mitigating aspects), we can watch the life proceed quite calmly and profitably despite this, while other, more favourable potentials are to the fore. When, however, this Venus potential for difficulty is activated by progressed aspect or by transit of a slow-mover (transits of the faster moving planets will only produce minor and shorter periods of bother) the native will undergo some important and memorable test in respect of the emotional life. Astrologers who can picture with accuracy an actual situation ahead do this by means of some additional psychic faculty which enables them to combine the basic astrological facts with clairvoyance. I do not deny this possibility. What I want to make clear is that *without* any such faculty it *is* possible to foretell general trends; the ups and downs, the expansions and limitations of life; enough to guide people without making them feel strait-jacketed by some wholly predestined pattern of events.

A client can be shown, if he or she is willing to profit by such advice, how a testing time ahead can, if rightly dealt with, represent an opportunity to deal constructively with strengths or weaknesses.

The intelligent but uninformed client will, very naturally, say, "You tell me my progressed Sun will be conjunct my Mars [Venus or Mercury or whatever planet]. Tell me what this means."

The truthful answer is roughly this. 'The Sun is at present stimulating or activating this particular energy factor to the maximum of its potential.' If this energy is clearly a strong, good force, it is a time of maximum opportunity in the relevant field. Even if the natal planet is far from perfect, it is a fact that if during your life you have overcome the natal faults of this particular planetary energy, you will have the opportunity of enjoying the best of whatever planetary energy is activated. If, on the other hand, you have let your moral tone get even flabbier than it threatened to be at birth, then you cannot expect to have much joy or profit from any stimulation of this vitiated force. Of course one refrains from saying this to the poor person who seems to have made a muddle of life. That would be cruel and useless. It is never too late to start improving on the basic pattern, and the Sun's stimulation of any force will bring opportunity.

The art of consultant astrology is based on a very complete understanding of what each planetary energy stands for in the individual life. However much you think you know about a planet in isolation, you can be completely stumped when meeting a highly complex planet in an individual chart. To give one instance, Venus in an uncomplicated chart will stand for nice, clean, straight-forward relationships. Such a Venus, when activated, will manifest in friendships, love, contracts-forming, group activities, and/or marriage. In quite another chart, one with a weak and afflicted Venus, activation by precisely the same aspect can correspond to emotional tests or perverted relationships of a possessive or obsessive type.

Finally, over long years of analysing charts, what have I found that I can unfailingly rely on in the interpretation of the progressed chart? Without any doubt at all, it is the solar aspects, especially when the progressed or converse Sun reaches the exact degree of a natal planet. And what is so satisfying to the astrologer is that they work without fail in traditional ways. Mars when activated brings increased energy, courage and initiative (within the framework of the potentials as a whole). Saturn activated brings hard work and serious endeavour. But before being too sure of the future, even in generalised trends, the thing to look out for is plenty of backing up. Even a single solar aspect is apt to wait for a similar aspect of the progressed Moon to trigger it off, and in that same month a succession of transits. Given a big enough pile up one is pretty safe in thinking a notable year is ahead.

But the last impression I want to leave with you is that astrology can be used for accurate forecasting of events. The true value of the progressed chart is that it shows which facet of your character, or which talent, is being activated. This can help the individual to go with the tide when it is with him and to refrain from unprofitable resistance and resentment when it is not.

11. WHAT IS THE ECLIPTIC?

I have puzzled over how to write this description in what I insist is not a textbook. So I warn all who need no information on this point to skip the following extremely simplified explanations which I use when telling children about the planets of the Solar System and their setting in the zodiac.

This is my method.

Find a large round, flat board, table or tray. Why a flat surface? Because a plane is a flat surface, and this is to represent the PLANE OF THE ECLIPTIC. A movable, portable board has the advantage that it can be tilted, and the plane of the ecliptic at any moment is always tilted according to the angle of the Sun to the Earth; and the signs of the zodiac are on its infinitely far-distant rim. Not in neat close goups, by the way, as some of the stars in the formation of each are immense distances nearer the Sun than others.

To start with, have ready some malleable substance such as Plasticine or Blu-Tack. With a marking pen draw the names of the signs of the zodiac round the rim and the Sun in the centre. Keep your blobs of Plasticine movable to represent the planets which go round the Sun. I have drawn them on the diagram in their correct order from the Sun, but with *absolutely no attempt at indicating the correct proportions* . . . as to size or relative distances.

The first use of this model is to *see* why astrologers say that the Sun (or for that matter any of the planets) are 'in' a particular sign.

Stand where you can pretend to be the Earth blob on your surface and, looking towards the Sun in the centre, move slowly round the Sun and watch how, as you circle it in an anti-clockwise direction, you see the Sun against a changing background of the signs of the zodiac which are drawn around the rim of your circular 'plane'. Watching the rim as you move, the complete circle round the Sun represents one year of Earth time.

Each planet goes round, or 'orbits' the Sun, and as it does so it follows an ecliptical and slightly tilted path, so that each is sometimes a little above our table or tray representing the Plane of the Ecliptic and

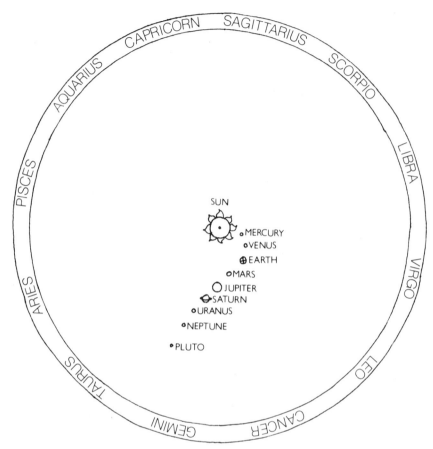

Diagram only. No attempt at scale.

sometimes underneath it. This tray or table image is useful for visualising, or explaining the planet going down through the tray and later coming back up again, as this is known as 'crossing the Plane of the Ecliptic'. Its distance above or below the tray is known as Celestial Latitude. If when reading the Ephemeris you see that a planet is in 0° of Latitude, it is when (in this imagery) it is bang on the tray (or Ecliptic); Northern Latitude is above and Southern Latitude is below the tray.

Once this image is clear in our minds, it becomes very obvious how eclipses and occultations occur. These terms are used when one heavenly body in the solar system is exactly hiding another from the point of view of Earth. Put your head down, level with the tray, and imagine yourself as the blob Earth, and you can see that if you move your Moon dead in line with the Sun, this is the position of an eclipse of the Sun, i.e. the Moon is blocking the Earth's view of it. But if you lift the Moon-blob up a bit, that is to say, give it some Northern Latitude, it will still be in the same position in relation to the degrees of zodiac round the rim of the tray, but not in the view-blocking eclipse position. Southern Latitude would have to be demonstrated with the help of a small boy under the table. If you are keen enough to elaborate your working model, you should mark 360° round the rim of your circle starting at 0° Aries, through Taurus and Gemini, through to Pisces. These are the degrees of Celestial Longitude.

Occultations are effectively the same as eclipses, but the term only applies, astrologically, to the blocking from the view-point of Earth, of one *planet* to another. The term eclipse is used for the Sun and Moon only. A normal conjuction is when two planets are in line with one another in Celestial Longitude, but at different latitudes (or distances above or below the tray) so one of them does *not* block the view of the other for the observer.

The Moon's Nodes, which many students find hard to picture to themselves, are also easily explained with the tray method. All planets and the Moon go round (describing an ellipse rather than a circle) at an angle tilted somewhat to the tray (or plane of the Ecliptic). In doing this they are sometimes above and sometimes below the tray. The degrees of the Nodes are degrees of Celestial Latitude (as seen from Earth) marking the point where the Moon goes through the tray (North or South) on its orbital journey.

Planets also have nodal points where they cross the path of the Eclip-tic, i.e. go through the tray one way or the other.

If you want to demonstrate to children where the path of the Ecliptic is, in the sky at a particular moment, you must hold your round flat tray tilted with the appropriate sign of the zodiac pointing up at the Sun and its opposite sign on your feet – i.e. in June when you know the Sun to be in Gemini, point that edge of the rim at the Sun and that of Sagittarius on to your feet. In your imagination see your tray reaching to infinity in an immense flat plane, right through the Earth at your feet.

Few people seem to realise that the bit of sky behind the Sun is the segment of zodiac the Sun is 'in' for the month. So it is the entire zodiac and stars that *appear* to go round the Earth every 24 hours, with the Pole Star as the pivot.

Another question which is often asked when a very bright planet is seen, is "Is that Venus or Jupiter?" The clue here is that Venus is never more than two signs away from the Sun, so it is either a morning or an evening star, according to whether it is in a sign ahead of the Sun (morning) or behind the Sun (evening)). Other planets can be identified easily if you see in your Ephemeris that they are close to the Moon, or, like Venus, in the sign (or two signs) after the Sun, when they will be visible after sunset.

137

This information is intended either for children or for those who are curious to know which part of the night (or day) sky is concerned in the birth chart.

Planets, or the 'wanderers' as they used to be called, do their wandering on or near to the plane of the Ecliptic. The Earth is one of these. It may muddle students at first when they read the 'Sun's Latitude' in the Ephemeris. This is not operative on our 'tray' imagery. We view the Sun from the Earth at different angles at different seasons and there is much more to it, but the explanation is too complex and technical for this book.

I have devised this tray or table image to help in visualising the concept of the whole universe with its concentric rings of orbiting planets as an enormous Flying Saucer. 'Unidentified Flying Objects' are described as being padded saucer-like shapes. Galaxies, too, are similar formations, made up of billion upon billions of universes. This shape, then, would seem to be the right one for space travel regardless of dimensions.

12. THE PRECESSION OF
THE EQUINOCTIAL POINTS AND
THE GREAT YEAR

The Aquarian Age

The points in the heavens known as the Vernal and Autumnal Equinoc-tial points are where (in spring and autumn) they can be seen exactly overhead at the Equator. At this time it shines equally on the northern and southern hemispheres and night and day are of equal length all over the world. The Vernal Equinoctial point is known technically as 0° Aries, not only to astrologers but to navigators, astronomers and all who deal with almanacs. As seen against a background of constellations, this point moves through the signs very slowly, so that it changes sign in, roughly, two thousand years, beginning a new 'Age'. It moves *backwards*, so that the movement is not from Aries to Taurus, but through Aries to Pisces. There is much talk at the present time of being 'in the Aquarian Age', although strictly speaking the Vernal Equinoctial point is still in Pisces. But as the constellations Pisces and Aquarius overlap, no one is quite decided as to whether in *this* connexion it is legitimate to use the 30° sign divisions, and say the Aquarian Age has begun. My unofficial opinion is that we can assume that it has. Indeed judging by the typically Aquarian happenings and inventions, it would seem to have been effective for some time. Science, space-travel, radar, all the modern trend of thought is characteristic of Aquarius, as also are humanitarian ideas and levelling out of class distinction.

It is interesting to try and relate the historical symbols used in former times with these Ages. The Piscean Age, for instance, coincided with the Christian Era, or first two thousand years of it. Jesus was called Icthus, the Fish; the early Christians used the symbol of the Fish and there was talk of Fishers of Men. In the Arien Age, from about 2000 B.C. the Ram or sacrificial lamb played a part in ritual, replacing the sacred Bull, Taurus of the preceding Age, which began about 4000 B.C. The Geminian Age, about 6000 B.C. had its cult of Twins, of which there are traces in Babylon, Assyria and Samothrace, with the accent on pairs of gods. The year 8000 B.C. tallies with the beginning of the Cancerian Age, Cancer being a watery sign which suits well with tales of catastrophe by flood. There is even a legend that our present Moon first appeared in the sky about this time (Moon rules Cancer). Still earlier is the Age of Leo, the beginning of which may be placed near 10,000 B.C. This is the golden Age that has left its trace in Sun symbols on Easter Island, in South America and elsewhere. Leo is the sign of the Sun and its metal is gold. These matters are mentioned in the belief that there is correspondence between the constellations (or their traditional significance) and the general history of our race.

The Great Year

It takes about 25,800 years for the point of the vernal equinox to travel back through the complete circle: this period comprising twelve ages is called the Great Year. Technically, this movement accompanies the gradual swing of the poles of the Earth in a full circle round the poles of the Ecliptic, a movement known as nutation. It is something like the motion of a humming-top which revolves faster than the eye can follow and makes at the same time a slow, swinging movement that is easily observed. It is one of these slow, swinging revolutions of the Earth that takes 25,800 years to complete.

Tropical and Sidereal Zodiacs

It is not strictly correct to speak of *two* zodiacs. The zodiac is a circular road in the heavens divided into twelve 30° segments, and the difference between Tropical and Sidereal reckoning is merely the starting-point on this same road. 0° Aries Tropical is the Vernal Equinoctial point, 0° Aries Sidereal is a somewhat arbitrary first degree of the constellation Aries and thereafter follows an equal 30° division regardless of the inequality in size of the actual constellations.

The obvious drawback of the Sidereal method is that its starting-point is steadily changing from an Earth or geocentric point of view. The more serious objection for a practising astrologer is that characterisations made by this method quite simply are not descriptive of the personality under consideration. An astrology of personality needs an unchanging circle (or cycle) of qualities as a background against which to judge the planetary principles or energies and the Tropical method supplies this. It is logical to pick as a starting-point the moment in time, corresponding to a position on the Great Circle, when the Sun crosses the Equator from south to north. This is the time of the Vernal Equinox and there is an invariable result on Earth in the change of season. To use the *constellation* Aries as a starting-point in astrology of personality seems as illogical as to say that spring *should* begin at the true 0° Aries of the stars and to attempt to grow crops out of season. If our whole earth with its seasonal changes, mating season, weather and crops manifestly responds to the starting-point of the so-called 0° Aries of the Tropical Zodiac, must human beings be so perverse as to imagine that they alone in nature can step out of line and remain unaffected by this universal happening?

It is a pity that there has been so much stress on the names of the signs, picturesque as they are; for it gives the impression that the group of stars so named has some kind of specific effect or correspondence in human behaviour; and this is fantastic in face of the real state of affairs, for some of the stars in a constellation are millions of light-years distant from others in the same so-called group. It seems far more logical to assume that the important factor is the circle and that the seeming significance of the zodiac, bulls, rams and the rest, is really a matter of the degree placings in whatever circle is under consideration. Even users of the Sidereal Zodiac of the constellations use a 30° division of the circle.

It is necessary to say a little more on this subject, although its bearing may not be entirely clear to those who have not received some training in astrology.

There is certainly no question but that the moment in *time* of the Vernal Equinox is significant. Mathematically it has been found to be a useful starting-point for calculation and calendar purposes. It is the point in *space* where the Sun in its apparent path crosses the Equator from south to north. It is known as 0° Aries and starts the Equinoctial or Tropical Zodiac that most Western astrologers use, since it is the zodiac of the calendar and almanac. This is the zodiac whose sign meanings are described in pages 31–76. There seems no doubt whatever that these sign meanings are valid in terms of human character. If, however, the Sidereal Zodiac is regarded as the circle for the Great Year, and it is possible to relate characteristics of the signs to a given epoch, this is to admit the validity of the signs of the constellations in this connexion and this is a point when supporters of the Sidereal Zodiac insist that you can't have it both ways. I do not agree with them. I hold that the circle itself has significance and the starting-point of one circle will have affinity with the starting-point of *any other circle*, and many circles are used in astrology, greater and smaller. It is a segment of 30° or twelfth part of the circle that has its own characteristics whether you call it Aries or the first thirty degrees of any given cycle of experience.

This is borne out in the interpretation of charts, where the starting-point may be different for each person. As any astrologer knows, if Leo was rising over the horizon at the moment of *your* birth, then for *you* Leo governs the first 30° of the chart, known technically as the '1st House'. Traditionally, '1st House' matters relate to first things and can be likened to Aries, the most personal sign, the starting-point, initiatory action.

Given this traditional relation of the first thirty degrees to Aries in '1st House' matters, regardless of the sign on the cusp of the 1st House, it seems logical to go a step further and take the point of the Vernal

Equinox as relating to beginnings and first things in Earth problems and call this point Aries, regardless of its correspondence to the Stellar Zodiac. In this way Aries becomes the name for beginnings.

The late C. E. O. Carter pointed out in his book *The Zodiac and the Soul* that the Zodiac portrays the path of the soul of man, that life is kindled in Aries, accumulates power in Taurus and flows freely in Gemini where ideas take shape. These divisions and their traditional meanings are indeed more significant than is generally recognised, since they stand for life itself at given levels. The circle that never begins and never ends is symbolic of life in any part of the cosmos. The very simplicity of their presentation in symbolic form indicates that the application is general. Like parables, they can be interpreted at more than one level and they are not less significant at one than another.

I suggest that confusion regarding the two zodiacs arises when it is not realised that everything living has its own circle, or cycle, which can be depicted as a zodiac with its significant degree areas and that if we relate beginnings to Aries and go on from there we have a key to the problem in whatever circle we are considering.

PART III

Consulting an Astrologer

1. THE CLIENT–CONSULTANT RELATIONSHIP

The newly trained consultant, like the medical practitioner, has to start on someone, but it takes time to build up a secure foundation on which his interpretations are based. A wise consultant will do the charts of as many as possible of his own close friends and family members, because it really is not honest to charge a fee until he has assembled tried and true indications on which to base his findings.

I begin a person-to-person consultation with a new client by telling him enough about himself to establish confidence that I am really talking about *him* or *her*. This is a wise precaution, as there are those who lie about their age so consistently that they give the wrong year of birth, and in that case the consultant will have calculated the chart of quite another individual.

Some clients need firm handling. There are strong-minded types who visit the astrologer with the fixed intention of being told what they want to hear.

The consultant should, above all, help to allay fears and inhibitions. To do this he must help each person to understand his own pattern. Not, I would stress, in order to manipulate life, for I hold the opinion that the happy individual is one who, in a subtle way, allows life to 'live *him*'. By improving the channel, or the instrument that the breath of life plays on, it will be found that events take care of themselves. The client should be encouraged to trust in heaven, which astrologically speaking means the heavenly or sky pattern, and to live the pattern the way it is meant to be lived. The astrologer should respect the fact that the 'way' and the 'pattern' are different for every individual.

In talking to the client about difficult factors in the chart, I feel that if I make a picture of the sort of actions and reactions that are typical of a particular aspect or group of aspects, it is up to the *thinking* client to imagine a way of adjusting the scales, as it were, to fit in with his personal possibilities and circumstances. Let no one imagine that I am the kind of clairvoyant practitioner who can see details, such as misdeeds or mistakes. But the client knows these facts for himself, and the astrologer can only help if the client treats him as a consultant. The client who shuts up like a clam cannot get the best out of an interview with present-day astrologers, who are quite a different proposition from certain psychic practitioners who prefer silence. If in doubt it is best to ask which is preferred.

I remember a conversation with one of the many clients who come to me with some sort of marital trouble. She was beautiful and talented, with a capable but somewhat critical look. I could sympathise with her urge to get back to a career. "Do you know that your main ability lies in your critical faculty?" "Yes," she said, "I was told that at school and university." I pointed out that it was just this critical faculty, so valuable in professional work, that was her problem. She would be excellent as a critic in the film world, or as a buyer for a firm where discrimination is needed; or perhaps at laboratory work where the capacity to niggle over details is appreciated. But in her case this strong critical faculty was running riot in domestic life and distressing her husband and children.

This is a very obvious case. But domestic friction often arises when circumstances prevent a powerful urge or talent from being employed constructively. The consultant astrologer can help by pointing out a suitable channel for the blocked energy.

Positive advice should be given. It is more palatable to be told how to use strengths than to be criticised about the effects of their *mis*application.

The late Professor C. G. Jung wrote much about 'meaningful coincidences' and synchronicity. I experienced such phenomena at the time when I did many brief analyses each day for the 'special offer' feature of *She* magazine in its early days. Each chart was a personal document, calculated from time, date and place of birth. I found that although the orders came in at random from readers of all ages, there emerged a pattern for the day or the week. My secretary remarked on the fact that three or four charts running contained almost identical problems.

Any practitioner, astrological or otherwise will know what I mean when I say that one gets accustomed to clients (or patients) with a particular problem or characteristic crowding in over a period in time. And it is also a fact that each practitioner attracts a clientele of a particular type. However skilled an astrologer may be, he cannot help all types of client.

Some clients come for a single consultation and never return. With others with whom one has greater rapport there is a yearly or longer cycle separating contacts and enquiries. Lastly, and happily most infrequently, there are the deeply disturbed folk who depend heavily on one and in such cases it takes time and patience to help the individual to a fuller discovery of himself.

The astrologer should not, I feel, give specific advice and most certainly should not attempt to impose his opinions. Any interview, however short, involves a relationship between two people, the consultant and the client. The impact of this encounter can prove constructive or destructive. My advice to young astrologers is to terminate any professional relationship that has the wrong 'feel' about it. There are those who ask questions that are unanswerable or who obviously expect a form of fortune-telling that the serious astrologer makes no claim to offer.

Few astrologers set out to act as therapists. Nevertheless, clarification of the natal pattern often proves therapeutic. A person who feels abandoned or deserted while in the throes of a compulsive or obsessive relationship can be greatly comforted by an analysis of the relationship which may show clearly how an irresistible, if temporary, magnetism is at work.

It can happen that over-enthusiastic friends or clients press someone to have an analysis. It is, however, preferable for the initiative to be that of the client himself. I am fortunate in that I seem to be sent, by recommendation or because the individual has read something by me, clients who are in sympathy with my approach. I may be over-sensitive, but if I am pushed at people I feel they will arrive in a "Bet she's no good!" mood.

The matter of selecting an astrological practitioner is important. I can be most fully of use only to those who look on life as I do. Many would resent the fact that I am primarily interested in spiritual progress, in evolution, and in the path of the soul rather than in mundane success. I warn clients who want business advice that I am *not* their best choice for this.

The birth chart of every client is also that of a moment applicable to many other levels of interpretation. Your child may be born at the same time that a business project gets going, or a car comes off the production line. Interpretation of the moment is adapted according to its application. Every moment is part of the Whole of which we are a part and to which the individual contributes for good or ill. This makes every client of great importance. By introducing him to himself and to the pattern entrusted him to fulfil and expand we can do much more than he expects when he – maybe condescendingly – visits an astrologer. We can introduce him, perhaps for the first time, to his basic potential, and – if he is prepared to accept the idea – to the life or 'soul progress' pattern which is his to do his best with.

Many people want to know if they will marry, be rich, avoid disaster. They think in big headlines, like the Press. They don't think, "Will I be nice enough to attract the man I want to attract?" or, "Will I work hard enough to get to the top?"

It is of no help and it can do positive harm to make pessimistic, negative statements in analysis. I have been horrified to read blunt and cruel statements given to some of my clients by heedless, power-conscious, badly trained astrologers. The classic case of this which occurred many years ago was that of a girl who had spent some years under psychiatric treatment. She came to me in great distress, asking whether it was true, what an amateur astrologer had told her, that she would never make a friend. As relationships were her weakest side, I do not question the reasoning of this amateur who had analysed an afflicted Neptune in the part of the chart to do with friends. I do, however, heartily condemn his lack of tact and humanity. In fact he was mistaken, too, for it is never safe to isolate an aspect and pronounce upon it. A single bad aspect can correspond to the occasional set-back, but no aspect of any chart constitutes a permanent blight.

The consultant has the power to help a fellow human being forward on his path or the reverse. There is need for kindliness and caution in dealing with an art that reveals a person to himself. In the above case I remember explaining to the girl that she also had a good Venus aspect which showed she could be a good friend and this quality could not fail to attract affection. No chart is wholly negative and the duty of the consultant is not only to clarify difficulties but to reassure the client regarding the potential of his positive qualities.

2. WHAT DOES CHART INTERPRETATION ENTAIL?

Planets and signs were characterised in Part II of this book. Some may have found such explanations rather technical, but no interpretation can be attempted or even vaguely understood without some knowledge of how each zodiacal sign and planet plays its part in the assortment of all that goes to make up an individual chart.

Millions of people have charts with similar basic ingredients. Perhaps the most important rule, therefore, is not to make *any* statement on the basis of a single feature, trait or aspect of the chart without first checking it against other factors that either support or contradict it.

To use my own basic mixture as an example, my Sun is in slow, practical, earthy Taurus: fiery Sagittarius is rising and intense, watery Scorpio contains my Moon. To complete the elements, my ruler, Jupiter, is in airy Libra. In assessing such a mixture the astrologer would have to picture how a basically slow and very determined Taurus individual feels when made to function through a lightning-quick and impulsive Sagittarian Ascendant. To do this we look elsewhere all round the chart to see which of these contradictary basic signs is backed up or frustrated by planetary energies.

We take the fiery Ascendant first. It is ruled by Jupiter in Libra overhead, so that friendliness and the need for approval are exaggerated. The fieriness is strengthened by the Midheaven being in fiery Leo. (Usually a Sag. Ascendant has a Libra Midheaven, but I was born in the Southern hemisphere which has the effect of reversing the angles between Ascendant and Midheaven). People often ask what difference it makes to be born in the Southern hemisphere, and technically it is just this fact of an altered sign on the meridian or Midheaven. To my way of thinking this makes a very big qualifying difference to the Rising-sign. I know that I am a far tougher proposition than relations of mine born in England, whose Rising-sign, like my own, is Sagittarius, but who have Libra – gentle, amenable Libra – culminating. This is not a subject that gets much airing, but as one who is directly involved, I throw it out for your consideration.

This fiery Midheaven (or career point) boosts the basic urge for self-expression and performing in public. My Saturn, too, is in fiery Aries, a competitive, me-first sign. And in truth I like to be first to experience this or that, first in the race, head of the queue. So, in spite of my Taurean Sun-sign being traditionally slow, there is nothing to suggest that my Saturnian braking system is applied otherwise than when I so choose . . . in respect of tempo, that is to say.

Next, we consider the Sun-sign – in my case, Taurus. What is the conditioning here? The ruler, Venus, is in Pisces (its exaltation) in the 4th House. What does this mean? It benefits home life and increases the already strong urge of Taurus for affection. But Taurus likes to give as well as to receive affection and Venus in Pisces is yielding to a fault; so here is a character who will go overboard with no restraint when emotionally involved. And with true Piscean self-sacrifice will enjoy caring for those she loves.

Mercury also in Taurus, in the 6th House, adds to the Taurus strength, manifesting here in service to others or healing. Or, since the aspects are harmonious, in good relationships whether working with others or employing them.

I have gone this far on my own analysis to try to demonstrate how to set out on a chart analysis. Contradictions work side by side and account for the myriad complexities found in every human being.

A person with seemingly gentle, conciliatory signs prominent can have a powerful energy factor, such as Mars in Aries, squaring the Moon. It will have to be gauged how a basically gentle person will channel an argumentative, battling force.

This is where face-to-face consultation is useful. I would ask such a client whether there are occasions when he or she feels rage or irritation building up. In some cases, tensions such as this can account for physical symptoms, skin eruptions or high blood pressure. And in the case of truly evolved human beings what is seen as violence in the pattern may manifest as violence in others with whom the individual is in close contact.

All this should show that, except in people with the mentality of a clockwork mouse, whose every response is automatic, the chances of getting an accurate character analysis from a computer reading is remote. In fact, it may help people who have been puzzled by one of these to transpose certain statements from active to passive connotation and vice versa. A doctor or ambulance man, for instance, may well read that he or she is liable to accidents or crises. True. But whose accidents? What crisis? Critics of astrology who complain of over-generalised statements will do well to reflect on this.

Even the trained or semi-trained student of astrology should be careful never to make pronouncements on the basis of the natal chart only. The chart should always be studied with the Ephemeris for the relevant year in hand, to see in the progressed or converse positions of planets when these go Stationary or Retrograde, and take note of the years in which planets move into another sign. Even when doing the briefest analysis, this procedure should be followed. Why? Because you may be fussing over a danger which never materialises. And what is the importance of a potential if it is never activated? Then again, there may be periods of several years when everything piles up.

The reader may be puzzled at this point as to how a single page of an Ephemeris can show portents for years to come. It just happens to be a fact that by the method of secondary directions, every day following or preceding the birthday represents a year. So, for the average lifetime, the astrologer looks at the seventy to eighty days before and after birth to check on the main possibilities of the whole life. The days after the birthday for what are called 'progressions' and the days prior to birth for the 'converse' directions. For the benefit of astrologers who have not tried the latter, or who may be doubtful of their efficacy, I can assure them that when I was approaching sixty years of age I reviewed my past life and checked known events with progressed positions. A few major events seemed unaccounted for astrologically until I looked at converse solar aspects for the years in question and found the appropriate correspondences. I came to the conclusion that these converse aspects operate in important inner or karmic experiences more than in outer events.

I have already written of the necessity when studying any chart to check where strengths and weaknesses lie and to note any outstanding lack or imbalance.

When writing or talking about the charts of small children, the astrologer should take great care not to sow fear in the mind of a parent. It is possible sometimes to invent stories that can illustrate the out-working of a dangerous aspect without being too definite. When in doubt, I advise portraying an energy combination at its highest and best potential. Remember that planets in combination are energy combinations and only secondarily 'events' . . . events that in fact may never happen.

It is quite normal to find a weak member of the planetary team. The runt in the litter, one might call it. It is a force that needs building up. The wise astrologer won't say: "This Venus or Mars (or whatever) is hopeless!" but he will point out that a certain energy factor – or quality or element – needs boosting, and it is up to the client to accept that this is so and work on it himself if he wants to be better integrated. The individual who studies his chart is less likely to complain, "Why, oh why does this happen to me?" and more likely to be interested in watching what actually happens, outwardly or in inner feelings and emotions, when a weak point in his pattern is activated. In this way he will gradually learn to become more self-governing.

Why do I prefer to work by personal consultation? This is because face-to-face consultations give one such a valuable check on one's interpretative skill. I never find that astrology is wrong, but I *do* find that some aspects appear to function so strongly as to dominate a chart, and am sometimes surprised, having studied the chart, to see 'what' walks in through my door. To check up constantly with live cases is discouraging to the use of set phrases or textbook interpretations. I have known astrologers to be so in love with their pet theories that they are furious to find themselves off target.

However, written work has to be done for distant clients and there *is* an advantage in not being side-tracked or over-influenced by appearance, manner or sheer personality. A penetrating and frank study, especially of the less harmonious factors, is perhaps best done this way, possibly as a preliminary to person-to-person discussion. Of course it adds to the expense for the client to have both, so I may be suggesting an ideal rather than a practical procedure.

The dabbler in astrology who draws up the occasional chart for friends is often a bit of a menace. He or she is in danger of making too much of a single feature and failing to synthesise the whole. An interpretation should be done with the realisation that what is under consideration is a cosmic moment. Who are we to criticise or belittle such a thing? One moment may be less harmonious than the preceding one, but to the individual to whom it applies it is all he has in terms of energy factors and potential. It is his framework on which he must build his life and create his future. For everyone's future is built or ruined by his reactions to the present – to the all-important NOW. The interpretation of a personal chart in a time of crisis, in so far as it stimulates or depresses, can tip the scales one way or another.

I would like a beginner consultant to do the birth charts daily – for a period – of every baby born in a given hospital. This would give him a clearer concept of basic sky patterns. He would follow the gradual formation, day to day, of important aspects – a tense Cross or harmonious Trine and would appreciate how these, in daily change of emphasis, form a similar yet subtly changing background for the quicker moving planets. He would learn the importance of accuracy. For only when given the exact degree of the Ascendant or Midheaven can it be observed that baby X born at noon has neatly avoided involvement with a difficult configuration (which of course is *in* the chart, but not emphasised), while her twin, Y, born half an hour later, is right in the turmoil, with, say, the tensest part of the Cross right on his Ascendant degree. And so on through that day and the next, *and* the next, the main pattern is very similar except for the fast-moving pointers geared to the earth's revolutions of 360° in 24 hours (approximately). These, like the minute and second hands on the watch, modify or exaggerate what is there for all as a background scene.

Any professional astrologer has to work to a time schedule. He has to talk to a client about his chart while realising within himself that it has taken him years fully to fathom his own pattern, if indeed he ever does so. So here is a recipe I evolved for quick assessment of a birth chart.

A doctor of my acquaintance, known as a brilliant diagnostician, once told me that when a new patient came to his surgery, the first question he would ask himself was, "Is this an ill person, or is he (she) basically a healthy one with an ailment?" The astrologer with life-long experience of charts should be able to make much the same assessment when confronted with a fresh birth chart. Accordingly, for a quick and comprehensive assessment of a natal chart, I proceed in the following manner and order:

1. Assess the basic characteristics and how the individuality (represented by the Sun-sign) is likely to work through a perhaps contradictory Rising-sign; then consider how this combination of signs will deal with the main lessons of the life, as indicated, broadly speaking, by the Moon-sign.
2. Study the balance of elements and qualities.
3. Study the aspect pattern. Is it (a) harmonious? (b) afflicted? (c) contradictory?
   If (a) is it so harmonious as to promote laziness?
   (b) is it so afflicted as to be unbalancing?
   (c) see what the contradictions consist of.
4. Study aspects, especially to Sun, Moon and ruling planets, noting how these modify the sign potentials.
   By now it should be clear what type you are dealing with. Continue by considering the fields of activity or 'houses' of the chart, remembering that the individual's attitude to his pattern is of greater importance than the corresponding events about which it may be wiser to keep silent.
5. Assess spheres of talent and good fortune and also spheres of hardship, frustration and the serious lessons of the life.
6. Finally check with the Ephemeris to see if the pattern unfolds and develops so as to further the aims and ambitions or the reverse.

I have left out the most important advice of all, which is to remember that your client is a sensitive human being, not a sort of guinea-pig on whom you try your skills. It is far better to seem to be a bad astrologer than to hand out a load of negative pronouncements.

Chart interpretation depends on the human intermediary. No astrologer can understand a client who is at a very different level of evolution from himself. So, if you consult an astrologer, it is well to realise that the variation in intelligence of interpretation between two practitioners can be as wide as that between mere 'waffle' and a lecture by a Senior Wrangler.

Is it possible to diagnose a split personality from a chart? If by this one means what is known medically as 'schizophrenia I would say "No". Yet it is certain that, being wise after the event, a state of schizophrenia would be found to have fitting correspondences in the pattern of the planetary aspects.

All astrologers have seen charts that divide into what amounts to two distinct halves. The birth month has nothing to do with this. I say this because people with too little information might start wondering about what are called 'dual' signs. Indications of a personality divided in itself show, in my experience, in a strongly-acting planetary configuration which is totally unrelated to the rest of the pattern. For instance, Mercury opposite Uranus, is itself an indication of originality or eccentricity, and neither of these two aspected by any other planet, so that they are unrelated to other energies. Such an aspect, when activated, could produce reactions totally at variance to the main personality.

I feel it to be important in my astrological work to remember that I am not a medical practitioner, and be reticent about what amounts to pathological imbalance. If more enlightened days arrive and the medical profession appreciates the light that can be thrown on a case by a skilled astrologer, much could be gained by an interchange of opinions. But until this day arrives the astrologer should be reticent in what he says to his client, or to the parent of a child whose chart he is studying.

Balance and Imbalance: The Elements

Experienced astrologers and astrologer psychologists find that in gauging the balance of the individual, perhaps the most indicative factor is seen in the elements. I am indebted to Stephen Arroyo and his book, *Astrology, Psychology and the Four Elements,** which is the first book I have read that deals with the elements and their varying balances and imbalances in detail.

In order of importance in assessing balance I would next take Qualities or Quadruplicities, namely Cardinality, Fixity and Mutability.

It is not merely a question of listing the *number* of planets in both of the above groups, as the Rising-sign and the placement of Sun, Moon or Midheaven far outweigh the remoter energy factors. What do I mean precisely? You perhaps have the Sun in Capricorn, an Earth-sign, and nothing else in Earth-signs. But the Sun is always of high importance and with that alone you will be well represented in earthy characteristics. In fact in gauging balance it is best to discount Uranus, Neptune and Pluto. These slow-moving planets stay so long in a sign that the effect lasts for a whole generation or longer and applies to every baby born in more than a decade. All members of an age group share the generational characteristics of Uranus or Neptune in a particular sign.

* C.R.C.S. (U.S.A.), distributed by L. N. Fowler & Co. Ltd.

What should be looked for? The *complete absence* of emphasis on an Element or Quadruplicity is something to reckon with. I always tell the client with, say, not a single planet or sensitive degree in, for example, Earth-signs, "You will find it difficult to understand the types who like solid results; who are good at practical work; sensible (*you* might call it mean) about money . . . because this is just not your scene." Indeed, if a person who completely lacks any one element tries to become a psychologist, he or she will have to rely solely on theory to empathise with an individual who is strongly of the factor lacking in his, the practitioner's, make-up.

Planetary energies can to some extent restore imbalance of elements. A well-aspected Saturn and Mars can give the energy capability and ability to finish a job, but while this may seem the equivalent of having strength in practical Earth-signs, it does *not* give the basic potential which, when absent, can deny fulfilment and even produce a feeling of guilt.

Likewise, and this I can vouch for personally, a well-aspected Mercury in an Earth-sign can give the impression of intellectual brilliance, but to be really at home in the academic field a person needs strength in Air-signs.

A powerful, expressive Mars in Airy Gemini, which permits its owner to go off pop when angry or impatient, can give the impression of Fire. But the basically Fire person has a warmth which a strong Mars working through a non-Fire sign would not give.

You may be fooled into thinking someone is strongly Watery. He is emotional, sensitive, but on better acquaintance you find the intensely blue eye is accounted for by Neptune rising or near the Sun . . . and a strongly placed and aspected Moon substitutes for what you thought to be Cancerian tenderness.

I consider that I have an even distribution of elements, so I list them as an illustration of how to judge lacks or overbalances.

In my chart Fire is adequately represented by a Sagittarian Ascendant, Leo Midheaven and Saturn in Aries; Earth has the Sun and Mercury in Taurus – Air has Mars and Jupiter; Water has the Moon in Scorpio and Venus in Pisces. I leave out the Extra-Saturnians as these would be the same for all in my age group.

How does this affect my life? I think that due to this even distribution I have not been aware of being swamped by powerful Water people, overlaid or crushed by Earthy ones, left way behind by the brilliance and speed of Air, or unable to participate in the enthusiasms and ardours of Fire . . . although this may come in old age. I have seldom had a severe clash with anyone or found myself totally unable to empathise; except with those for whom relationships are a chronic trouble.

We all judge others by ourselves. How else should we? But long experience of analysis can bring understanding of very different points of view, and the consultant learns what very different approaches there can be to problems.

Difference in tempo of living often relates to the elements. Speed is natural to strongly Fire and Air types, and aspects such as Mars rising close to the Ascendant degree, or Mars in strong aspect with impulsive Uranus, are found in the charts of racing, danger-loving types. Earthy types on the other hand have affinity with the slow rhythms of growing things, even if contradictory factors in their charts make them plant a row of cabbages as though the devil were after them.

Regardless of tempo, Earth strength manifests in a need to see results. The seed of an idea has to be seen to grow and bear fruit. Theory has to be tested. To the Air person, the theory is satisfying in itself. (But here again I speak of Air undiluted – and in balanced people this would not be so. The absent-minded professor is rare enough to remain a comic figure.)

As a practitioner rather than a theorist, I value truths in astrology that will not let me down in my professional contacts with clients. One such proven truth certainly lies in the effects of imbalance of elements; especially in temperamental clashes.

Incidentally, if the signs are transposed into the Sidereal Zodiac, which is the visible sky zodiac of the constellations, these reliable indications are thrown out of gear. Small wonder that the Siderealists dismiss elements and quadruplicities as nonsense, for they cannot use them with confidence, as is possible when using the tropical zodiac.

The Quadruplicities: Cardinal, Fixed and Mutable Signs

The effects of imbalance of quadruplicities are very easy to spot in human behaviour. An excess of planets in Cardinal signs (Aries, Cancer, Libra and Capricorn) gives restlessness – need to 'do' something about it. Fixity (Taurus, Leo, Scorpio and Aquarius are the Fixed signs) shows in rigid obstinacy and there is a type of looks that I associate with Fixed signs. The Scandinavians have an expression about people with strong characters having 'a bone in their nose'. They must be visualising Fixed types. Mutable signs (Gemini, Virgo, Sagittarius and Pisces) *in overbalance* produce the type of person who yields too readily and gets pushed around. When this is the case, intelligent adaptability has degenerated into weakness.

The late Dr. Carl Jung would have appreciated the synchronicity in what I am about to relate. A client arrived just as I had got to this point in my first draft of this chapter. I had not done her chart, as she wished to speak of problems other than astrological. Her main worry was that she was not 'doing enough'. She felt utterly frustrated by the fact that she did not know what her life's work was, and illness prevented her from being more actively helpful to others.

I calculated her chart on the spot to find that she had no less than eight planets in Cardinal signs, forming a double Grand Cross, within which the restrictive planet Saturn was in the same degree as Mars, the main energy factor. Both were in Aries. So here was excessive Cardinality (restlessness and urge for activity) with the brakes full on, limiting her strong Mars potential for action and initiative. For the interest of fellow astrologers, as if this was not enough, Jupiter was opposite them in Libra, exaggerating the whole thing. Never have I seen a better example of excessive Cardinality, and her parting remark, "What if I can *never do all I feel I should be doing?*" was an illustration of the unfulfilled potential if ever I saw one.

A case of similar imbalance of excessive Fixity was described under the Taurus heading as an instance of longevity.

Planetary Disposition

The disposition of the various planetary energies* in the personal chart can also contribute to balance or imbalance. Each of us has a team of forces – or energies – at our disposal. Each planet represents a different type of energy. We do not need our Mars courage and initiative while lying sunbathing by a pool, although we might suddenly need to summon it up if a toddler falls into the water. We call our Venus into action to ingratiate ourselves with someone or to make friends, our Saturn when we need to be stern, forbidding or self-controlled; and so it goes on. So where does balance come in?

The chart of a birth moment will show if, regardless of what we consider to be 'our' sign, any particular planet is overstressed. It may perhaps be strongly placed in its own sign and have many aspects from which it gains extra energy. I can spot an over-strong Mars energy a mile off. The individual will be insistent, impatient for immediate attention, aggressive (although possibly politely so), over-ready to take action or interfere. On the credit side, such a person will cope competently and, if need be, courageously in a crisis. Saturn in excess can be stern, coldly cruel, fanatically punctual . . . or in some cases depressive and pessimistic. Jupiter in excess shows itself in foolish optimism or exaggerated joviality.

The whole balance of a chart can be put out if one of the members of the team is weak, like the weak link in a chain. For of what benefit is it to have the potential for, say, painting, if application and ability to stick to the job is lacking? The variety of planetary possibilities is endless. Your aggressive small boy may have a strong Mars in analytical Virgo so that his aggression manifests competitively in compiling longer lists than his friends of the cars, footballers or Judo experts that fill his mind.

A weak Saturn, among other defects, can mean no sense of time. And of what use is talent if the individual is late for interviews, rehearsals and so on? In this way the imbalanced chart may show talent and energy with

* Full planetary descriptions in Part II, Chapter 6.

small possibility of it being employed productively. Even in an otherwise Saturnian chart – one with Capricorn as Sun-sign or ascending – the potential is not necessarily fulfilled. A basic seriousness of purpose will prove inadequate if the native is unable to exercise discipline on himself or on others, should he be in a position of authority.

The art of interpreting the birth chart depends on ability to synthesise the various energy factors. I advise students to develop a sort of built-in checking system. If tempted to say "A Scorpio! Proud, intense, power-ful, passionate . . ." look quickly at Mars, the ruler of Scorpio, to see how the Scorpio energy of this individual with the Sun in this sign (or rising) is *in fact* channelled. Is it channelled easily, strongly, confidently, or is there some impediment or some twist? If the latter, then there may show a very recognisable pattern of inner conflict where powerful energies boil up but are hindered of outlet. Such a person will not behave as a textbook Scorpio, yet his behaviour is the direct con-sequence of his thwarted Scorpio depths.

Imbalance in general in the chart (and I am not referring to mental imbalance so much as imbalance of energies) means that one energy is not backing up another and so not enabling a basic potential to be satisfyingly fulfilled.

It is not only beginners who run up against astrological puzzles.

I once heard the late Charles Carter, author of many authoritative books, confess himself puzzled by the chart of a young Sun-Leo. This youth, it seems, lacked confidence. He was shy of girls and prudish to the point of hesitating to enter a shop and buy himself underpants. Very un-Leo-like.

At this period in the early fifties, psychological know-how had scarcely begun to infiltrate into astrological circles. As a very junior student I hesitated to suggest that the explanation lay in the fact that far from letting down astrological thought in being an atypical Leo, the youth was in truth *over-sensitive concerning his unfulfilled Leo potential*. For if a sign is strong, as Sun or Rising-sign, the basic urges run strongly along the lines of the sign in question. In this youth's case it was Leo. But the ability to develop and enjoy a potential may be weak . . . *was* weak in this particular case. His phobia and embarrassment were all the more acute because basically he was a Leo who was 'letting down the side'. Had he been basically a shy Virgo or a sensitive, timid Pisces, there would have been no inner conflict. Obviously not all Pisceans are timid, but even tough-seeming ones would have a basic appreciation of reticence or shyness.

There is a real danger, when interpreting a chart, of confusing poten-tial urges with the possibility of actual achievement and fulfilment. As I have illustrated in the case of the shy youth – a Leo is not necessarily a confident leader; a Cancer is not necessarily tender and protective, and so forth.

Major psychological complexes arise when one cannot fulfil a basic urge which is at work in the unconscious. So before saying rashly, "You are a confident, natural leader," to a Leo, look carefully at the whole chart to see if this basic potential is supported. If there are strong indications of frustration, such a statement could be far from true. It would be natural for an afflicted Leo to be highly aware and sensitive about his failure to lead. The study of contradictions is necessary, for it is in the accurate gauging of complexity and imbalance that we can help the individual to increased self-knowledge, and through self-knowledge to integration and self-government.

An important fact to bear in mind in analysis is that factors in a chart do not cancel each other out. It is true that helpful factors mitigate unhelpful ones, but it is faulty thinking to consider a human being as a consistent conglomeration of his various ingredients. We are all a mass of contradictions in infinite variety.

I have written thousands of analyses and have continually varied my methods in an effort to keep a fresh approach. I like to start with a synthesised impression of the person as a whole before considering the effect of each member of the planetary team in turn. Each of us is a whole only in the sense that a team is a whole . . . a unit. The emphasis of certain signs provide the overall picture, within which the planetary components play their various parts, so giving it its special character. At a glance it can be seen if there is a preponderance of heavy Earthiness or other element or if there is balance. Or it may be that Cardinality, Fixity or Mutability colours the whole.

I try to get the feeling of balance in respect of signs, through the elements and quadruplicities, and then give attention to each planet in turn, noting its element or quality. (By the way, a quality, astrologically speaking, is the same as a quadruplicity and it's shorter to write.) As with a team, a single member can let the side down or score the goal that brings success.

Once the individual grasps the idea that in different circumstances he can call on different members of his team, he finds it fascinating to check and test this out against the chart. Which planet was in fact activated when you had that accident or when you had to cope with danger? When action in a crisis is called for, what kind of a Mars energy can you call up? Have you a resourceful, cool Mars to summon to your aid or do you just flap? The clever man covers up his deficiencies and most of us substitute conventional language when referring to a sympathy we don't feel. This could be described as Mercury (communication) covering up for Venus (heart).

Integration is desirable in all team work, and what is this astrologically if not the conscious use of *all* our planetary forces in efficient group effort?

Integration

The well-integrated person is one who functions wholly. In other words he uses all his powers in a harmonious harnessing of their strengths. There is no shrinking from life, which he allows to 'live him' . . . and this means accepting himself for what he is, warts and all. Is not this what is meant by the injunction to 'love your neighbour *as yourself*' which implies self-love that cannot be excessive if we love our neighbour to the same extent? We are not asked to love him *more* than ourselves.

Is the astrologer serving any useful purpose in studying a life pattern? Or is he encouraging morbid introspection? Morbid introspection has become a cliché. What about healthy introspection? A review of our qualities in the spirit of a general reviewing his troops – to see if they are up to the standard of tackling what lies ahead.

This kind of critical inspection is made possible by the birth chart. Of course we will find *something* unpleasant. We all have a 'shadow' of some kind, and it is healthy to face facts and acknowledge that just as we seldom, if ever, meet anyone who seems perfect in every respect, so, when we meet ourselves face to face, analytically, there is no denying the faults. Intolerance of failings should not, however, go beyond a healthy determination to overcome them, just as satisfaction with talents should externalise not in smugness but in the will to put them to good use.

Faulty integration of imbalance in the individual occurs when he hates a part of himself and thrusts faults and weaknesses into the background, imagining that by so doing he can lead a successful life with what remains. The fact is, he cannot. To go back to our military image, the General cannot fight with half his army because some regiments are less efficient than others. We must not imagine that Heaven has made a mistake in creating us as we are. It is up to us to look in the mirror of self-analysis and come to terms with what we see. No shoving of skeletons in cupboards. No pretence and no excuses.

One point I am anxious to make is that imbalance can and does occur regardless of the birth month or the Rising-sign. And so can extraversion and introversion. Indeed, the most complex pathological introvert may be one who has unfulfilled extravert potentials and vice versa. What is important to see in either case is whether a main potential is blocked. The blocking may appear to manifest in frustrating circumstances, whereas in truth the so-called circumstances are an externalisation of complex energy patterns in the individual.

So, at the risk of repetition, it is quite erroneous to think that astrology says that if you are born under, for example, LEO, you *are* sunny, confident, commanding and all the rest. What it *does* say is that you have through your Leo Sun the basic potential for Leo characteristics, which the rest of your birth chart with its different energy emphases will implement or frustrate. It is no good telling a frustrated Leo that a modest violet also goes to Heaven. He loathes modest violets! But ask him if he unconsciously feels himself to be bigger, more commanding than he actually is in this life . . . suggest that in a past life he has been a ruler, and something in him will respond. He goes away feeling that at last someone really understands him.

The opposite also applies. The potentially shrinking, reserved introvert thrust into an extravert, positive, self-expressive job is subjected to intolerable strain.

Is there a remedy for imbalance and lack of integration if this is strongly shown in the birth chart?

Clearly, in extreme cases of illness, deformity or neurosis one cannot just hand out brisk advice on learning to cope. Such cases need gentle, specialist handling. But for the average case with a slight lack of integration of existing energies one can advise on how best to jolly along the negative side by skilful use of the positive.

A therapeutic application of astrological techniques lies in a positive dealing with the 'whole man', and not in the attempted amputation of some feared or imagined 'evil' part.

3. DIFFICULTIES – DISASTERS – DEATH

Many questions are asked about disasters, accidents and death. I have been asked how much an individual's chart is influenced by the containing 'world' chart. Can personal trends be swept aside by larger world calamities and disasters?

The world chart, as one might call the ever-changing pattern of planetary aspects in the framework of the zodiac, will, in theory, draw into the disaster only those whose personal charts have points of correspondence with prevailing disaster aspects. If there is no connexion the individual will be unaffected; or, as can happen, emerge from a disaster unscathed.

It is also asked if more personal disasters, such as deaths in the family, can be shown in the personal charts of members of the family. Here, I feel that much depends on the impact that such an event would make on those bereaved. The long-expected death, by whatever means, of someone very old could show as a happy release in the chart of a relative on whom the burden of nursing had been heavy. The death of a husband or a child taken in seemingly full health would surely show as a shock and disruption.

Are tragedies foreseeable? What is termed a 'tragic life' would certainly contain the potential for this in the natal chart. But just as a doctor will not commit himself about life or death situations, the wise astrologer will not spread fear. For, in fact, while he may see a difficult aspect ahead, he cannot know the specific events it will correspond to. All he is sure of is that the individual will be tested in some way which, after the event, will be seen to fit the threatening aspects. Evolved people may work off times of difficulty in some *inner* test rather than in any obvious disaster.

People's minds jump readily to death and disaster as an interpretation of an approaching difficulty. Experience has taught me to think with Mark Twain, who, I have heard, remarked that he had been through some terrible things in his life, but that most of them had never happened!

In any wide-scale disaster only a percentage of people suffer. It is certainly true that fear is a waste of time and energy. "The coward dies a thousand deaths, the brave man one," is a truism I admire, although I don't suppose for a moment I would be unafraid in a moment of danger.

Sidestepping Trouble: To what extent is it possible?
We are being badly misled if we imagine we can side-step trouble through knowledge of our charts or the help of an astrologer. Of course it is true that with insight and foreknowledge of tests ahead we may negotiate them better. Every day can be lived better or worse.

But a client mustn't expect to be given clear directives to questions such as, "Tell me about my chart so that I won't be killed" – or "Tell me my aspects so that I won't marry the wrong person" – or "Tell me my little boy's chart so that he may be a genius!" Potentials for any of these things show in the birth chart, as do potentials for accidents and tensions, and the astrologer can warn of a difficult or testing time ahead, but I absolutely deplore the idea that we should advise any side-stepping process or indeed give the idea that evasion is possible. In olden days knights in armour rode out expressly to meet dangers and challenges, and the whole idea of life was to be as brave and chivalrous as possible. In the present time there are dragons just as formidable as any who lurked behind a mediaeval tree. They may have changed shape, or attack on different planes, but the same qualities are needed *in us*. Courage is needed to face an operation or health problem; self-control and patience can be practised in every bus or taxi queue. All these give opportunity to meet life as it is; not to evade trouble or annoyance.

Are the trends in the chart something over which one has no control? I repeat that I do not believe that trouble or disaster can be avoided by taking evasive action. Do you remember the story of the farmer who was plagued by a leprechaun (which my dictionary tells me is an Irish sprite)? Evidently this farmer didn't know how to treat leprechauns, and the teasing grew to such an extent that he decided to leave the district. As he was moving off in his wagons a neighbour called to him, "Be ye flitting, Will'm?" and the leprechaun stuck his head out of a churn and answered, "Aye, we's flittin'!"

The answer lies in ourselves. We attract events that are in some way part of us, and if we don't like the pattern, the remedy is to change ourselves, which is not something that can be done overnight. I am sorry to sound so 'improving', but it really can be said that we can control our lives to the extent that we gain control of our actions – or reactions. Meeting trouble with courage can be the making of a person.

A so-called 'bad aspect' is primarily a difficult energy combination which seeks an outlet. Analysis of the particular energy which is at work at a given time is preferable to seeking information with a view to evading the possible outcome of what look like dangerous or tiresome energy combinations.

At the emotional level it can help a man or woman to be shown the brutal truth of the unreality of a relationship that has become a torture. Suffering may be the order of the day, but progress and a higher level of consciousness can be achieved by thinking of tests and troubles as something we have been born to cope with. The precise test needed to prove ourselves will be put in our path, and if we can say "Let's tackle it!" that is the positive attitude.

If after all this, you still think you can use astrologers or astrology to help you to side-step difficulties, either shut up your astrology books and never consult an astrologer again, or have a shot at turning what is seemingly negative into something positive – a destructive energy into a creative one. It is nearly always possible to make some choice in this way, and it seems to be a fact that if a potentially dangerous energy is *used*, it is less dangerous. This is seen in the charts of doctors and nurses who have difficult or violent aspects in the part of the chart to do with health – aspects which bear on the illness or injury of those in their care rather than their own.

Especially in analysis of children's charts, the astrologer should point out how the energy of an aspect can be made productive. But for everyone it is a fact that energies need outlet: the work of the astrologer should be to clarify such energies, which can be studied through familiarity with the different planets and the potentials of their inter-relationship by aspect.

Accidents

Is it possible to foresee accidents ahead? Personally I wouldn't bank on it. In a fully progressed chart – which is not, unless specified, part of a basic character analysis – periods likely to produce events of a certain nature can be seen. But people vary so greatly in the way they react to identical circumstances that one cannot be accurate as to the exact nature or outcome of aspects or events. Given the same aspect (but against its individual background) one person may have an operation, another a car accident, a third may be involved in caring for others with these troubles. In all cases, however, the period of time when some such happening is in the picture is foreseeable. It is of comfort to those in trouble to be told that the tiresome phase has an end as well as a beginning.

What signs or aspects are associated with accidents?

The late Charles Carter wrote a short book on the subject of the astrology of accidents,* and no doubt much has since been written on this subject, which I will not repeat or quote as I prefer to stick to

* C. E. O. Carter, *The Astrology of Accidents*, Theosophical Publishing House, N.C. 1961.

experiences I can vouch for personally. The worst car accident, which involved a client of mine in a succession of operations, came at the time of a traditionally favourable aspect to her unaspected Mars. Mars is the planet to do with physical courage, and this series of events certainly involved a considerable testing of this quality. In her next life, no doubt she will be born with a stronger natal Mars which needs no such testing.

My daughter cut off a toe in a rotary mower in a year when her main progressed aspect was one of renunciation. Well, she certainly renounced that toe. And, basically she has an impulsive and independent character which contributed to the event, as she had omitted to wear protective boots.

Ethically, an astrologer should never blurt out that at a certain time in his life, little Johnny will probably have an accident. All children have accidents and mention of a specific one could implant fear in the parents' minds. If a chart is accident-prone, it is a good idea to suggest that the child concerned be taught to cope with crises of one sort or another. Just as the charts of doctors, nurses and, especially surgeons, contain a sickness or ill-health potential, so do they often appear to be accident-prone. Such people fulfil the aspect constructively by coping with accidents and injuries and this seems, very rightly, to protect them from personal injury. The inference is that the aspect has to work, but not actively and passively simultaneously.

So, really, it boils down to the fact that it *is* possible to tell from the birth chart when accidents or mishaps are likely, but whether it is a good idea to issue warnings is quite another matter. I am against creating fear, and unless consulted by a client who realises that he is accident-prone, I keep quiet. People react differently in tense moments, and self-control varies. Where one will hit out, physically or verbally, another will refrain. After years of learning the hard way, an accident-prone driver may become aware of his faulty reactions and master the impulse to press the acceletator. Or a person prone to violent argument may come to recognise in himself the state of irritation that leads to trouble, and decide to control himself.

The astrologer can point out times of tension, but it is not safe to conclude that an accident or other violent outcome is inevitable.

Death

Astrologers differ, as indeed do most people, in their ideas as to what can or should be said about death. Eastern astrologers think nothing of it, which seems to me to be a healthy attitude, if the client also holds it. But European clients would be decidedly upset if one replied when asked if a certain month would be good for changing residence that they needn't bother as they'd be dead anyway by then.

Death was taken for granted as a common-place family hazard in olden days. Perhaps this is why in old-fashioned books on astrology, one finds death the interpretation for almost any unfortunate aspect.

I have been asked many times by clients if I see their death ahead. And in close on thirty years of practice of course I have had clients die. But I must disappoint you if you think I can give any clear indication on this subject. What I have found is that deaths group very neatly in respect of my own chart. When researching for this chapter I was interested to find that no less than five of my clients died in 1964 and never more than one in any other year. Charles Carter connected the quincunx aspect with death, as this is the angle of the Ascendant degree to the cusp of the 8th House (the so-called House of Death). And sure enough 1964 was a year when my progressed Sun reached a natal quincunx aspect between Uranus and my Mars/Pluto conjunction. Sorry to be technical, but I have always found some 8th House involvement when deaths occur.

The day of death is shown in a variety of ways. My own husband, in his mid-eighties, died in a month when his progressed Moon was conjunct Jupiter . . . an indication of expansion and fulfilment, and for him this is exactly what it was . . . death for him was a wonderful release from pain and infirmity into lightness and freedom. His death showed in my own chart in a transit of Saturn over my 8th House Neptune. Very appropriate, as all astrologers would agree, the 8th House being the part of all charts to do with death, and Neptune having to do with escape, including shifts of levels from one plane to another.

An elderly client, a very active person in public life, on committees and so forth, asked me if I could give her any idea how long she had left to live. Her doctor had already told her it was doubtful that she would live another year. She was particularly well balanced; the sort of person one could talk to freely on any subject, even her own death – so I told her that I had never yet been able to spot the exact moment of death. In her case, she had a difficult transit of the Uranus/Pluto conjunction over her Mars. I told her that this time of tension was due to happen three times in the coming year and that her guess was as good as mine as to which of these three transits would be the most operative. In the event, in her weakened state, it was at the time of the first one that she died. Let me make it clear that in earlier life she, or anyone else, would have weathered this and worse. Astrologically speaking, as one gets old and frail, it takes less in the way of bad aspects or transits to correspond to death than it would in full health. So to give the impression that this or that aspect or transit means death would be crazy.

After years of looking at charts of people who have died, I would say that times of danger or tension are indistinguishable from times of death. A really critical year, with illness, whether the person succumbs or not, shows in a prolonged build-up of aspects backed up by difficult transits. Indeed for notable events it is this sort of build-up that should be looked for, in good times or bad, before jumping to conclusions on the strength of a single indication.

In the case of a huge and dire build-up, what does the astrologer say? I can only answer for myself. To me, astrology is *not* fortune-telling (or often enough misfortune-telling), and, if the trends show tensions, storms or fine weather, I make no claim to see more. It seems wrong to me to predict illness, death or violence. With an evolved client such a prediction could be incorrect, anyway, as any aspect (or for that matter, pattern in a tea-cup or the cards) *can* manifest at inner levels, and the individual in a time of potential violence and stress may find himself coping with emotional storms or the illness of those with whom he is in close contact. Who are we to judge with certainty the stage of evolution of anyone who consults us?

As to death. Have you considered to what extent our present life *is* death? Every moment we think of ourselves as living, a part of us is perishing. Particles of skin slough off, and while these are replaceable, it is an established truth that every day ten thousand brain cells die and these are irreplaceable. So in a real sense death is NOW . . . as it will not be when we are free of this tiresome, heavy, 'dying' body. The 'cross' for everyone is surely his descent into matter, and so-called death is truly a birth back into reality and permanence.

I had one elderly client who was terrified of death and dying. "I've been so wicked!" she told me. But in fact she had led a perfectly average life and been far more charitable than most. Her chart was a strong one, with (for the benefit of readers who welcome technicalities) Aries rising and ruler Mars squaring the Moon in Scorpio. Saturn in her 6th House in Virgo squared her Sun, so ill-health and depression in old age were not surprising. But there were splendid aspects too and no evidence of wickedness. I came to the conclusion that she was resonating to some past life where she had laid about her and done (or ordered) some violent killings.

I decided this was a good line and I stuck to it. When she rang up in a state of genuine panic about dying, I told her with the confidence of strong intuition what I felt sure could be true, namely, my opinion that she *had been* wicked in some past life (I had to pander to this idea as she was so keen on it) and her fear of death was a simple memory of having died with so much on her conscience. But this time, I stressed, there was none of that to fear. "You've got a hangover, my dear! Forget it! This time round you'll get a lovely welcome!" Indeed I promised to lay on a loving reception committee, so sure was I that this would be done.

There is an end to this story which is strictly NOT for sceptics. She died suddenly and painlessly, and one night as I was in that state between sleeping and waking, the telephone seemed to ring and I heard her voice. She thanked me for helping her over and said it was now her turn to help me. I felt both happy and comforted by what had seemed a very real conversation.

4. HEALTH AND PSYCHOLOGY

Can astrology throw any light on illness? Do certain illnesses attack those born under certain signs?

It is easy enough to trace illness in the chart after the event, and there is a correspondence between planetary aspects and the physical condition, but this does NOT, in my view, justify the use of astrology to predict specific illnesses. I have described elsewhere how twins with identical bad aspects have not suffered identical ills. The fact that certain parts of the body are associated with certain signs does not mean that people born in a given month are prone to a particular complaint.

Psychological troubles are often rooted in the far past. The book *Many Lifetimes*, by Joan Grant and Denys Kelsey (Gollancz, 1974), tells of the successful treatment of troubles stemming from misdeeds or misconceptions some thousands of years back.

Astrology and the birth chart fit very well into this concept. The theosophist/astrologer, Alan Leo, writing in 1908, observed that each horoscope marks a step in the progress of the soul. By its representation of the character and environment of the soul, it shows the stage reached by the individual in a particular birth. Indeed the nativity indicates what we have sown in the past and *how* we are going to reap what we have sown. Being set up within moments of birth it *cannot* represent anything created since birth. However, when it comes to difficult aspects I find that, given a combination of intuition and experience in interpretation, one can make pretty sure surmises as to why and how this or that difficulty in circumstances or temperament was generated and by what sort of action. In particular charts, imbalance can be seen to have its uses. Why is it said that genius is akin to madness? Surely in many cases because the genius dares to *use* his imbalance in some art form, or in creating what is at first dismissed as a crazy invention. We should remember that the 'imbalanced' moment that marks the birth of a genius or 'nutcase' is in itself just as much a spark or moment of the Creator as is the moment that corresponds to the birth of the evenly balanced average person. It takes a more highly evolved soul to animate a 'mad' moment brilliantly. To say that a mad, unbalanced moment produces a million way-out types and one genius is another way of saying that advanced souls are rare.

For those who react badly to the word 'soul', read PSYCHE . . . the part of you purported to be studied by psychologists, although many of these are incapable of contacting their own psyches, let alone those of their patients.

Projection is an age-old concept which Professor Jung defined clearly in modern idiom. One of its workings is by means of an inner mechanism which compels a man to blame his neighbour for what he dislikes most in himself. We all do this to some extent. In the long run, it is only when we are reconciled to and accept our own Shadow side that we find wholeness.

Astrology can be of great value here; for studying his own pattern a man can analyse why he so dislikes this or that fault in his fellow. It will unfailingly be found to correspond to some basic potential. The evolved man with a violent pattern will detest violence and cruelty. "Know thyself!" is still the best advice towards the attainment of wholeness in individuals or nations.

People ask if it is possible to determine times of year when we are more than usually prone to illness. This is a reasonable question, for surely each year the Sun appears, geocentrically, to travel the same journey through the signs, and the individual can be told which of his planets and what favourable or unfavourable configurations are activated by the passage of the Sun in which month of every year. But there are many other factors, so I am not suggesting that each of us experiences a recognisable cycle every year. In my own case, a record kept has shown that my relations tend to die in late summer and clients have told me that it always seems to be in a particular month that they fall ill. Sun-cycles are easy to follow, but it doesn't end there. Every planet has its cycle and particular correspondences. To follow and record them all would involve longer work than most professionals would wish to tackle and could result in unhealthy introspection. I would certainly not undertake it.

Healing

Is astrology of use in this field? Sometimes, very definitely. Among my clients I remember a woman who had recently completed several years of treatment for depression. The indications in her birth chart, and especially in the progressions for the years in question, were most helpful. I asked her if her trouble had been acute for five years, and she said, "Yes, exactly five years." I was able to show her in the Ephemeris for the year of her birth that in fact a stationary Mercury had, as it were, stopped dead right on her natal Saturn five years back and was only now moving off. As Saturn is the planet of restriction, heaviness and karmic tests, and Mercury has to do with all forms of communication, mental or physical, this very neatly fitted her circumstances. What helped her most was to see this in diagrammatic form, in the printed columns of an almanac. The fact that I had pin-pointed the start of the heaviness reassured her that I could be right in telling her that the end of this heavy patch was approaching fast.

It is in cases like this that the astrologer has the drop on the therapist who has no such means of seeing both past and future from a simple diagram. A doctor sees the patient as he or she is at consultation – in pain, discomfort or in floods of tears. Very often he has no means of knowing what the norm of his patient is. The astrologer, on the other hand, can and should remind a distressed client that he/she is not normally at this low ebb, and can talk about the happy, positive potentials that will be activated again, given time. "Let me remind you," he could say, "that you are normally attractive/happy/talented/healthy/beautiful" – or whatever applies – "and that the present depression or painful time must be thought of as a storm-cloud you are travelling through."

We all need occasionally to be reminded of our potentials. I have seen clients surprised and pleased to be reminded of how they are at their best – a best they may be despairing of recapturing. This is highly therapeutic when done sincerely and truthfully in reference to the truths of the birth picture.

This sort of therapeutic clarification is not fortune-telling so much as a permissible form of prediction, in cases where the start or end of a bad phase is evident in the progressions of the chart. What is more tricky for the consultant is when a chronic state is indicated. This has no clear beginning or ending and, as for the medical practitioner, the wording to the clients needs careful thought.

The so-called norm to which the client returns is different in every case, and in the astrological chart no aspects are wholly 'good' or 'bad'. Even when considering the health conditions, a 'bad' aspect can be constructive if taken as a challenge. There are energy forces at work in the individual which clash. The result is felt physically, emotionally or in difficult circumstances. If the individual is a strong enough character, he or she will more readily accept set-backs as hurdles to be overcome . . . boulders in the path that have to be surmounted. The lesser character quails at the thought of an obstacle. He fails to recognise that the view is often improved after a stiff climb.

As to using astrology for diagnosis, general medical techniques are so thorough that it would be far better to rely on these unless one has access to a practitioner of so-called 'fringe' or alternative medicine. In this last field it is Radionics that springs first to my mind, where diagnosis is needed for any living things, from crops to humans. I am informed that David Tansley's book, *Dimensions of Radionics*,* is one of several available which give a clear and up-to-date statement of this subject.

* Health Science Press, 1977.

I think the time is coming when medical practitioners of many kinds will appreciate the fact that the astrological chart is a useful aid. The ability to understand a birth chart would be of great help in assessing a patient. An educated look at the chart and he could see at a glance . . . "H'm . . . yes . . . too much Fixity. Constipation? Retention? Rheumatism? Inability to let go . . .": that kind of thing; or he could see the nervous stress and strain accounting for dyspepsia or high blood pressure.

But why use a laborious technique when more instant means are available? I think most doctors of my acquaintance would be impatient of what astrology would add to their own disciplines. Not including, I hasten to say, those few who have already studied the subject. Astrologers vary in competency, and it is rare to find one who combines interpretative sensitivity with a seer's ability to detect disturbances in the physical or even the etheric body. But astrology at a more usual level of ability can be of value as a backing-up factor to diagnosis. I would readily work in with a doctor or psychologist, as indeed I have done many times. Astrologers could very definitely be of use in a team effort over difficult patients, for the chart can show, almost at a glance, what it could take the psychologist years of questioning to elicit. By this I do not mean to imply that sessions with the psychologist are not of the utmost value. I *do* mean that astrology can provide an almost miraculously short cut to the understanding of the pattern of the psyche under study. Astrologer and psychologist or doctor should work together with benefit in a more enlightened future.

A highly sceptical old 'general practitioner' back in the thirties confessed to me that a young astrologer had pinpointed past (and, as it so proved, future) occasions when his own mentally disturbed son suffered major breakdowns. I would stress, however, that a recurring aspect seldom operates identically, so it would be wrong to assume that because the activation of a bad aspect had corresponded to a mental breakdown its repetition would coincide with a second breakdown. There would be some appropriate set-back – appropriate to the planets and fields of activity, that is to say – but in my experience it is more usual to find a repeating aspect operating differently each time. And for this reason I heartily disapprove of computer readings being applied to health. Any generalised analysis of signs or planets in relation to health is deplorable. It cannot in truth be said that there is a specific aspect or sign that unfailingly corresponds with this or that illness or deformity.

Of course, after the event one can relate *any* disaster or illness to the personal chart. Such studies have been done, and much has been learnt. Factors in charts have been seen to connnect with this or that disability or epidemic, but even with knowledge thus gained of what has been shown to have a correspondence, I would be horrified for any reputable astrologer to predict a disease for a new-born baby. To sow fear in the heart of anyone is evil and must be avoided at any cost. This is accepted in the medical profession, whose members refrain, when the occasion demands, from expanding on the prognosis of certain states of health. And so, indeed, the astrologer, if he invades the medical scene, must respect a similar code of ethics.

At the moment of birth of a severely handicapped child, others in the world are born with no affliction of a physical or mental kind (although certain circumstances or brutal relations may provide a vivid and more than adequate substitute). So it is not only ethically wrong but probably erroneous to describe certain aspects as productive of this or that affliction. In short, generalities in respect of health can only be dangerous. A difficult aspect in your chart, when activated in different years, may coincide in one year with a burglary and in another year with a health condition. Given the increased frailty of old age, a difficult patch will more readily manifest in physical suffering or disability than would the identical aspect in full health in youth.

It has been long established that each sign of the Zodiac has affinity with a given part of the body, starting with Aries at the head and ending with Pisces at the feet. A section indexed as 'body areas and signs' in Derek and Julia Parker's book, *The Compleat Astrologer* (Mitchell Beazley, 1971) is particularly informative in this connexion. All the illustrated books about astrology indicate how the twelve signs are related to different parts of the body. For example, Taurus is connected with the throat. Many singers have the Sun in Taurus or Tauris-rising, and their throats are particularly strong, while other Taureans with less well-aspected charts suffer from throat trouble. Again, Gemini has to do with the chest. You may be a strong Geminian with a good chest who runs races, or an afflicted Geminian with bronchitis.

Depression

I have found this to show in the individual chart in difficult aspects from Saturn to the Moon or Mercury. Emotional or mental moods come under these two planets. So if asked whether the astrologer could trace moods in the chart, I would say that moods, feelings and attitudes to life are what is *best* shown in the chart. Actions, after all, are conditioned by the amount of control we have over our moods; and outer circumstances may be right outside the control of any individual.

People who suffer from depression can sometimes be helped if they are shown that it is not the whole of them that is affected. I tell such people to try to see the mood or depression as a dark cloud that for the time being hangs over them. "You are not that cloud! The real you is travelling *through* the cloud [or the tunnel, or the fog or whatever imagery you care to use] and will come out into the clear all the quicker if you can manage not to identify wholly *with* the cloud."

I do not set out to be a healer, but my work as an astrologer has turned very largely into therapeutic work, because I don't think the side of astrology which deals with prediction is either reliable or, except in specific cases, useful. I am not interested in studying the chart from a health point of view so much as seeing it as a whole, from the point of view of balance and integration of the various energy fields. This question of balance is dealt with in the chapter on elements.

You will read in technical books (which this is NOT) that the 6th and 12th Houses have to do with health matters. It is true that a planet introduces its particular energy into the field of the House which contains it. Mars in the 6th could either mean energy going into healing or health or welfare work, or if afflicted, the heat and aggression of Mars could correspond to burns or injuries through battle or accident. But it could mean many other things, and 'service to others' which is certainly a 6th House matter, can also apply to military service, which no one can deny is a service to the community.

Then again, each planet can be studied in several ways. You may look at your chart and see absolutely no planet in a particular House. But this doesn't mean that this empty House is a dead note in the chart or that nothing can be read about it. Each sign has a 'natural' House. What do I mean? I mean that, say, Venus, which may be found in any of the twelve signs, will also have, through its aspects and total qualities, some bearing on its two natural signs, Taurus and Libra, and also on the two Houses 'natural' to these two signs. These are the 2nd House (which is akin to the second sign, i.e. Taurus) and the 7th House (which is akin to the seventh sign, i.e. Libra).

So, you see, it is never just a question of seeing what is in your 6th or 12th House in order to judge your health, but of taking in all these connexions. If you do all this, checking backwards over your known past life and health, you will get a surprisingly true picture. Accurate forward assessment is much harder to do as there are so many possibilities. And to do this in respect of health would be like reading a medical dictionary. I'm sure we have all done this and been appalled to see how many fatal diseases we have!

Small animals, domestic pets in particular, are 6th House things. This confuses the issue if you want precision: you may feel like asking if the lady in your consulting room is a nurse or medical practitioner, only to find she breeds Pekes . . . or cats. And who will be ill when *her* 6th House planet is adversely activated? She or little Chu Chin Chow? No. The astrologer can help in a given situation, but he is not a magician.

This is why I often use a system of educated guessing as to what misdeed in a past life has created the sort of difficulties, temperamental or circumstantial, that obtain in the present life. If I hit the nail on the head, it doesn't worry the client at all. After all, it is something that, psychologically, he or she has lived with, that has been part of him and his reactions since birth. He is used to it. He feels, "That makes sense of what I've suffered. I wish I'd known of that possibility before." One woman said to me, almost with tears: "Oh goodness! Why couldn't I have talked to you twenty years ago when I was so worried that I couldn't have children?" Frustration in this department was clearly shown. Mind you, a specific thing like this is easier to see in retrospect, and I would not consider it right to suggest that a woman could not have a child, although I would try to get her more relaxed and accepting about the matter by pointing out that delays were indicated, if in fact this were the case.

One can see very clearly in a chart the periods when a particular facet of the life is activated, whether a potential for joy or for sorrow.

A helpful thing about an astrological reading that forecasts a particularly testing time ahead can be that the family, on re-reading, can get the whole thing in perspective and avoid the self-reproach, "Where did we go wrong?" There is considerable therapy in clarifying a man to himself. I once asked a client if he was aware of saying the wrong thing rather too often to be comfortable. "Only too frequently," he agreed. His very meekness illustrated that he was highly aware of this fault.

In writing about a child with this sort of aspect – I recall that Saturnian severity afflicted the Mercury potential for communications – one could speak more freely. "You see this aspect? This is what makes it so easy for you to be rude or unkind. But now you know you have this aspect, you can practise overcoming it. Determine that you won't give way to an automatic reaction. You aren't a clockwork mouse!"

Saturn is often operative in temperamental or other difficulties. It has to do with hard work, duty, sternness to oneself or to others, and the limitations that come through work or through disability. I analysed a small boy who has Saturn in the 6th House. His mother says he can be a proper little hypochondriac. And indeed this position of Saturn can be interpreted this way – taking a dismal view of any little ache or pain. But this is not the only interpretation. It can mean karma to be worked off in matters of health or service. I told this child's parents that he should be encouraged to work for others in the future, in medicine, healing or any appropriate work of service to the community or the animal kingdom.

With her permission I would like to quote what Dr. Zyp Dobyns, a brillian American astrologer/psychologist, has said about astrology:

"It offers a personality system based on an external frame of reference which is superior to the arbitrary systems manufactured in such abundance in the field of personality study. It is almost certain to be the universal system of the future. It offers a symbolic blue-print of the human mind and destiny which cannot be manipulated by the subject wishing to fake good or fake bad, which is relatively easy to do in many psychological questionnaires. It offers insights into areas of which the subject himself often knows little or nothing – into his repressions, never consciously verbalised – values never consciously verbalised, ambivalences and conflicts projected into events and relationships never consciously faced. It offers clues to unrealised potentials, to early traumatic events depth therapists might wish to explore . . .''

and Dr. Dobyns ends with the expectation with which I heartily concur, that counsellors of the future will use the horoscope routinely "as we use background data on the subject".

In the above quote I find the bit about 'faking good or faking bad' of particular interest. It is not possible to fool a well-trained astrologer or to persuade him that you are bristling with potentials that simply do not appear on the chart.

The aim of the psychologically oriented astrologer should be to assist the integration of a human personality through better and fuller understanding of its component parts. For while there are separate meanings to each sign and planet, the importance of astrological analysis (and I mean analysis by a fully trained person-oriented astrologer) lies in its capacity to pin-point a strength or weakness and to judge the possibility of fulfilment of the basic potentials. Only an educated study of the whole pattern can show whether, say, two contradictory factors such as a Sun-sign and a very different rising-sign are healthily backed up by planetary energies so that each potential has outlet. Many people have a sense of guilt that they are not making the most of their lives and talents. These are the ones who will be found to have inadequate backing or energising of a potential.

And one mustn't make the mistake of thinking that fulfilment always equates with external success. A gentle, introverted type whose aim in life is to knit or be domestically occupied may also suffer frustration and a sense of inadequacy in her own field. Psychosomatic illnesses can spring from seemingly unimportant inadequacies as easily as from a bigger and splashier failure.

Psychology helps a man to face the whole of himself and to become a more integrated being. Astrology helps in that it affords an accurate picture of the various energy factors and strengths or weaknesses in need of adjustment. Imbalances of all sorts are shown to a nicety. (See also Balance/Imbalance.)

It is well known that neurotics tend to live in the past or the future and as little as possible in the present. So good, healthy participation in the NOW – making use of immediate aspects and circumstances, even the testing ones – is not only the right way to cope with life, it also makes very good sense healthwise. We remain psychologically healthy if we try to meet difficulties with courage and resource. If we accept trouble and tackle it resolutely, we learn something, whereas if we lie down and die we learn nothing. It can be said that difficulty and pain is worthwhile if it educates us to be better integrated and happier in the long run. People think a lot about training muscles. They run about, ride bicycles, do exercises to keep fit, yet think little about training for *life* – for meeting trouble, sorrow, or coping with tiresome people. Moral muscles have to be developed if we are to be able to react well to trouble.

Talking about keeping fit, can the chart show anything useful about overweight problems? It is said that many planets in the Venus signs, Taurus and Libra, indicate a tendency to put on weight; possibly because these signs are prominent among easy-going, laugh-and-grow-fat types. I have definitely found that Jupiter, planet of expansion, expands the figure, among other things, when it forms aspects to the personal chart. This may be because increased prosperity makes it possible to eat more richly. Jupiter and Venus are both fun-loving and opposed to limitation and sternness, and I have known many a generous Sagittarian or Piscean who bulged a bit at the seams. On this reckoning one has only to wait for a limiting Saturn transit to find it easier, if not compulsory, to tighten one's belt. The urge to slim, which calls for discipline, or the necessity to slim due to lack of money or food is typical of a Saturnian patch, and the exact opposite happens if Jupiter is making his presence felt.

So if you want to slim, you either have to pull up your Saturnian socks and exert self-discipline, or wait for Saturn to loom up and do it for you by means of physical or emotional testing. Laugh and grow fat is a Jupiter truism.

To sum up, astrology is not healing, but it can provide additional knowledge to a healer especially as concerns the time factors. Given the medical facts it could be of value to a doctor to plot the course of an illness and note when recurrence or relapse is indicated for his patient. But this is secondary in value to the light that can be thrown on the whole temperament and potentialities.

I would warn people against seeking advice from the astrologer as a means of compensating for their incapacity to adapt to a particular life situation. By all means ask advice in order to clarify or mirror a problem. But don't expect him to solve it. Today's astrologers do not talk in terms of 'prognostication' and 'fate'. What can be seen in the personal chart and its progressions is the activation of a particular facet of the character or energy factors. Old-fashioned astrologers used to predict dire illnesses, accidents, mishaps or even misdeeds with positive relish. In certain cases they would prove to be right . . . the average run of humanity reacts automatically and makes small attempt to be self-governing. Instinctive reaction is natural enough, but the evolved man or woman is in command of reactions and such a type is less easy to assess. I read of an advanced Yogi who deliberately chose the worst aspected times to tackle work in order to prove to himself that he was above the level of automatic reaction. It is obvious that our health and whole nervous system can benefit from right and controlled reaction.

To check on our own reactions could prove instructive. For example, in a bus or car, when held up, do we fret and wear ourselves out, or do we refuse to be disturbed by circumstances beyond our control, and quietly adjust our plans? If someone we deal with is truculent, do we automatically take offence or do we make allowances and refuse to be put out of temper? If the surgeon says we need an operation, do we give way to fear and resentment of our hard lot and add to our difficulties with mental tensions, or do we accept the news as a challenge to courage and make up our minds that Heaven will use the opportunity to make us well?

This may seem to stray from the question of health and astrology, but it doesn't really. Adverse prognostication or bad aspects may concern health or varied circumstances. We cannot change the fact that we are being tested one way or another, but we can modify all ills if we train ourselves to extract maximum good from any situation. This is very hard for the pessimist to do, but the healthy person is one who learns to make constructive use of high-powered energy activation. The natal chart is a starting pattern. It is not a strait-jacket in which we are confined for life.

5. CLAIRVOYANCE – DREAMS – SENSITIVITY

All manner of unusual experiences come the way of the astrological consultant, and there is always the possibility that he will get out of his depth when psychic or paranormal events are concerned.

Dreams are a case in point. Their interpretation may necessitate seeking assistance from a person more qualified to judge their significance. I myself, on more than one occasion, was fortunate enough to receive valuable advice from a psychologist friend. I learnt, for example, that alarming or evil dreams can be turned to good if they can be grasped, accepted and digested. Thus, a friend once dreamt of a snake which curled round her leg. She heard a voice telling her to grasp it – or, in psychological terms, to accept her 'Shadowself'. She was able to comply, and as she did so, the snake shrank to a tiny replica of itself in pure gold. In this connexion I recall an injunction (although not, alas, its origin) to try to keep the *transformed image* of what is evil. However, I am certainly not suggesting it is easy to 'retain' or even to recognise the reality of the 'gold'.

Some dreams are revelations. I have had clients who remember being taken to what they call the 'Halls of Learning' while asleep. I think I did this myself without remembering much about it, as at one stage I used to wake up hearing the ends of lectures ringing in my ears. The result of this is that knowledge of hitherto unknown or unfamiliar subjects starts dripping as if from nowhere into the waking mind. Without realising it, you yourself have prepared your mind for such knowledge. A door has opened. In your own way you can become a channel for what some higher source wants to put through you. The channel is clear or semi-blocked according to how much your ego gets in the way.

In the astrological chart a faculty for clear dreaming usually shows in a strongly aspected Neptune and/or in accentuation of the 8th or other occult House of the chart. I have known dreams of clients to confirm an astrological analysis. To one client I wrote the following: ". . . Here are complications. Uranus [her ruling planet] is strengthening the determined independence of Aquarius and there is a coldness and limitation indicated by Saturn. Your emotional reactions are tied up with power and severity. Your Moon and Saturn are both in Fixed signs, and this seems to me to have made them set like concrete. Your poor Moon-self, which normally has to do with the sensitive *feeling* in all emotional contacts, must literally be chipped out of her prison before she can function."

In reply, this client wrote, "I have had recurring dreams of being entombed." She went on to tell of her childhood, spent in male company since her mother died, and she, like her brothers, was expected to rein in all emotion and 'keep a stiff upper lip'.

Just as everything in both your astrological natal or progressed patter is YOU and not something 'out there' influencing you, so everything in your dreams is YOU. You may be dreaming of someone else or of a difficult situation or even about animals or inanimate objects. In all cases, my psychologist tells me, it has to do in some personal way with your reactions or emotions. Wild animals, it seems, represent passions or sex urges. So if you dream of a leopard, it is the untamed and maybe beautiful animal side of yourself. But equally it could be an image of vanity that is projected, and of course, other interpretations are possible.

In the last year of my old husband's life I dreamed I was walking down a street and came on a dear old St. Bernard dog sitting by the roadside. He looked so sad and worn that I sat by him and comforted him. On waking I recalled the above theory. "Well, that's me! That's my poor old body, I suppose getting tired like the old St. Bernard." I related this to my husband, who, I must explain, dearly loved his whisky although the doctor limited him severely. His reaction was that the amount of spirits I was allowed to carry to him wouldn't tire anyone, let alone a St. Bernard.

As to unsought sensitivity – when I had a question and answer column some years ago, a girl wrote to me, "How can I convince my family I am not mad because I am aware of the spiritual plane?" – I am sure many readers will sympathise with this girl, but again others, differently constituted, would side with her family in disbelieving what she tells them she sees or hears. I wrote to her that she must accept the fact that she, with her sixth sense, had been born into a down-to-earth family and there was nothing to be done about convincing them.

People with misunderstood gifts of this sort do best to keep fairly quiet about them. In time the situation will sort itself out. There is a comforting saying – 'When the pupil is ready, the Master appears', and those who feel alone in their awareness should read the massive literature now available on psychic subjects. And I don't mean trash. The College of Psychic Studies, 16 Queensberry Place, London S.W.7, is the place to help or advise sensitives. Once you meet others who are like you, you will have no need to try to convince the unconvincible.

An eerie experience was reported to me some years ago, which interests me more now than it did at the time, because I have since come across similar cases. A girl told me that sometimes on looking at her reflection in the glass it was as though she looked at a shell, she herself being only faintly visible. At such times she saw her family or friends as total strangers and went cold all over . . . with a prickly feeling. Since then, I have discovered that in the old days, sensitives made use of mirrors for some form of scrying; so the girl may have been resonating to some former-life experience.

A much more recent client of mine, who developed considerable yet unwanted sensitivity, found that she too 'saw' in mirrors. This, in fact, was a case of 'possession' and the image in the looking-glass showed her if a 'goodie' or a 'baddie' was operating.

My answer to the first girl may interest any reader who has similar experiences and feels fear. I wrote: "This shows a considerable degree of sensitivity and can teach you that you (the inner YOU) are a higher self animating a body. For a flash when you seem to lose the familiar image of yourself, you are the true instead of the temporary down-here self. Don't be frightened. But if the sensation continues to alarm you, I suggest that you use your imagination and see yourself to be protected in a beam of light. Have no doubt: there are those who will give help in moments of fear . . . but it is for us to establish contact and ask for help."

An astrologer does not need clairvoyance, but continued study of astrological charts tends to develop intuition and the ability to 'tune in' to clients' problems. Clients are often ready with stories of what this or that clairvoyant has told them, which has not come true at the time promised. The answer to this, as I suggested earlier, is that the client has projected so strong a wish that the clairvoyant has seen it as a thought form and has predicted an event whose only solidity was in the mind of the client.

Does distortion happen in astrological interpetation too? Yes, unhappily it does. This is why it is safest for the one analysing the birth chart to stick to broad 'keyword' descriptions of planetary energies activated, without promising concrete events. It is logical that if an imaginative client is living night and day in some emotional dream or fantasy, that this will show in the progressed chart. The vivid interior life of the mind and emotions, which is so powerful that it is medically acknowledged to cause psychosomatic illnesses and disorders, is extremely hard to separate and disentangle from outer and more visible events. I have known a major progressed aspect to correspond to the subject matter of a play in the case of a playwright, and with the dramatic role occupying the mind of an actress. "What absolutely horrifying things were happening then?" I asked the late Diana Wynyard. "I was playing Medea!" was the reply.

Most of us are only conscious of ourselves as physical beings. We tend to disregard steady, but largely spiritual progress or character improvements and only remember under the heading of a *good time* some concrete fact, like winning the pools or getting a proposal of marriage. The most significant moment in life – a flash of real consciousness or sensitive vision – comes and we may still say, when asked by the astrologer, "A good month? . . . oh no, nothing important happened then." This event, important to our inner or higher life, simply has not registered in our 'body' mind. However, it is impossible for the best astrologer in the world to cover all possible interpretations at all levels of consciousness for each configuration that is activated.

Work done with trained psychologists – in my case these have been Jungians – has been of inestimable value in understanding clients. The psychologist is trained to analyse and study each potential and to be unshocked and unperturbed by suggestions as to how this or that combination of energies may manifest. As clients, therefore, they are a joy. Most people have rows of sacred cows. This or that subject, one feels it instinctively, must not be mentioned. But in talking to a psychologist all doors can be opened.

An astrologer does not need to be psychic to practise successfully, but the sensitivity and perception possessed by the true psychic are useful additions to astrological training. Astrology can be learned by anyone with the necessary will, intelligence and application. I have noticed on the other hand that genuine clairvoyants and sensitives do not need a training in astrology to be aware of astrological pointers when referring to the client or someone involved in the client's life. I have known one to peek into her crystal ball and say, "Who is the Aries man, dearie?" or "Watch out for that Cancer woman – she's jealous!" and she was right. It was an Aries man I was thinking of. But the fact that they 'see' the correct sign without any calculation or chart means neither that they are good astrologers nor that they are bogus. Their intuitive knowledge backs up the astrological tenet that the sky pattern keyed by astrology is fundamental. It is a truth, and as such can be stumbled upon along different paths. An advanced psychic does not need to study astrology for his work. Neither does a trained astrologer need to be psychic.

Clairvoyants can be most valuable in clarifying generalisations made by the astrologer. A clairvoyant friend of mine visited the house of a client of mine whose chart showed an afflicted 12th House. (The 12th House of the chart has to do with prisons and institutions among other things.) Without knowing what I had seen in the chart, she told this woman and her husband that the house they were living in had had a dungeon in past times and that they had been the gaolers in a former incarnation. I had not been so specific, but these facts fitted perfectly with my own findings.

Sensitivity can be studied in the birth chart largely through the placing and aspecting of the planet Neptune. Given a strong Neptune, emphasis on the Water-signs (Cancer, Scorpio and Pisces) in the natal chart, tends to the visionary and intuitive type of psychic. Air-sign psychics (Gemini, Libra and Aquarius) are the strongly communicative ones, either in writing or by the spoken word. I have noticed that Earthy sensitives often like to use some sort of physical aid, such as in Dowsing or Radionics, or they work directly on the physical body in the techniques employed by Physiotherapy, Osteopathy and Chiropractic. It is well known that leaders in these fields have a remarkable sensitivity or psychic faculty which leads their hands to the exact vertebra or pinched nerve or muscle spasm. One does not think of practical Earthy types as sensitives, yet in their own field they are supreme. For example, Taurus, an Earth-sign, can be very much at home in the world of music, where sensitivity is productive of audible if not tangible results; while analytical research is typical of careful Virgo. At the risk of taking these generalities too far, I would add that the warmth of Fire seems to produce sensitive astrologers (Leo, especially around the 27° mark, is well known for this) and surgeons and other 'healers with the knife' are typical of fiery Aries, or a strong Mars.

Finally, an admixture of Libran balance is helpful in the healing arts as it adds to the potential for restoring either mental or bodily balance and alignment.

6. THE PREDICTIVE SCENE

Many people think of astrology purely as prognostication. And, in a sense, if character dictates one's destiny, I suppose they are right. It is certainly a fact that by changing ourselves we can change our lives – whether for better or for worse.

When I see a strong indication of sudden disruption, such as can be expected with a strongly Uranian activation, I believe in sticking to keywords (Appendix) and saying, "I haven't a clue exactly what will happen, but don't count on everything going to plan when Uranus is involved."

The moral of this seems to be that it is best to be vague. I have found that, since the individual knows his own circumstances, a vague indication can be applied where it belongs by the client. He will be grateful to the astrologer for clarifying a situation that is, in detail, totally unknown except to himself. I hold that faulty attempts at greater accuracy can be remembered as inefficiency.

A sense of fate or destiny in a personal chart I have found to tie up with the planet Pluto. Indeed, when Pluto is strongly placed, near to the Sun or the angles, the containing sign is indicative of the career to which the native is drawn.

It is understandable that the Church condemns the 'fated' side of astrology. The philosopher and mystic know that as soon as a man achieves a measure of self-government and grows into the consciousness of his higher self (or Deep Centre, or 'I', or whatever you care to call it) he ceases to react as an automaton to the impulses that are stimulated in him in reaction to planetary tensions. Our birth chart is *not* the blueprint of a limited fate to which we are subject. Its value is to show us the energies or working tools at our disposal.

Total freewill does not exist either. We can only function within a certain framework – the framework of our parentage and birth circumstances. But developing from this framework we can and do make our own future. What happens tomorrow is the result of what we do today . . . using the talents and temperament we are born with.

The sort of questions that bother people are 'How much is one ruled by one's stars? Can we change our fate?'

The modern psychological astrologer simply does not talk in terms of 'fate'. In the old days, of course, astrologers did just this, and issued huge warnings of 'evil' events or actions. I don't suggest that life is all roses, and sometimes they were right, although not wise. It is unhelpful and defeatist to suggest the worst. It is better to advocate the desirability of self-government, and point out that planetary forces are, in this context, energies which can be used or misused.

Obviously, people can't change their normal reactions overnight. A habitually bad-tempered person will react violently when provoked. But I have said enough about the desirability of self-government. There is much in us that we can't change – our parents, our looks (much), basic poverty or riches, health, the structure of our bodies. But we need not be content to put up with traits in our character that bring us unhappiness. If you wonder what this has to do with destiny, I answer that it has everything to do with it. The birth chart shows character difficulties which are ours until we overcome them. Valuable people are those who get results in spite of opposition. It is not destiny we have to fight. It is ourselves. I once read an article in a Sunday paper about people who 'believe their future is locked up in the Stars'. I believe no such thing. It is a ghastly thought that anyone can be so spineless as to think he must stay the way he was born, characterwise. Admittedly the birth chart shows the starting pattern, but this is the basis on which we can build our lives.

Today's well-trained and well-educated astrologers don't talk in terms of fate and predictions. What interests them is the activation of this or that personal energy or emotion.

Sometimes the scene looks gloomy. If a thoroughly difficult natal aspect is activated, an old-fashioned astrologer would confidently predict an 'evil' action or event. In many cases he could be right, more especially for the below-average citizen who goes with the herd, while priding himself on being individualistic. While the controlled person stays in command of himself, you can rely on the former type to be violent when angry and use bad language when thwarted.

I hope to have made it clear that I deplore the popular concept that astrology is primarily fortune-telling. Far the most valuable use of the birth chart lies in the psychological field. It can help us to know ourselves, faults and all. As the Chinese say, "The man who knows he is a fool is not a great fool."

There is still much confusion of astrology with sundry fortune-telling techniques, and unhappily there are practitioners who pander to the demand and actually advertise their services as such. This is against the law and to my mind it is a good thing that it should be so. As I have said, exact prediction by astrology can only apply accurately to those who live at the level of automata.

What *can* be foreseen?

It can be read with accuracy what *type* of experience an individual will undergo and the period when it will happen, but it cannot be foreseen how the individual will react. Of course, some astrologers combine clairvoyance with astrology, in which case there can be remarkably accurate predictions. Nostradamus was such a one.

The urge to see into the future is very strong in human nature, and while I make no claim to know what is in store, I know that it can be seen in general if the future will be tense, stormy, heavy or clear. I would never talk of illness, death, and I have already said that aspects which traditionally correspond to physical violence or accident can also work out at a mental level in emotional storms or tensions.

The truth is that it is *people* who are predictable when you get to know them. You know what your son will say if he cuts himself or trips over the cat. At least you think you do. But if he decides one day to be more of an individual, you could be wrong.

To know in advance when we shall be put to this or that kind of a test can be a good thing if only to prepare us against reacting automatically. But attempts at exact prediction are dangerous, either because the prediction will be based on the lowest, most automatic level of response or, if the consultant is clairvoyant, on our own thoughts and wishes which may be so vividly projected as to make a clear picture. Thus, people get told what they want to happen rather than what is actually in store. The astrologer who relies on his charts is less likely to mislead us in this way.

Warnings can create fear and I don't approve of them. I can only remember once feeling a warning to be in order. It was a chart for a girl born in the fifties. She had a group of 5th House planets indicative of sex complications. Almost to my surprise I found myself warning her that if she wasn't careful she could have an abortion. This I would not normally dream of saying to a young girl, but the chart showed me so plainly that this was a possibility that I felt it had to be said. Her answer was prompt. "I expect you are used to being told you've hit the nail on the head. I'm only sorry to tell you the advice about abortion is too late. I had one in the year you've just mentioned when you asked me if things had been chaotic. . . ."

Welcome as well as unwelcome times can be forecast. The fact remains that what cannot be seen is how the individual will react. Winning a fortune may ruin a person as effectively as facing a crisis or even bankruptcy may be the making of him.

One last point. No two consultants are alike. Personally I don't like being asked to help people to make decisions. I even state that specific questions will not be answered. I don't want to offer solutions to questions that should be sorted out by the individual himself, even if he makes mistakes. At least they will be his own. And how better to learn? . . . An observation that applies no less to the consultant, who should always aspire to raise the level of his or her performance.

7. HEREDITY

Can inherited tendencies run counter to birth-sign qualities, causing the individual to be pulled in two directions? This question, which is often put to me in one form or another, assumes that an astrological description begins and ends with the Sun-sign. Let us create a possible astrological family picture. . . . Father could have a Cancer Sun, a Sagittarian Moon and the sign of Libra rising. Mother might have the Sun in Aries, the Moon in Aquarius and Sagittarius rising. Their child, allowing for strong heredity, might well have the Sun in Aquarius, Moon in Libra and Sagittarius rising.

In this example Sagittarius seems to be the link between all three charts in spite of the fact that it is in no case the Sun-sign. The father's manner and response to life (his Moon-self) will correspond to the child's personality (Rising-sign) and there is the further strong bond of the child's Libran Moon-self being on the same vibration as the father's Ascendant or Rising-sign. The parents have a happy link in that the Moon in his chart is in the same sign as his wife's Ascendant sign.

This is all terrifically simplified, but it illustrates how heredity is displayed through very dissimilar charts. Note that all three are born in different months and so, by popular astrology, 'under' different signs. The true picture shows a considerable sharing of signs.

As to being pulled in different directions, although this can happen, it would not be that heredity is pulling against astrology, but merely that opposing factors in the chart portray a complex character. Heredity and family likenesses are portrayed with great clarity in the charts of several members of a family.

This fixation on the Sun-sign crops up again and again. I get asked, "If a child has the same sign as one of its parents, has it more of the characteristics of that parent?" The answer is very possibly but not necessarily. A mother with Sun in Taurus who has two children, the one with the Sun in Taurus and the other a February-born Aquarian, might be more in sympathy with the second child because of quite other points of similarity in her chart and his. A shared Sun-sign undoubtedly gives shared basic characteristics, but these may be hidden by marked differences shown by other factors. . . . Or it is put to me that "surely upbringing and heredity are what matter and not planetary positions? I don't like the thought of planetary influence." Well, I don't like the word 'influence' either. It suggests that some planetary fairy is waiting round the corner to put a spoke in our wheel. I try to put the thought across that all life is one, and whether we like it or not, we are part of that life. Each of us is the living embodiment, not of a sign, which would lump us in with one-twelfth of the population of the world, but of a moment in time and space (each moment having its own characteristics). It is up to us to develop that moment as best we can in our lives. Upbringing, heredity and so forth can be identical for two in a family who prove to be unequally equipped mentally and physically. What differs is the incarnating individual.

Where one member of a family takes strongly after another, the charts will mirror this. A strongly different type marrying into a family can introduce new sign emphasis along with the new blood, and subsequent descendants will be born with signs and aspects which were formerly not found in the family.

Some families have very marked family traits, and you hear people say "I could spot that Jones chin anywhere. . . ." Astrologically, likeness can be traced in the decided features of the 'fixed' signs (Taurus, Leo, Scorpio and Aquarius), or in the hearty laugh of strong Jupiter aspects, while the melancholy pessimism of an afflicted Saturn can distinguish members of an entire family regardless of birth months.

Family pride is an admirable quality and it can be this that makes questioners sound so cross when they ask, "Surely heredity is stronger than the Stars?" This question seems to presuppose that if one factor works, another doesn't. In actual fact, the birth charts of an entire family over several generations give an accurate picture of the hereditary position. New blood shows, as I have said, in new aspects or hitherto unfamiliar signs which start recurring in subsequent generations. Royal families are; happily for astrologers, well documented and it is easy to trace that our own royal family in Edwardian days was largely Sagittarian. King George VI married his lovely Scottish wife, Elizabeth Bowes Lyon of Glamis, who, with the new blood, introduced a new sign emphasis and subsequent descendants have been born with Leo and Scorpio characteristics. This beloved granny has Leo as Sun and rising sign, and the Moon in Scorpio.

A family only notices this sort of thing as the children mature. The astrologer can see the facts in the birth chart of each baby as it arrives.

If astrology were based only on the twelve signs, its findings would indeed clash with the findings from a study of heredity. But have you ever known anyone who was not a mixture of qualities? Far from being describable by the characteristics of a single birth-sign, we are a mixture of traits and a positive cocktail of signs and planets.

The value of the astrological approach is that one can see in diagrammatic form just where and in what field of activity family traits recur. However, each pattern is individual; sometimes similar to, but never the same as that of another in the family.

8. CHILDREN

Analysing a child's chart is a serious matter. The astrologer should beware of letting his imagination run away with him. The child will grow up. He may find and read the analysis done for his parent. Imagine his or her reactions on reading comments like 'violently dangerous', 'accident-prone' or 'possibly psychotic'. Even if we think such descriptions to be true, they should be kept to ourselves. Responsible present-day practitioners feel that their task is to point out to every client (or child of client) the highest rather than the lowest in himself. To give life, in words, to a dangerous or violent potential is, to my way of thinking, a way of fostering some negativity that, with care and understanding, might be turned to positive use.

It is a moot point whether missing qualities can be satisfactorily built up. If a lack is spotted early by means of the birth chart, the parents can help with suitable training, being careful not to force or impose their will or tempo of living on a child purely for their own convenience. It would be sad indeed if there were no possibility of improvement during the life. Obviously this is what incarnation is all about – to make progress with the tools at our disposal. Education and influences during childhood can clearly do *much* to help or the reverse.

An analysis of the chart can only help a parent to deal with a difficult child if wise use is made of the knowledge. A parent who throws the facts of difficulties of temperament in the child's face could do terrible harm. Quarrels in a family are often due to lack of understanding. An impulsive, fiery child cannot see why a sensitive, emotional parent is hurt by an outspoken remark. A slow, gentle child will feel upset and bustled if urged on by a quick, impatient parent. It is idle to think that children will take after their parents and act as the parents think right. A child is born with his own problems, to work out at the tempo natural to him or herself.

Astrological knowledge is of value to a teacher, who can see precisely why one child in a class is a trouble-maker. The chart shows what lies behind a child's naughty or destructive moods. A tiresome child often has a higher potential for either good or evil. His energy potentials are

188

powerfully seeking outlet. The wise teacher or parent will find out the type of strength which seeks expression. It can be helpful, also, to know if a child tells lies out of cunning or cowardice or because he is exercising an unusually fertile imagination.

I do not suggest that parent or teacher or anyone in charge should just sit back and put up with any nonsense in the sublime trust that here is a small genius. I do suggest that they investigate by the means available, such as through astrological techniques which will in the right hands provide the means of studying the energies that lie behind a child's naughty deeds. I am quite confident that the astrologer can describe the main energy forces, strengths, weaknesses and basic drives of the individual. With the advantage of hindsight I am able to confirm that the young people whose charts I drew up and analysed at their birth did in fact grow up into the types envisaged. But it is not possible in these days, where job possibilities are so widespread, to pinpoint a career. Gone are the days when a young gentleman was pitchforked into the Army, the Navy or the Church . . . and young ladies had no career at all, and virtually no education.

One of the most difficult things in these materialistic days is to hazard a guess as to whether artistic tendencies or mystical or inspirational leanings will occupy the main stream of the career life or be an absorbing sideline.

It is important for those with the care of children to know where the strong trends lie. The child can then be helped towards a career which will fulfil and occupy his or her needs for energy outlet.

Curiously enough it is the faults which provide the more obvious pointers to these needed energy outlets. The chart of a child who tells untruths may disclose that he is subjected to over-stimulation from Neptunian unreality. The parent in this case should be warned, "Here is an over-active or even morbidly vivid imagination. Rather than repress and scold, try to encourage the possibilities." Here could be a potential Ian Fleming, Agatha Christie or Conan Doyle. All these used a vivid imagination to make their fortune.

Is the child aggressive or brutal? Does he take a sharp weapon and carve your best furniture? The obvious thing is to train him to use a knife constructively. He may one day be a skilled surgeon, carver or hair-cutter. Every energy worth having seeks an outlet, so if misuse of it can be dangerous, there is all the more need to educate it to productive use.

This does not only apply to children. Much can be learned by the astrologer through ascertaining just how a client with what looks like a cruel or violent pattern utilises these strengths or how they manifest. For example he or she may work on the staff of an accident ward or casualty station and deal with accidents continually. In that event their work would represent the right or legitimate use of a violent streak in their own charts.

A child with such a pattern responds eagerly and comes alive when there is a challenge to cope with. Most parents are familiar with the plea, "Can't I have the hammer and nails – the axe – the razor blade or whatever. . . ?" The wise parent lets him have the weapon, under supervision. This is the kind of urge which, if suppressed, may emerge in later life in more violent or anti-social episodes.

This principle applies to us all. We should try to make constructive use of the energies at our disposal . . . especially the energies which other people think of as faults. An intolerable chatter-box in a quiet office may be in her element somewhere where her gift for 'communication' is needed.

Chart comparison is usually thought of as useful for adults. But if your child is at a school where a particular member of the staff makes him feel completely cowed, or brings out latent aggression or timidity, comparison of the two charts may show that the teacher has an afflicted, stern Saturn in the very degree of your child's Sun or other sensitive point. If so, the child will feel a sense of restriction, inadequacy, resentment or anger, whereas with another teacher these sensations will not be aroused. Mind you, it might be a bit tricky finding out the teacher's birth data. Easier, perhaps, to remove the child from his care!

Introverted Children

A parent wrote to me of her little daughter whom she described as a 'loner' because she was 'different' from other members of the family, and asked if astrological analysis could help.

Parents of what they feel to be a 'different' child should try to appreciate the fact that we are all 'different'. It is wrong to try to change a child or make it adapt to a tempo of life which is alien. Like flowers, some children blossom early, others late – some grow or learn fast, some slowly. If a child doesn't readily make friends and play, she may be what is called introverted rather than extraverted, but she is none the worse for this. If the position were reversed and she were the only extravert in an introverted family, she would also be found to be strangely 'different' from her parents and siblings.

I suggested to this mother that her introverted little girl would come into her own when old enough to protect or mother other shy children. This sounds rather as if I think there are no introverted boys. Of course there are, and gentle, caring qualities in men need, if anything, even more sympathetic handling. Introverts of either sex need more encouragement and affection than do the little extraverts who make friends and join in with group activities without hesitation. But it is a mistake to think they will be happier if forced to be what they are not. "I don't want to go to the party!" may be a genuine objection which could be respected.

What are the astrological indications of extraversion and introversion?

A reliable judgement can only be reached through study and assessment of the balance of elements, qualities and the whole aspect and sign pattern. Most people are a mixture of the two, and it is *wholly misleading* to say that this or that sign is introvert and that others are extravert. On reading about the signs it is evident that IF it were possible (which it is NOT) to be the embodiment of any sign, it would be very simple. One would just state baldly that "all Leos are extraverts . . . or that all Pisceans are introverts'. But what about the unfulfilled Leos and the unfulfilled Pisces?

Psychic Children

In these materialistic days, it is more than ever important to watch for manifestations of clairvoyance or other forms of psychic awareness in children, since these gifts soon wither, if they are not actually destroyed when exposed to a climate of 'adult' scorn. (See also under NEPTUNE, page 100, which has to do with all kinds of sensitivity.)

If the parent fails him in this way it may have the effect of distorting the child's whole attitude to truth. His truth is not believed, so why not tell a lie?

He or she may come up to you in the garden or park and describe something or someone – invisible to your eyes. What to do? Swallow your disbelief and say, "How interesting! Tell me about it."

When my younger daughter was about six, we were staying in the most unlikely place for a psychic or spiritual experience – a Bridge Club which happened to be handy for the children's school during a bad bombing period of the War. I went upstairs to say goodnight and she said, "A little man put his head round the door and it frightened me." As she was so young and there were men staying in the club, I bristled. "What did he look like?" "He was about so high and was dressed in brown with a little pointed cap." "Was he an elf?" "I don't know." "Well, you're very lucky. I've never seen any of the little people. If he comes again, say 'Hullo, what do you want? Who are you?' Perhaps he'll talk to you." And I went out thinking that if she'd made it up it would soon be forgotten.

About a week later I suddenly thought of it when saying goodnight to her. "Have you seen that little man again?" "Who? Elf?" "Oh, he's Elf, is he?" "Yes, I call him Elf and we have long conversations. You'd better say hullo to him. He's here now." I said "Hullo" to an empty chair. "Not there! . . . *There!*", pityingly.

Looking back, I don't think that Elf was truly an elf belonging to the Fairy Kingdom, although I believe that this exists. I think he was some close friend or guardian spirit who wanted to talk to her and chose a form that wouldn't frighten her. They appear to have had interesting talks. She had recently lost a beloved uncle in the war, and I said one day that we mustn't be sad about Uncle Owen because it was nice for him not to be in the fighting any more. Again the pitying look. "Oh, Mummy, you don't have to tell me what happens when people die. Elf tells me all about that." And he did. She was as knowledgeable about other-worldly matters as anyone who gets information straight from the horse's mouth.

Elf visited her regularly for five or six years. Only once during that time did she see fairies. It was all the more convincing because it *was* only once and I was with her.

We were resting on a hot afternoon in early summer near a horse-chestnut tree in full bloom. Suddenly she grabbed my arm. "Look! On the branch there. Dancing!" "Goodness gracious, are you getting all fanciful and thinking the chestnut flowers are fairies or something?" "Don't be silly! I can see the flowers. There *are* fairies." "Well, tell me what they're doing." She said, "They're dancing all round in a big ring . . . and one in the middle is better dressed than the others. She must be the Queen." She couldn't have made that up. The bit about the one being better dressed came out so spontaneously. She told me they went on dancing and finally . . . "One's leading off now . . . Now the Queen's gone . . . Now the last ones have gone." And that was that. Never again in her childhood did she see fairies, although Elf visited her for years. When she was at boarding school she saw him for the last time. She was then nearly fourteen. Apparently he told her she wouldn't see him any more, but that if she ever needed him she could "call on him".

Having said earlier that an afflicted Mercury or Neptune can operate in an over-vivid imagination and at worst result in the individual telling lies, I feel I must add that my daughter's chart shows no signs of a vivid imagination, and she reports very factually about things. She is now the mother of psychic children and has the problem herself of sorting out whether they are being over-imaginative.

Character Formation

It has been said, "Give me a child before he is seven and I can form his character." What arrogance! And were it true, would not all children brought up in an institution be identical in outlook? All have the same conditioning.

Your child's basic potential can be read at birth. It is surely obvious to all parents of more than one child that a similar upbringing and conditioning doesn't make them identical in outlook.

Some children have difficult patterns. There are as many difficult charts as there are difficult people in the world. As many violent aspect combinations as there are fatalities, accidents, cruelties. We can't deny this, but parents of difficult children can be taught to recognise the

various traits and shown perhaps how best to educate potential
weaknesses or dangerous traits to good use.

It is highly gratifying to see children grow into the pattern one has
tried to describe when they were in their cradles. It can be grotesque to
see the chart of an innocent baby displaying potential egoism or cruelty.
"Here is someone's beloved little baby and here am I seeing a cruelty
aspect and difficult or dramatic karma to be faced. How am I to wrap up
this information?" What would I have thought if harsh words were said
about my babies? Oh! the tact you have to use. And yet one must get
across to parents something that will be helpful when difficulties arise.

It is in this connexion that I have developed a technique which
involves at any rate the idea of reincarnation. I say a 'technique', because
it has developed into this out of the convenience of being able to talk of
the worst potentials in the past tense . . . as something built up in a past
life which now forms the framework or basis of a new life. When you see
a shocker of an aspect in a newborn baby's pattern, no one in his senses
is going to say, "This child *is* cruel!" Obviously no baby has had time to
create such a potential. Where does such an aspect come from? It can
only be related to him or her through some antecedent cause.

When I see a difficult aspect, then, I make an educated guess as to how
that child in a former existence could have acted in order to make it
necessary to return to deal with a particular chunk of karma. And since
karma works for good or ill, it is evident that beauty, talent and productive qualities are also the fruit of former lives. What we sow we reap.

Physical Handicaps

It can be of great help to the parent to understand the temperament and
behavioural attitudes of however badly handicapped a child. All who do
healing work seem to agree that it is best not to dwell on the difficulties
or deformities of the physical body. As an astrologer I try, in the case of
terrible afflictions, merely to give a picture of the more inward qualities.
If the parent finds it possible, he or she can be helped by holding to the
idea of the soul of their handicapped child, who, for this life, has to
inhabit a poor twisted or otherwise inadequate physical frame.
Temperamental problems and frustrations are often stronger for being
suppressed, but the astrological pattern interpreted in the right context
may disclose lines of education or recreation best calculated to relieve
them.

Any parent wanting astrological advice about a handicapped child
should make no secret of the problem. I know of no precise aspect that
indicates specific disability. True consultative work is much more
valuable if you do not expect the astrologer to be some sort of magician
who will know precise details from the birth chart.

The astrologer with concern for his client would hesitate to state a
suspicion that there could be crippling disablement, in case this had not

yet manifested – as could be the case following an accident – yet the potential would be in the natal chart.

Readers, if any, in these more enlightened days, who are anti-reincarnation should skip this paragraph about *autistic and mentally retarded* or defective children. The possibility is that the soul, imprisoned by day in an inadequate or faulty body, may be an exceptionally advanced one who, formerly lacking some important human quality, has elected (or been advised) to incarnate under this limitation. A proud, uncommunicative ruler who failed utterly to 'share' may be born unable to communicate or to share in cosy family life, while longing to do so. The precise karmic cause is different in each case. The only point I want to make is that what appears to be a backward or 'simple' child or one lacking in affectionate impulses may in reality be the most evolved member of a family.

Your Own Attitude to Children

How you relate to children can be studied in your birth chart in the 5th House, examining not only planets in this part of the pattern but (as you may have no planets here) the planet which rules the cusp of the 5th House. Your Moon too has relevance to your attitude and conditioning to motherhood, and Venus to the affections in general. I have known an afflicted Saturn in the 5th to correspond to active dislike of children; but this same Saturn can also mean hard work involving creative efforts which are not necessarily offspring of the body. Saturn can also manifest here in some sense of limitation or delay in having children.

It would be very wrong to suggest that a bad aspect to the 5th House means that the individual is cruel to children in this life. He or she could be paying off some karmic debt from the cruel old days when children were deliberately farmed out to wet-nurses, who may have had milk but not of the human kindness variety. Many old souls have something to adjust in respect of children, but there is no reason to suppose that the individual with a potentially stern aspect (or a violent one) to the 5th House is at the primitive stage of baby battering or neglect in his present *persona*.

The 5th House is the field of creativity, so the potential for this is concerned as well – as are children and child-bearing. I have known an afflicted 5th House Saturn to correspond to hard work in the theatre or entertainment world. The man who spends leisure hours rehearsing a choir might well have this sort of indication of hard work involved with pleasure. Saturn gives a sober attitude to the concerns of the section where it is found in the chart, so the person with Saturn in the 5th House may prefer constructive work to what he would consider senseless parties.

If you suspect that your attitude to children is faulty, the astrologer might find the reason for it; or discover why, when dealing with a class or group of children, you find it difficult not to pick on a particular child. Even to realise the possibilities could help you to guard against what you realise is an unfair, yet curiously uncontrollable, reaction.

Concerning Adoption

I have only once been asked to help with the decision of whether or not to keep a baby. It came about this way. It was twenty years ago that Janie first wrote to me. I was at that time writing a question and answer column about astrology for *She* magazine that gave people a chance to contact me. Janie was then a schoolgirl with a crush on an older girl, and something I had written about chart comparison intrigued her and she persuaded her mother to bring her to see me in London. The mother, a very understanding woman, sat in another room.

I felt drawn to the girl. Romantically her pattern had similarities to my own but was more complex.

In particular the potential of a Venus-Saturn opposition threatened emotional problems. But when would it be activated? I saw that in five years' time the Sun would progress to a good aspect of both these planets. But experience has shown astrologers that when a highly testing aspect receives a beneficent solar stimulation, it may be the best possible time to come to grips with a basic difficulty; but this does not turn a basically bad aspect into a good one. I felt sure she would be in some sort of trouble and said, as casually as possible, "You may be tested in some way on the emotional front in about five years' time. If you need advice, don't forget you can contact me."

This fitted in with a natal aspect suggestive of delays in educational matters, so that if she went to university, this test would possibly arrive just at a time when it would be most disruptive.

I heard nothing more for a full five years, when a long letter arrived. "Dear Miss Lind," she wrote, "I doubt if you will remember me . . . I remember you very well and especially one thing you said to me – that in five years' time I might have a problem to solve and that I could, if I wished, come to you for help. I nearly came at Easter but somehow felt that the problem I had then was not the one I was destined to come to you about. I hope that doesn't sound too superstitious." (Astrologer readers may agree with me that this is typical of the girl's Capricorn self trying to cope with her Piscean romanticism.) She continued, "I have very little time for a decision which must be irrevocable. . . ." She did not state the exact problem, so I wrote back that I would set out her fully progressed chart, but that, in this instance, she must ask specific questions. This is in flat contradiction to my printed instructions to clients which state that I don't deal with specific questions. But in this case it was a particular problem arising in relation to a foreseen time of testing. In order to be of help I had to be put more fully into the picture.

Given a full and free set of questions based on facts, my answers could be based on the astrological correspondences.

Her second letter gave the full story, that while up at university she had embarked on a stormy relationship with a fellow-student and become pregnant. The young man wanted to marry her, but she, with admirable good sense, did not want to marry a man who had proved to be of difficult, even violent temperament just for the sake of the proprieties. She tried unsuccessfully to abort.

A little girl was born and Janie wrote that prior to the birth she hated the baby she had grown to hate the father, among other things for having disrupted her career. (Her ambitious Capricorn Ascendant thwarted, due largely to her Sun-Pisces muddling romanticism.) After the compulsory wait, to comply with adoption law, when the mother is given a chance to get to know her baby, the inevitable happened and she wrote, "Of course I got fond of her. She is so beautiful. Her father visited us and I was moved [Piscean sentiment] to see him holding her, but quickly realised I didn't love him and couldn't marry him. So what to do? My mother wants me to keep her but I am afraid of the responsibility of bringing her up alone. . . . Would anyone marry me if I keep her? It seems selfish to give her up and refuse my responsibilities for the sake of my freedom, but wouldn't she have a better chance in life with adoptive parents? I'm not even sure that I am concerned with the unselfish alternative. It horrifies me that I miss her so little in the time she has been with a foster-mother. [Here speaks Venus opposite Saturn.] Some of my relations are dead against my keeping her. I hope you will be able to shed fresh light on it all."

I thanked her for writing so fully. Here follow selected bits of my reply:

"I have done your progressed chart, your baby's chart and a comparison between this and your own natal pattern. It is interesting to see the links between the child and your own difficult aspects. As I see it, the whole difficulty is a karmic thing you had to go through, and I'm afraid I feel bound to tell you that if you shirk it now, the whole test will only recur in more painful form, in this life or a future one. You must realise, if you can, that this is an important test for your whole future. In my view we do not live once but many, many times, and the pattern we bring with us is one we have created. Your chart shows much good. Reliability, ambition, brains, ability, affection, dynamic energy, sensitivity, charm and sweetness. But there are also difficult aspects suggestive of romantic escapist urges. In short there is a conflict between good and bad, reliability and heedlessness, sensible and scatty, straight and crooked.

"It is your emotional life that has the potential for trouble, and, as was foreseeable in 1960, this potential was activated recently. People who have no knowledge of the deeper realities will advise you to forget it all; to palm off the baby and start again. But where will this get you? Back to square one, with the whole basic problem to face again. Get it into your mind that the important thing in life is inner progress – call it soul progress if you like. It is not just a myth that we account for each thought and deed. Not that anyone punishes us. Oh no! We punish ourselves. We create the circumstances for our next lives by our deeds and misdeeds. So, just as you have, undoubtedly, sown the seeds for this silly mess in some past life, so now you have the opportunity to straighten things up. And to do this you have to act selflessly, thinking of your baby rather than yourself. It's up to you.

"Don't be afraid you will lack love. If you live according to the laws of love, you will attract love. But guard against weakness when it comes to sex impulses. If you don't take care, you could be a pushover for anyone who stimulates your love of pleasure. And don't listen to every clairvoyant or fortune-teller you meet! You have shown good sense in not marrying a boy you don't love. You have Capricorn common sense. But do try to control automatic responses. You've read *A Midsummer Night's Dream*. Titania was bemused by the love philtre and mistook Bottom – perfect name – with the ass's head, for her true love. This is what so many girls do out of sheer need for fulfilment. They project their ideal on to the nearest available male, only to wake up with the ass's head next to their own on the pillow.

"But don't become disillusioned or bitter. Keep sweet and loving. For the moment stop thinking of what life may or may not hold for you. Work hard for your exam and care for your baby with your mother's help and try to *become* the sort of person the right man will be proud to love – not just a pretty kid who stirs his senses.

"Your baby has a clever chart. She is not the sort to be given away like a pound of tea. Imagine her in eighteen years' time – beautiful, proud-making, belonging to strangers. No! It's unthinkable.

"This is your chance to make something out of a difficult situation. All my good wishes and good courage!"

What happened next? It was several years later that I got a letter from Janie telling me how immensely grateful she was that I had persuaded her to keep her baby. The girl's mother, too, clearly a remarkable woman, wrote to tell me . . . "Our lives are transformed."

Would I always advise this way? Obviously not. Each case must be studied and considered on its own merits. Adoption or abortion may be advisable in certain cases. But here, I knew from her chart, was a worthwhile girl whose pattern showed she had certain emotional tests coming to her and it was up to me when specifically asked to advise, to try to get her through her tests with flying colours and above all not to evade the issue. Anyone with a knowledge of karma knows that evasion is just a putting off of the evil day, if not an active creation of fresh difficulties to be faced on top of the old ones.

What can be done when an adopted child's birth time is unknown?

Personally, I set up a roughly calculated chart for sunrise, so that the Sun marks the cusp of the 1st House. Except for the Moon, which travels 14° approximately in 24 hours, the planets will be in their correct signs, and degrees and aspects can be studied. What cannot be studied from such a so-called 'solar chart' are the very important 'fields of activity'. So you might see that a child has a limiting Saturn but not know which field of activity it will limit or inhibit and your interpretation is likewise limited.

As years go by, if you keep in touch with the child and have time to study events, you will probably be able to make an estimation of the Ascendant or Rising-sign.

I have a friend for whom I have studied the charts of her several adopted children. I remember that one girl had a difficult progressed activation of Venus coming to her at the age of seventeen. This could be seen regardless of the missing birth data. I said to her mother, "Do let me know when this time arrives if there is trouble and don't go blaming yourself for bringing her up wrongly, because this is quite evidently something karmic which she has to go through."

Exactly when she was seventeen her adoptive mother rang me to say how right I had been, not only to warn her but to assure her that it was a necessary test for the girl and not wholly her [the mother's] fault. After this event the girl's mother came to see me and together we came to a pretty sure conclusion as to the hitherto unknowable Ascendant.

Choosing a child by means of his birth chart is a possibility. But no astrologer is infallible and, as with marriage partners, I feel that the use of the chart, in comparison work and so forth, is better used after the event. I think that instincts and circumstances should be allowed to influence the situation and the selection. When younger, I wrote with some force how valuable the knowledge of the child's chart would be in selecting a child to fit in with the adoptive family. I still think the chart would be invaluable, but would encourage people to trust their hearts before anything else.

9. ANIMALS CAN HAVE CHARTS TOO

People ask questions such as, "Would I find it easier to understand my animals – I have three labradors with very different characters – if I had their charts done?"

My reply is that yes – animals have different temperaments which can be studied in the birth chart. If you breed animals, the charts can tell you at birth which will have the best temperament for shows or which will make the best pets or guard dogs. And if you have other animals, it can be told at a glance by the astrologer which puppies in a litter will get on best with your cat. A most important factor, this, where the cat is confident that she owns the place.

Some people are surprised that an animal can have a 'horoscope'. But since the chart of this is the pattern of the moment, such a moment can be the starting moment for anything or anyone; so it is not really strange at all. Before welcoming a new animal into my household I check carefully that it will get on with my family and with other animals. A kitten given to my grandchildren was checked thoroughly to ensure that she would make friends with my Cairn terrier and vice versa. I did a chart comparison as I would do it for humans. So confident was I that they would become friends that I took him on a lead to fetch her home, carefully telling him that it was *his* to look after. Two years later the terrier was killed in an accident and Della, the cat, mourned for days.

Of course in talking of the chart of a pet, one would not say, "This poodle has the potential of a Prime Minister, or this cat could be a clergyman". But within appropriate limitations, the same pattern can be studied for animal or child for qualities of steadiness, affection, obedience or eccentricity, over-independence and dangerous aggression.

I have seen shocked faces when I say I choose my dogs by their birth charts. As though 'man' – exalted man – were the only living thing worthy of connexion with a cosmic plan. It is time it was realised that a chart of a birth or a beginning is relevant to all living things and even to inanimate things or projects that have a starting moment on which to base a calculation.

Some animals are difficult to mate It could save time and money to know beforehand if a pair is compatible. Or it can happen that a bitch likes the dog and still fails to produce pups by him. The whole question can be satisfactorily studied through comparison of the birth charts.

It might be important for owners of zoos to foretell an animal's temperament. So far, I regret to say, I have not numbered any enlightened zoo-keepers among my clients, and wild lions or giraffes have not approached me either. But a friend of mine who breeds horses consulted me a few years ago about a show jumper bred on her estate, so that she knew the exact time of birth. She sent me dates of events for an entire season, and I commented on Beauty's chances for specific days. It proved pretty accurate. The only win coincided with a day when Beauty's finances were favoured, and a day with restrictive aspects proved to be a day when the event was cancelled due to bad weather.

And what about horse-racing? Can astrology win us fortunes? The serious answer here is that far too many calculations are needed to build up a helpful picture. Charts of all the jockeys and their runners, for a start. My advice to anyone interested would be to concentrate on a single horse, jockey or trainer . . . not to mention the punter's own chart for the day of the race. All too complicated for my money. But for an owner to know an animal better, it could be very helpful in more than one respect.

10. RELATIONSHIPS

Compatibility

Incompatibility is the cause of much human suffering. In many cases the difficulties stem from childhood. There may have been fear or hatred of a parent. Perhaps the nurse or schoolmaster did something unspeakable. Or the problem may be of more recent origin, involving, let us say, a clash of temperament or some traumatic encounter. In any event, the astrologer gets consulted on all manner of issues which revolve around the hub of *relationships*; and usually one in particular. However, it is not always easy to get the birth data required to make a full assessment of the situation. And in any case a matter of ethics arises. I state clearly that I will not analyse one adult for another. Clients sometimes ask me to analyse a friend (or enemy) but this I refuse to do without the written consent of the second adult.

Nevertheless, all relationships can be studied by means of comparing one chart with another. It can be seen if the difficult side of one chart impinges on the other. All of us have imperfections or 'shadow' sides of our nature, but by no means everyone feels the impact of this. We are different people to someone on whom our Saturn seems a heavy weight and to someone else who is linked to our more light-hearted energy forces, say Venus and Jupiter.

Compulsive, emotional relations that lead to intense suffering can be analysed to the benefit and comfort of the sufferer. Even if he (she) has been let down by the beloved, it is comforting to wounded pride to be told by the astrologer that the dynamic link that drew them together was no figment of imagination; indeed, that the emotional testing entailed may have been integral to the fulfilment of a basic character pattern. If this is so and a break occurs, this doesn't necessarily mean that it was a mistake to embark on the affair. It is very wrong for a practitioner to issue huge warnings against marriage or partnership. At a deep level a main purpose of life is to acquire wisdom which usually can only accrue through experience.

An important function of the person-oriented astrologer is to provide a ready ear to the troubles and sorrows of the client. How much can one person understand another? Through the charts, the astrologer is in a good position to explain to his client why he is 'misunderstood' by his partner, but while clarifying the temperamental differences in a way that may satisfy himself, he must not imagine that a man or woman in love will accept more than he or she wants to believe either about themselves or the partner with whom some problem or rift has manifested.

Just as introspection can be unhealthy when carried to extremes, so I believe it to be a mistake to try to explain a person to themselves beyond a certain point. Each of us has to travel a lone path. As Kahlil Gibran wrote in his memorable little book, *The Prophet* (Heinemann, 1926): 'Let there be spaces in your togetherness.' So possibly it is wiser to be thankful we can't fully understand those we love, still less those we are trying to help. If a parent finds his or her daughter impossible in some respect, it is wisest to steer clear of the very basic incompatibilities. It may well be the parent's own dark side which provokes stress and it would do no good at all to expose something which would not be accepted. Nor would the average person want to examine his own murky depths when what he is hoping to hear is how terrible his child (or partner) is. The parent unconsciously seeks justification for a critical attitude. Some sort of reassurance of incompatibility is a wiser course than over-frank delving into whys and wherefores and rights and wrongs. The astrologer's function is not to play God so much as to help sympathetically. The problem cannot be solved, but light can be shed on the reasons for temperamental discord.

We all know the fatal attraction that can exist when two people seem drawn together with no possibility of harmony or happiness. And what about types who make your hackles rise even from a distance? What makes for sympathy? Or antipathy? Why love or hate at first sight? To say sweepingly that natives of signs in square aspect (that is to say, born exactly three months apart) never agree would be wrong. The assertion is, however, based on a profound truth. The person vibrating with Fiery frankness (Aries, Leo, Sagittarius) is unlikely to see eye to eye with another who quivers with Watery sensitivity (typical of Cancer, Scorpio and Pisces). But it takes two whole charts, not merely a comparison of Sun-signs, to show where balance or imbalance, sympathy or antipathy, will occur.

Have you known someone to have a stultifying effect on your personality – in whose presence you can't utter? At a guess I would say that the charts would show his limiting, restrictive or stern Saturnian energy working in the same zodiacal degree as your Sun (self-expression) or your Mercury (Communicative energy). Or have you responded instantly and rashly to a magnetic attraction, knowing well that there was nothing else in common but an overwhelming and temporarily delicious body urge? A comparison of charts could show that the sole strong link was your carnal Mars in the degree of his magnetic Uranus.

You hear people say, "I was born under Libra (or Taurus), so Venus is MY planet." I can assure you that Venus is everyone's planet when it comes to forming relationships. All of us have our team of energies. All the planets were present at your birth whatever month you were born in, rather like the good and bad fairies. Only the individual chart shows which were playing which role for you. Planets are described loosely as beneficent or maleficent, but a venal Venus can be a bad fairy and a serious Saturn entirely a good influence, contrary to uninformed popular opinion.

Integration cannot be perfect if one element of energy is weak or out of balance. While I do not suggest that the basic nature can be changed, it is true that increased self-knowledge can help the individual towards self-government – becoming the sort of person he wishes to be. This in turn will improve his ability to relate happily with others.

Love and Marriage

The astrologer must absolutely not sow seeds of anxiety or fear in the head of a young person who has hopes about marriage. At the risk of being thought a poor astrologer I would withhold certain information.

New Age astrology should be free of fatalism. If we see charts with a potential for divorce, who are we to say "Don't marry!"? Much better let people get on with it and work off the karma. This may be what they have incarnated to do. We cannot (should not) tell them to avoid this trouble. In fact, my favourite sage has said that marriage is never wholly a mistake, even if it comes undone. And here I can quote from a known instance. I did a girl's chart and found so many good aspects that I wondered if I was ever coming to a bad one. At last I came to a close square of Venus (relationships) to Neptune (renunciation – when in bad aspect). More, this Neptune was in the 7th or marriage House. I recalled that my sister with an afflicted Neptune in the 7th had lost two husbands and I wondered if this girl too would be widowed. But Neptune has to do with all renunciations and not just with losses through death – and after some years of marriage her husband left her for another woman. Foreseeing trouble, should I have warned her or advised against this marriage? No! This would have deprived the girl of several happy years and her three children. My feeling is that the couple had to come together *and* later to part in order for her Venus-Neptune square to be fulfilled. It was clearly part of her emotional karma. I hold that astrologers should take the karmic factor, or at any rate the client's developmental needs, into account, and attempt to clarify the situation, not pontificate upon it and make premonitory noises. In this case it would have been legitimate to say the girl had the potential to be disappointed by a partner . . . but to go further than that and sow the fear of widowhood . . . ? Unthinkable!

When working on compatibility between two people I would look for planetary links at all levels. The physical basis of sex and instinctive attraction, the body links, are an essential factor. At the mental level, too, there should be enough harmony and compatibility to engender mutual respect. At first sight either sex may exert a physical appeal. Beauty, glamour, a fine physique can sway the young adult into a certainty of 'this is the one'. But without true *liking*, as opposed to a sexual urge, the marriage will founder. I like to see a good link involving Venus for true love, and involving the Sun, Moon and Ascendant for basic harmony. Mars has to do with carnality, and Uranus with personal magnetism – although at a high level of consciousness Uranus can stand for true awareness. The 'fatal' Marilyn Monroe type of sex appeal I have found in the charts of beautiful women with Mars in close aspect to Uranus, and twice at least where the Sun has given basic detachment from an Air sign, and Scorpio rising adding intense emotional impact.

Such a person is by no means debarred from a true love link, but attraction involving *only* the magnetism would be unlikely to endure, yet while it operated it could involve the 'hooked' partner in considerable distress.

Mars is the energy most associated with sexual potency and carnality, and on this reasoning the sex act is a Mars function. I would certainly study the aspects and placing of Mars in both charts when looking for sexual compatibility. A classic link is for the Mars of one lover to be in (or in close aspect with) the degree of the other's Venus. But again I would stress that the body link on its own is not enough on which to base a lasting relationship, although a pleasant little sexual tug might well be felt by each partner in the presence of the other, even after a separation of years. However, given plenty more harmonious basic links, this aspect is a splendid one for body closeness.

If Venus predominates in a relationship, the sex act can be light-hearted, happy and pleasurable. Venal, in fact. Laughter between lovers is a lovely thing, and some involvement of Venus and Jupiter will promote this quality. But again, if this is not backed up by more solid links, it could mean that here is someone with whom you can have fun – temporarily.

I wouldn't think of Saturn as an energy involved in the sex act, even though I realise that in a Saturnalia there was something called the 'lustful goat' which reminds me that in Victorian times, many a father performed the sex act purely functionally to engender a child.

Uranus, on the other hand, has much to do with sex. Instant attraction of the 'across a crowded room' variety is very Uranian. But perversity. impulse and unconventionality are also under the Uranus heading and while, given plenty of other links, Uranus can add the electric spark that is galvanic and irresistible, it has more to do with affairs than with marriage. Such links need other basic ones if permanence and true love is aimed at.

Does Neptune belong in this line of thought? We use our Neptune energy to escape from the mundane into relms of bliss. And to those in love what greater bliss than the perfect sex act? It is rare that Neptune bliss and shifts of level are found in the sex act, but when they are . . . Hemingway in his novel, *For Whom the Bell Tolls* (Cape, 1941), described the perfect orgasm – 'the earth moved'.

Pluto definitely has to do with sex. With my belief in reincarnation I have come to call it the 'karmic sex' planet, as I find Pluto to be so involved in the 'sense of destiny' felt when two people recognise a deep sense of having known one another for ever. Because of the intensity of emotion aroused unconsciously as well as physically, the ties formed when this planet is activating the chart are felt as compulsive. This is doubtless why Pluto is associated with divorce, because under its stimulus the urge is to throw everything overboard and start again with the one for whom the compelling karmic tug is felt. Pluto is agreed by most astrologers to be associated with Scorpio and the 8th House, both of which have to do with sex and fundamentals.

What about the Sun, Moon and Ascendant in chart comparison? These are concerned with the basic potentials of the chart and harmony between one or other of these is essential. I have spoken of the Elements and Quadruplicities (or Qualities) in Chapter 2 and I consider it takes an overwhelming number of harmonious planetary links to compensate for the more basic clash of, say, Fire in one partner and Water in the other. Links between the Sun and Moon and Ascendant show in family charts. Siblings who share an Ascendant often look alike, just as one child in a family with a surprisingly different ascendant from Signs current in his family will look and behave differently from the others.

So far as sex is concerned, I am steering clear of over-simplification regarding Signs. It is nonsense to give people the idea that because their Sun is in this or that *Sign* they will be more or less passionate. As you read in the section called Balance and Imbalance, the worst complexes arise when a potential (of a basic sign) is unfulfilled. So, as long as it is understood that I am NOT saying that you are sexy or unsexy if born under a certain sign, I will go as far as to state that in my experience it IS folk with many planetary energies working through the Fixed Signs (Taurus, Leo, Scorpio and to a lesser degree Aquarius) who get most steamed up over sex. And women with Fixed Signs are the ones who go on about having given their all, when, to tell the truth, it was they who ached to give it in the first place.

The Air Signs are the coolest, but to make up for this they are very attractive. Their baffling detachment can be teasing. Their love of travel and communication helps them to get around. For these, there is much in the placing of Mars and other planets that can warm up someone who is potentially cool.

It is said that the 'animal' signs are carnal. Which are they? Aries, the Ram, Taurus the Bull, Leo the Lion, Sagittarius the Archer who is half man and half horse, and Capricorn the Goat. This leaves out Scorpio, so it is certainly not an exclusive list. And I would add that many with a strong need for love may not be sex-driven so much as emotionally hungry or longing to give affection, or have babies.

Extravert, out-going people often have the reputation for being sexy, when perhaps all it amounts to is that they talk more easily about it. The extravert will advocate frank talk or education in sex for everyone. The introvert praises the modesty of those who maintain what *they* feel to be a respectable silence on the subject. Who is right? As always each judges the other by himself and makes a virtue of his own attitude.

Any counsellor or analyst should be careful to appreciate and understand either attitude. As so often in life, it is not a question of right or wrong but of different attitudes to behaviour springing from quite different feelings and motivation.

For those in love or contemplating partnership who ask me "Will we get on all right?", the thing I look at immediately is Saturn in both charts. If your Saturn, which is your serious side, agrees with your partner's Saturn, which is representative of his idea of what should be taken seriously, it will augur well for some combination of work. Contrariwise, if a man with an afflicted, phobia-ridden Saturn partners a woman whose Sun or Ascendant degree is in the degree of this heavy (or at worst coldly cruel or restrictive) Saturn of his, she would feel no confidence in his presence. Her whole personality and vitality are restricted. Another woman who aroused quite a different side of this man's nature would not find him cold or restrictive at all. This is why it is so important not to put labels on people or group them under generalised headings. We are all multiple personalities, our reactions varying according to whom we are with. This is why I stress the importance of there being agreement – or at least, harmony – on what is taken seriously.

It is revealing to study the charts of two people who have divorced. It will be seen what drew the two together, and often enough a sex attraction is accentuated for a few years; quite enough to allow them to enjoy each other's company for a time. Then, when this died down, there was not enough harmony in the basic approach to living and not enough interests in common to perpetuate the bond.

In doing the comparison of two people one must see how many permanent links there are. You can expect to find some harmonious and some inharmonious ones, but be on guard if what you find is a lot of disharmony and just a few compulsive temporary links. (Temporary links are those between the progressed chart of one to the natal or progressed chart of the other. This means that the affinity will be short-lived and the pair be left with inadequate basic ties.)

In the case of true and lasting happiness one finds anything between twenty and fifty permanent bonds of shared interests, energy outlets and attitudes to life. Here too the temporary accentuation by progressed charts at the time of meeting will serve to bring the relationship to the boil, but without the fear of lovers becoming strangers again when the first raptures subside.

A small research project carried out in the Faculty of Astrological Studies in its early days found that in sample charts of happily married couples, the Sign Pisces figured strongly in those of the women. This is easy to understand, as Pisces is the most adaptable sign (unless strongly counter-balanced by the rest of the pattern) and for a woman with Venus in Pisces it would seem natural to fall in with her husband's plans and wishes. Indeed I have found that some Piscean wives even come to look like their husbands in the long run and imitate their expressions and share their views. Pisces is largely an unselfish, self-sacrificing sign. Venus is in its so-called 'exaltation' in this sign.

In the normal course of events, when people fall in love, I would think there was something very half-hearted if either needed convincing by an astrologer. After the event, the study of the two charts can aid mutual understanding, but if either were so undecided as to need persuading, I wouldn't give much for the couple's chances anyway.

Planetary oppositions – your Sun opposite his Sun and so on – are a close yet challenging bond – the bond of polarity. When you reflect that the sign opposite the most personal Ascendant and 1st House of the chart, is the 7th or Marriage House, it is obvious that the polarity link has a bearing on marriage or the 'other person' in any contract or situation, whether partner or enemy. Oppositions are important in the natal chart of the individual, too. They constitute a challenge for the person to accept and understand different sides of his own nature that are in a profound way complementary. Thus, in the marriage of truly linked souls, one often finds the birth dates six months apart giving this polarity link. It helps to orient the individual away from the egoistic self and to accept and 'know' either his own complementary self, or the complementary factor in the close partner. In this way the opposites are in a subtle sense united.

I am NOT saying that all marriages where the partners' birthdays are six months apart are bound to be God-given successes. The plain truth may be that the two are drawn together by this factor and later on the incompatibilities of other features in the two charts prove too great and the marriage or partnership breaks up.

A remarkably close link is where the Sun and Ascendant of the man is in exact opposition to the Sun and Ascendant of the woman. This would only happen where both were born at sunrise, when the Rising-sign and the Sun-sign are one and the same. But normally, for interesting and stimulating partnerships, some differences are needed if the relationship is not to become a mutual admiration society. In difficult marriages it must not be forgotten that the purpose of the marriage (karmically) is to work through a difficult combination.

Shared degrees are important. They indicate shared experiences for the simple reason that if a transit (or passage of) a slow-moving planet is approaching a shared degree it will involve both persons according to the type of planetary energy in both patterns. If you look at charts of family or friends to see why a particular person just happens to be around at dramatic moments: births, deaths, marriages, accidents or illness, he or she is there as if in answer to a summons; you find that you share some zodiacal degree that has been activated by a strong transitting planet or the hovering of a powerful Stationary planet.

So, if you have come to the stage in a relationship where you wonder if he or she is 'the one', remember that it is logical that there should be this degree sharing. Otherwise, when something vitally affects one of you, the other may not be in the picture. Of course, even when degrees are shared, circumstances may separate. He might be a sailor or she touring the world, but if you are really close, any dramatic event will involve you both, whether geographically apart or not.

Notable exceptions, if you are thinking in terms of happiness, are what can be seen in the case of close but disastrous partnerships. There are also partnerships in crime. And partnerships that come under the love-hate heading. In these, study of the comparison will probably show that a violent or dangerous configuration in the one chart exactly combines with important energy factors in the other chart.

The amateur astrologer or student will now ask, "Why don't you give chapter and verse? What planets on what other planets? Be more specific, for goodness sake!"

The truth is that this would be misleading. I could quote exact cases of partners in crime and hundreds of readers would find that they, too, have planet X on their husband's or wife's planet Y and would feel fear . . . quite unnecessary fear (for the rest of each chart would be completely different). In any case, you are YOU, and no specific aspect or combination of aspects with your partner is going to turn the two of you into a Bonnie and Clyde partnership of crime.

In working alliances a harmonious bond involving Mars energy and Saturnian thoroughness and reliability is of more value than any venal, good-time link. The good fellow in the pub may not be nearly as useful in the office as the penny-pinching type who adds up meticulously and spots errors with his irritatingly critical approach to life. A study of his chart with your own can show whether or no you will be so madddened by his personality that you can't bear him around the place at all, or if his accuracy will benefit your business beyond your wildest hopes.

All the facile rules and statements about who gets on with whom should be put in the dustbin. It all depends on what you want the other person *for*. The perfect secretary is not necessarily the right wife for you or vice versa. The comparison of two charts would save you a lot of heart-ache if it showed, for instance, that to engage Miss X on to your office staff would be to expose yourself to her sexual dynamism, which is not only of a high order but directly linked with your own impulsive energies. This is an instance when trouble could with benefit be guarded against. Of course you may be looking for trouble! If so, this warning is not for you.

People are vulnerable to those they love the most. They go through agonies wondering if they have said or written the wrong thing. It can be comforting to be shown the reality – or even the brutal truth of the un-reality – of a relationship. The astrologer is accustomed to being con-sulted in times of both joy and sorrow. A man arrives full of the joys of spring and says, "I'm going to marry Mary-Jane. Will you please compare her chart with mine?" Later he comes and says, "I *am* married to Mary-Jane." Things are evidently not all he hoped for and he wants to know why.

A delicate situation for the astrologer arises when two people intend to marry and the charts show a potential burden of the one on the other. I feel strongly that the astrologer has no business to say, "Avoid this trouble!" It is not comparable to avoiding taking into your office an unknown secretary. In this case the couple have met and fallen in love and wish to marry, but difficulties show in the comparison. After working on a particular analysis by post, I rang the man and asked, "What is there about your fiancée that could constitute some sort of responsibility or burden for you?" "I can answer that very quickly," came the reply. "She is a paraplegic and I have to push her about in a wheel-chair." This proved to become a very happy marriage. You can't just assume that a burden is unwelcome. By asking what the burden consists of – and remember it may be just an age gap – the astrologer can avoid being tactless or wounding. A partner may be deaf, or an invalid, or have some affliction that in no way affects the emotional richness of the partnership. Think of Robert Browning, the poet, who married Elizabeth Barrett. He fell deeply in love and eloped with her at a time when she though herself to be an invalid.

You will agree, I am sure, that it is not the job of the astrologer to make decisions or to try to bias those concerned in their choice of partner. I think it legitimate to analyse each chart (with the permission of both) and let each partner read the other's frank analysis. I would not go further than this. I would insist "You know this person. It is your problem – your decision." Even if things turn out ill, there is nothing so effective as learning the hard way, through one's own mistakes, misdeeds and misconceptions.

In the case of another couple I analysed, both had violent, passionate natures. The two maps were conflicting yet strongly linked. Their affair had followed its stormy route for more than a decade . . . bust-ups alternating with passionate reconciliations. I told them that these storms were indicated and that in a very real sense they suited each other, as one was as passionate as the other. I said that if, in the end, they married, at least they would be going into it with full knowledge of the possibilities. I am told they did in fact marry. I pray they are happy.

There are thousands of happily married couples whose Sun-signs are said to conflict. An unhappy marriage is far more likely to show something totally unrelated to the Sun's position, such as the husband's cold and stern Saturn being in the degree of his wife's Mercury (communications) so that he would tend to throw cold water on her every idea, and she would feel constantly rebuffed.

I am not saying that Sun and Moon links are not important. They are of vital importance, and it is true in theory that some signs harmonise and others clash. What is NOT true is that any individual reacts simply and solely to one sign.

Chart Comparison

The following interpretations are intended to demonstrate how the astrologer sets about the comparison of basic energies. Obviously, individual interpretations have to take into consideration that either person may be a saint or a villain. It is important to see if a particularly difficult grouping of energies in one chart inpinges on the other. A well-aspected, civilised Mars energy represents a quite different energy force from an aggressive Mars which forms part of a violent grouping of energies.

In the following please note that A and B are interchangeable as male or female.

1. *A's Moon conjunct B's Moon.* Similar automatic reactions and response to life. Emotional harmony. In the Astrological Experiment quoted in *The Interpretation of Nature and the Psyche*, by C. G. Jung and W. Pauli (Routledge, 1955), this was the most common factor to appear in the charts of married couples.
2. *A's Ascendant conjunct B's Sun.* A's ego is boosted by the sight of his own more superficial characteristics demonstrated in confident, basic fashion by B. There is also harmony through shared interests, and the companionship of shared problems.
3. *A's Ascendant conjunct B's Moon.* A's temperament and personality will satisfy B's unconscious demands of life and accord with his or her emotional reactions.
4. *A's Sun conjunct B's Moon.* An obvious link of A's positive self with B's negative response and receptivity. A profound link and one which has a physical application.
5. *A's Sun trine B's Sun.* Harmony through a sharing of the Element. Fire to Fire, Earth to Earth, etc. Sympathetic ideas and reactions. Similar tempo of living.

(If A's Sun is sextile B's Sun, the elements differ – but if the linking aspect is exact by degree, there will be a sharing of experiences when, as will inevitably happen, both Suns are activated by transit.)

6. *A's Venus conjunct or in good aspect with B's Sun, Moon or Ascendant.* A's urge for relationship, harmony and the expression of affection is stimulated by some facet in B's total personality.

The above are highly significant links. Midheaven and Descendant are also vitally important but only if the birth time is known to be accurate. But all aspects must be listed and considered if a true picture is to be formed. Difficult minor aspects can add up to intolerable strain and stress if there are too many of these.

Magnetic links and physical attractions occur when:

7. Mars, Uranus or Pluto aspect Venus, Moon or each other or the angles (these last only if birth time is exact).
8. Neptune is involved with sensitive degrees of the chart. If aspects are inharmonious, illusion or secrecy or sensationalism may play too big a part. The one whose Neptune is involved exerts the fascination over the other.

Links of friendship. Many of these are helpful in marriage as a backing to the more fundamental links given above.

A link that is common among friends of the same sex (and I am not here referring to homosexual bonds) is a sharing of Ascendant. This is often more obvious than a shared Sun-sign and the feeling is of having 'something in common'.

Shared mental interests show in general compatibility of the charts plus harmonious links between 3rd Houses, Mercury and Jupiter. It is also a fact that sextile aspects, both in a single chart and between two charts, have to do with mental interests.

Happy social relations are likely if A's Jupiter harmonises with B's Moon, Venus or Ascendant. A in such a case (if he has a good natal Jupiter) provides enjoyment, relaxation, luxuries or just sheer fun for B.

Shy people lose their timidity when in company with a friend or partner whose good Jupiter coincides with their own Mercury or Ascendant.

More serious sides of the nature are in harmony if Saturn in the one chart harmonises with Saturn in the other, thus linking what each agrees should be taken seriously. Clashes here could account for life-long feuds involving basic principles. One can laugh it off if a friend has different amusements from your own, but it can cause a real rift if he is a Communist and you are a Conservative, or he a Catholic and you a free-thinker.

How to handle comparisons. It is usually those contemplating marriage or partnership who ask for astrological advice or guidance. I have heard astrologers say that there should be thirty or more planetary links and the greater proportion of these harmonious. If this principle were followed, no doubt the divorce rate would decrease. But just as one can see in some charts that the native is never going to be wildly successful, so in others it is evident that troubles will occur in the emotional field. Certain natal indications only need activating to result in breaks, divorces or other outcomes of a turbulent love life. What is the astrologer to do when faced with a chart that contains such a picture? Advice against marriage would fall on deaf ears but as I have said, I don't approve of giving advice.

A final thought and summing-up. At the risk of repeating myself: Any markedly difficult configuration in one chart is likely to affect the life of the partner if it corresponds exactly to sensitive or prominent degrees. For instance A may have a violent T-square or grand Cross. (A T-square is to have one planet opposite another, both being 90° from a third. A Grand Cross is what it sounds like – two oppositions forming a cross.) To have such an aspect is fairly common and certainly not enough to condemn one to celibacy! But if B's Sun, Moon Ascendant or Venus falls in the exact degree of a malefic in such a configuration, he or she is likely to be hurt by A, or at least to share in his most testing and hurtful life experiences if they decide to join forces.

Inter-family Analysis

I get told somewhat plaintively that astrologers are for ever giving advice on who not to marry, but surely incompatibilities also apply to parent and child? Can it be shown why some children are easier to bring up than others? In one case a mother found her two Taurus children easy and the Cancer one difficult.

Only by setting out the charts for the whole family could light be thrown on just why this was the case. The mother had come to her own conclusion that Cancer must be a difficult sign. This is NOT the case. Every chart has its good, positive side and its difficult, negative side in varying balance. It could be that your child's worst feature is a badly aspected Moon and that this falls right on the degree of your Sun or some other sensitive point. In this case it will seem *to you* that when he or she is being horribly unreasonable, it is aimed right at you. It could be that it IS.

I have found recently what seems to me a very labour-saving method of studying a whole family's charts: and I am told, to my great satisfaction, that Stephen Arroyo has reached the same conclusion. This is a study of Houses. My way is to set out each chart separately, but thereafter to work on a single analysis incorporating them all. This can be done by looking at each House in turn and seeing, for instance, who has particular emphasis in the House under consideration. It is easy by this method to see if one of the family impinges on another and in which field of activity the main strengths or faults of each occur. It would have saved me time and trouble if I had employed this method years ago when I was consulted about a case of juvenile delinquency. I was, however, not asked to do the parents charts.

The mother of a fifteen-year-old boy asked me to anlyse his chart as he had started stealing. The chart showed the potential for difficulties in the home, so I asked, as tactfully as possible, if all was well between the parents. The answer came that the marriage was unhappy, and "I am only sticking to my husband for the sake of the boy". This praiseworthy effort was clearly proving disastrous. In the absence of a loving home background, the boy was stealing in an unconscious attempt to compensate for a lack.

I am not suggesting that an astrological analysis will improve a situation. This could happen only if the increased knowledge of another person – or child – helped to smooth the path.

The study of two charts is great fun as well as being very revealing. You'd think I'd be sick of the subject by the end of the day, but I often lie in bed looking at the charts of friends and relations . . . seeing why one old aunt always brought out the devil in me, while another made me feel loving and wanted; why some long-past love-affair still has the power to evoke sensuous memories, while another is deader than mutton. What never fails to amaze me is the exact correspondence with facts. In two charts where the only harmonious link involves Neptune and Venus you find, perhaps, that the two play in the same orchestra. Musically they harmonise yet loathe each other outside the door of the concert hall. So, once again, let no one be taken in by the oft-made statement that "Leo can't get on with Scorpio". That is a mere one-hundredth part of the total picture. Fields of interest, love, business compatibility can all be studied, and for any of these studies the whole chart is necessary.

Applied with skill, chart comparisons can throw light on any sort of relationship or combine. Complete harmony should not even be looked for, but I strongly suggest checking that the worst in one chart does not trigger off the worst in a possible associate.

Professional Links and Business Considerations

When comparing your chart with that of your doctor, surgeon, dentist, lawyer or astrologer, it is often found that Saturn is involved. Saturn is too often mistrusted as a malefic, but in the above links there is no need to jump to the conclusion that this is a bad thing, which it could be in a domestic partnership. In a professional tie-up Saturn plays a different role. If you are the patient, you are almost certainly a bit of hard work for your practitioner . . . some sort of a 'worry' to him, and therefore it is appropriate for your Saturn to impinge on his pattern. It could be on his Mercury as constituting a problem he has to think about. The reverse also applies. If *you* are the astrologer, don't in such cases say, parrot-fashion. "Her Saturn is on my Ascendant (or whatever), therefore I must avoid having anything to do with her." That would be faulty reasoning. Saturn is likely to be involved if you are working especially hard on a patient or client.

I don't imagine many people actually see the charts of their doctor or lawyer before seeking help. If they did so they might be surprised at the heaviness of the links between themselves and the most trusted practitioner.

As a consultant astrologer, and knowing my own planetary degrees by heart, I automatically see a client's chart in relation to my own. I often find their difficult aspects combine with my 6th House Mercury. (Mercury has to do with communications and the 6th House with health and work for others.) This does not mean that they are wrong to consult me, or I wrong to accept them as clients – on the contrary. For the brief time of our association it is up to me to carry their burdens or to suggest a remedy. I find it natural that a client's afflicted Saturn is on the consultant's Mercury or Ascendant if through his training and personality the latter can be of help.

As in the case already mentioned of the devoted husband of a crippled wife, it is of importance to think carefully of the nature of any relationship before summing up adversely on the desirability of an association. Just consider how many devoted mothers spend years in caring for a sick child. In such cases a heavy Saturnian link is sublimated into responsibility from which they would not ask to be relieved.

In everyday life it is a happy thought that there is always someone to whom even our worst is not apparent, which is why, although A stimulates the best in us, B arouses a devil. Comparison will show our harmonious aspects to coincide with important points in A's chart, while in the case of B our violent aspects clash with his. We may be old enemies from some past life. So while most people will see us with detachment as some sort of an integrated whole, Mr. A sees only our agreeable side and Mr. B hasn't a good word to say for us!

In a promising partnership it is found that planetary energies in the one stimulate dormant potentials in the other. There is an instinct in male and female, often unconscious, to seek as partner one who supplies a quality which is lacking in him or herself. This is one explanation of what I have already mentioned – married couples with Suns in opposite signs.

Teamwork in communities or groups succeeds where each is expert in his allotted place. Clashes occur where two fight over the same function. Similarly, when searching for the perfect partner it is not vital to find similarities so much as complementary qualities.

If you can lay hands on the late C. E. O. Carter's *Principles of Astrology,* *

* Theosophical Publishing House, 1925.

which incidentally was my bedside book for years, and turn to Chapter Six, section 3; 'Disposition and Temperament', you will find an admirable dissertation on the conflicts in a single chart which are also applicable between two charts. For example, he demonstrates how a man may be at war with himself by reason of a Fire Ascendant rushing his sensitive Water Sun into impulsive action; and how high spirits can clash with common sense in the case of a Fire Ascendant and an Earthy Sun; and so on through all possible natal combinations of elements relating to Ascendant and Sun in the same chart.

When applied between two charts, serious conflicts arise only if the preponderance of an Element or Quality builds up through further combinations of energies and aspects. One partner may be helped to integration and fulfilment by complementary qualities in the other. The powerful link between the Sun in one chart right on the Ascendant degree of the other might be especially valuable where the basic individuality (the Sun) is in need of support, as in cases of inner conflict between the Sun and Ascendant Signs. But in a full comparison, every small link must be considered and weighed up. The last straw can tip the scales.

The birth chart can be studied in order to gauge the individual's ability to handle *business or money matters*. Taurus, Virgo and Capricorn are three down-to-earth, materially conscious signs but, as always, only the whole, calculated chart will give a reliable picture. To have the right basic potentials is not enough, as these may remain unfulfilled. Even the dedicated financier may be successful or unsuccessful. For a study of business acumen, one must look for good indications involving the 2nd House of the chart and/or good aspects to the ruler of the 2nd House, not excluding indications of good sense and reliability.

Choosing staff. Can the astrologer help an employer to choose staff? Are there reliable indications of conscientiousness?

Given full birth data, which unhappily is not always available, a well-trained astrologer could be of help. An astrologically trained personnel officer could check for clashes of temperament. I myself look for good aspects to Saturn as an indication of thoroughness and punctuality and sense of responsibility.

The business itself can have a birth chart, if the moment of its inception is known. The charts of prospective employees compared with this will disclose if an individual will serve the company well or ill. Similarly, a ship's chart can be set up from the moment of launching, as can anything that has a known starting moment. Marc Edmond Jones has rightly called astrology the 'science of beginnings'.

Perhaps the most frequent demand among my clients is to know if partnership would be profitable with Mr. X. In such cases one must study everything in each chart to do with money and career. I remember doing this for a woman who was absolutely sold on the idea of going into partnership. She was sure she would make a fortune. I hated having to disillusion her. I was not seeing anything dishonest or criminal in the man's chart; it was clear, however, that the two people were inharmonious where money was concerned. "It's only in relation to money that I see clashes, so I am certain that whatever you do in a business partnership with this man will be costly or come to nothing."

She wrote a charming letter back saying, "Well, at least I can't say I haven't been warned. But I'm taking no notice. I've already put a lot of money into his properties."

It was years later that she told me that every penny was lost. Why had I been so sure? The ruler of her 2nd House was in 90° (Square) aspect to the man's gambling potential, which in his case was seen in an exaggerative and rash Jupiter in his 5th House, which squared his own 2nd (Money) House. I saw no need to look further.

In this way one can study any activity involving two people to see if their attitudes to a given subject harmonise or clash. Friendships, enmities, fascinations, revulsions, business or artistic or literary interests . . . all can be studied.

Back to *employees*. All of us, when we engage someone to work for us . . . what do we want to know about them? Firstly we want to check that their mere presence will not constitute an irritation. Energy and initiative is important according to the work involved. For this we look at Mars. Without a reasonable Mars there will be dithering and inability to cope in even a minor domestic crisis. An over-aggressive Mars is undesirable too. But we will look also at Saturnian qualities. Is this person reliable? Sober? Thorough? Or has he an overdose of Saturn? Can he or she turn coldly unpleasant and unapproachable?

A person can be admirably qualified and still be a pain in the neck to someone else. Uncongeniality can make an association very trying.

Dangers of Inexperienced Judgement

How can you get charts compared? Can an amateur astrologer help? Well . . . certainly not a beginner. It needs a mature grasp of what each planetary energy stands for in the context of the individual charts, and not as read in textbooks in isolation. And certainly not from computerised readings. (Computer calculation is quite another matter and most useful.)

In this of necessity skilled application of knowledge it is important that the concept of wholeness and integration is borne in mind; and even more important is the fact that a more or a less evolved individual can animate the same chart. The more evolved type does *not* react automatically. It is only the man or woman who reacts automatically who will be predictable when anger or other primitive energies are excited. If this were not a fact, murder would be more rife.

The inexperienced astrologer or amateur is prone to warn without real need. No two charts are wholly in harmony, so beware of magnifying the odd clash. If two people are aware of holding opposing views in some directions they can agree to differ while enjoying each other's company in other ways. Relationships can and do flourish in spite of differences.

For some years I was secretary to a surgeon. Our charts combined well except for the fact that his Saturn (serious views) was right on my Uranus (unconventional ideas, such as astrology). And right to the end of his life he referred to my more 'way out' activities as 'Crocodiles'. I didn't try to convert him.

In social life we know pretty well which of our friends will get on with which others, and it is always for a complex of reasons. Occasionally, however, we come across a person who draws some people like a magnet and yet is violently disliked by others. The chart of such a man would probably show that there is an abrasive side to his dynamic, magnetic pattern. Those whose charts in no way correspond to his difficult con-figurations may flatter themselves that they are tolerant and detached . . . wiser, maybe, and more Christian than those who seem conscious only of his 'impossible' characteristics. The truth may be, quite simply the so-called tolerant ones have nothing in them that reacts to his par-ticular brand of disharmony.

PART IV

Matters Arising

1. QUESTIONS COMMONLY ASKED

There are certain questions that are very often asked. Some of these come from people who are puzzled by what they read under the heading of astrology or 'horoscopes' in the popular Press, and many of their misconceptions spring from the common assumption that astrology is based solely on the date of birth and position of the Sun in a particular Sign of the Zodiac. But it is not only these casual readers who have posed the questions which follow; so they are worthy of mention. All the answers are my own opinion based on experience. I make this point as astrologers as a body are not single-minded on all subjects.

Why are birthdays around 21st–24th of any month sometimes listed under one sign and sometimes under another?
This is very simple to answer. In no two years does the Sun enter all the signs on the same date. Thus someone born on 23rd August in one year may have the Sun in Leo while his neighbour born on the same date in another year would be a Sun–Virgo. The only way for such borderline people to make sure of their Sun-sign is to consult the almanac or Ephemeris for the year of birth. There is a paragraph headed TIME WHEN THE SUN AND MOON ENTER THE ZODIACAL SIGNS IN 19—. Usually between July and November the dates of the change are later than in the earlier part of the year.

Shouldn't the moment of conception also be charted?
This question is dealt with in PART II, 8, IMPORTANCE OF THE BIRTH MOMENT. But how many parents could pin-point the date, let alone the moment of this event? And it must be remembered that the moment of coitus is not necessarily within minutes or even hours of the moment of conception, so to say the least of it the suggestion is not practical.

What about premature births or those artifically induced? Is the birth-chart valid in such a case?
We are not in a position to judge to what extent accidents can happen. What we consider an accident (or what may seem deliberate changing of a natural time-sequence, as in artificially induced birth) may be heaven's

way of ensuring that a child incarnates at the moment he is intended to. I myself am confident that the actual moment that a child draws its first breath is the moment to take as its starting-off point in a new sphere of experience; and valid therefore for calculation of its birth-chart. Life is what actually happens and bears little relation to what people expect or think ought to occur. And to the baby concerned, regardless of what has gone before, the significant moment is the one when he enters on a conscious and independent existence.

Birth Planning. Could one arrange the birth of a child in such a manner that its character and talents would be guaranteed?

This would be impossible, since it is the *momentary* set-up that matters. Moreover, it would be a very serious responsibility. If you planned successfully for a child to be born in a given month this would not guarantee any particular talents or qualities beyond those general to everyone born with a particular Sun-sign.

One could of course choose years or periods when the slow-moving planets were in harmonious relation – but your hopes could be wrecked by faster moving factors and you would run the risk of producing a little Hyde instead of the planned-for Jekyll.

This question ignores altogether the consideration that the spirit which comes into birth, or into the circumstances which the chart depicts, is a positive, individual and to at least some extent a self-determining entity.

What about heredity? Surely this is stronger than the Stars?

This question seems to suppose that if one factor works, another doesn't. In actual fact, the birth-charts of an entire family over several generations give an accurate picture of the hereditary position. This question is also dealt with in Part III, 7. But, in brief, a strong characteristic in a grandfather shall we say a Moon-Jupiter conjunction, indicating an exaggerated response to life may well repeat itself in one but not the other of his sons and in four out of seven of his grandchildren. An astrologer, instead of saying that such and such a child takes after his grandfather, would be able to isolate the actual quality inherited; but he would by no means be surprised if the child was totally unlike the grandfather in almost every other respect. Any strong family trait is traceable through a family by means of the birth-charts and usually one or two signs will appear again and again as Sun-sign, Rising-sign or Moon-sign, providing, as it were, a common factor of interest which sums up what people think of as a family likeness.

Can we get free of planetary afflictions, or, if the chart is a difficult one, are we doomed to difficulties all through life?

This rather depends on the extent to which we are automatic in our reactions. If we are completely automatic, which I dare hope no human being is, then every time a difficult aspect is set in motion it will externalise in some mishap or malaise. Likewise if we are completely automatic and unthinking, nothing will be learned from the event and it will recur at the same level of experience instead of repeating on an upward (or downward) spiral.

Happily, most of us are more or less evolved, thinking beings capable of learning from events and arming ourselves for the future. It seems to me that the more we can accept that outside events as they impinge on us are in some way related to our own character-potential, the more we can do to modify our own experiences. It may seem far-fetched, but I believe that we experience nothing by chance, and whatever we go through can be related to our conscious or superconscious need to undergo a particular experience. We do not necessarily make the best use of such experiences as they arrive, and this is where free-will comes in. It exists, but strictly within the framework of our potential.

We can certainly improve our lot by our attitude to life and control of our reactions.

Can Astrology help us to avoid disaster?

In some ways this question is like the one above, but it has a different angle as it suggests that a good astrologer might help us to side-step trouble by listing good or bad days. In very minor and mundane ways something of the sort is possible. For instance, I once went to inspect a second-hand car and decided instantly and impulsively to buy it. I found on looking at the Ephemeris that it was in fact an excellent day in relation to my own chart and in particular to my Mercury (travel). The car proved a success. Had it been a 'bad' day, I feel that I should have felt doubtful about the whole transaction and my 'intuition' would have told me not to buy.

I do not advocate dependence on 'the Stars'. Far better give our own intuition and hunch a chance to develop than step behind some bead curtain to seek advice on every minor problem.

Speculation and the luck element. Are there Lucky Stars?

Astrology hasn't yet, as far as I know, made the fortune of any astrologer. There exist astrologers who give advice to business firms and advise on investments, but it takes a lot of skill to sort out the one foolproof aspect from the several doubtful ones. The fact that people pay money to receive this advice suggests that something of value can be produced. I do not attempt this work.

Where horse-racing is concerned, many astrologers see quite clearly *after the race* just why such and such a horse won. Few will venture to utter on the subject beforehand.

As to lucky stars, lucky signs or the reverse, such expressions seem to assume that some heavenly body is benevolent or hostile. This is nonsense. There seems to be a myth about 'unlucky Capricorn'. No doubt this arises because Saturn is the ruling planet and it is known that difficult aspects from Saturn bring tests and difficulties; but a well aspected Saturn gives high probability of worldly success.

Of course some people are more fortunate than others or have carefree temperaments. This is shown in the personal chart in a variety of ways and has no relation to generalities such as the Sun-sign or ruling planet.

Jupiter is the planet associated with luck and unearned benefits. Well aspected in the right part of the chart it can work strongly. When badly aspected there will be an urge to 'try the luck' without much prospect of success. A sound financial position is far more likely to result from knowledge and caution; and these I would associate more with the sign Taurus strongly placed, or even with Capricorn, the so-called unlucky sign, as coolness and ambition (characteristics of Capricorn) play a big part in financial deals.

2. VARIOUS TECHNIQUES AND BRANCHES OF ASTROLOGY

Apart from natal astrology, which can be termed the psychological approach, other techniques such as Mundane or Electional Astrology can be practised. I would like to make it clear that I have not specialised in either of those mentioned; Mundane Astrology because it calls for historical and political knowledge that I do not possess and Electional and Inceptional Astrology because I mistrust anything that tends to build up the astrologer as an oracle. The most admirable human beings are those who have courage and initiative and who contribute something to the world. These do not run continually to oracles for advice on what to do and when to do it. Moreover, the suggestion that success will come only if a venture is embarked on at an auspicious moment is tantamount to saying that failure will follow if the advice is not taken. This leads to the creation of fear and superstition.

On the other hand, if the knowledge is applied wisely, it is valuable to have some idea in advance of tensions in our personal lives or in world affairs. The *general* use of forecasts of periods of high tension would help everyone, including politicians, to plan for the future. Demand for *exact* prediction is futile.

It is always possible – and indeed great fun – to do brilliant 'backwards' astrology and to see correspondences afterwards between chart and event and this leads some people to suppose that, if the astrologer has the skill, he can see the future in detail. It also leads some astrologers to stick their necks out and make predictions which do not come off. It would be more satisfactory all round if they aimed at general storm warnings instead of trying to say which tree will be struck by lightning.

Mundane Astrology

This is a most important branch of astrology as it deals with the effects on the world in general and countries in particular of ease or tension as shown in the aspects of planets to one another.

As I said earlier, it has been proved that aspects have an effect on radio weather and it may well be supposed that they are reflected in natural phenomena such as floods and earthquakes, or in collective human behaviour.

The technique can be applied to political questions, and just as in personal charts the prevailing aspects have effect in proportion to the extent that they do or do not touch off sensitive spots in the individual chart concerned, so also do they seem to affect charts drawn up for the beginning of reigns or republics, which serve as the 'personal' chart of a country.

It is evident, however, that the practitioner of political astrology must be something of a historian and be well up in world affairs.

Electional and Inceptional Astrology

As already mentioned there are those who consult astrologers with a view to selecting a favourable moment for the start of some new project. This is termed 'electional' astrology, while 'inceptional' maps are quite simply those drawn up for the known moment of the launching of a ship or of a car coming off the production line.

The first is a perfectly sound idea but the choosing of such a moment is no easy matter, for if the astrologer seeks for a single highly auspicious factor he still cannot change the rest of the planetary set-up. Moreover, one could not defer action indefinitely because of difficult aspects between the slow-moving planets in operation for months on end; and it would be inconvenient to hold a company meeting or launch a ship in the small hours. The best one can say is that during every 24 hours there are moments that promise better than others, or that harmonise better than others with the individual chart of someone closely involved.

Horary Astrology

This has been described as the branch of astrology which answers questions by means of charts of the heavens calculated for moments when pressing questions occur in the mind; or alternatively for the moment when such a question is put to the practitioner.

My objection is that, apart from the whole thing savouring over-much of fortune-telling, I cannot see how such a moment is satisfactorily arrived at.

It is only fair, however, to state that this branch of astrology has been practised from very early days. It seems that it flourished in the Dark and Middle Ages most probably to the detriment of more serious work. William Lilly is said to have perfected the art at the time of the Restoration.

I remember that my friend, the late Joan Rodgers, whose work I admired, considered horary astrology well worth studying. I suggest that certain of the pointers for judgement of an horary map are worth remembering in the study of individual problems. But in general I find present-day astrologers tend to agree with the above findings. The late C. E. O. Carter is informative on the subject in his early writings.[*]

Astrology and Palmistry

It is well known that no two sets of finger-prints are alike, so that police forces of the world can use them confidently for identification purposes. It would not therefore seem a very outlandish idea to go a step further and to look for an individual pattern in the hand as a whole.

The print of the hand, like the astrological chart, is interpreted by traditional methods. A character portrait emerges from study of the palm or other pattern indicators similar to that which arises from the chart; and palmists use the planetary characteristics in their work. The mounts of Venus, Jupiter or Saturn in the hand, if well developed, give pronounced characteristics of these planets which tie up with indications in the natal map, so that a person with a pronounced mount of Jupiter may have many aspects to this planet or Jupiter will be found to be strongly placed or maybe the ruler of the chart.

Palmistry, like astrology, is based on rules which can be learned and it is a mistake to suppose that psychic gifts or gypsy blood are needed. Probably the continuous study of personalities and the sensitivity needed for understanding tends to awaken intuitive thought or even second sight. It is hard to gauge where clairvoyance begins and one may think that the clairvoyant would do just as well with a crystal, a tea-cup, or other point of focus. True seership or clairvoyance is a gift in itself; but, as I have suggested, a latent trend in this direction often develops with the concentration necessary for study of palm or chart.

I would imagine that the palmist tends to make more use of psychic ability than the astrologer, who has a greater wealth of exact detail and calculation on which to form his conclusions. Certainly in astrology the time factor is more readily observable. I imagine the palm of a baby is not so easily read as the birth-chart, and it is a fact that the palm changes during the life as character develops. The hand-print of an adult, therefore, is comparable to the progressed rather than the natal-chart.

Astrology and palmistry in no way conflict and both support the view that each of us has a separate and individual pattern. We are not, as some educationalists would have it, uniform lumps of clay which the right moulding can transform into Grecian urns; some of us will be suitable for delicate porcelain and others for more utilitarian usage.

Medical Astrology

If, as I have suggested, the macrocosmical zodiac has its correspondence in the human microcosm, it is reasonable to suppose that every aspect of life is open to astrological interpretation and that the planetary movements, as they impinge on the sensitive points in the receiving set of

[*] E.g. *The Principles of Astrology*, Theosophical Publishing House, 1925.

the natal-chart, will be seen to have their repercussions in matters of health as well as events and moods. On the other hand, medical science has advanced far in methods of diagnosis and it is to be doubted whether the astrologer's contribution would be of assistance in this field. My own feeling is that only in real problem cases would the astrologer's insight into the total picture be helpful. Much of interest, however, could be accomplished through co-operative work.

To take an example, a young person is suddenly afflicted with fits. Medical science tests for tumours or lesions in the brain by means of electroencephalographs. Nothing operable is found and drugs are prescribed to control attacks. Control is achieved and the patient ceases to be of medical interest and returns to the home circle.

In such a case the astrologer would have valuable data to work from; the exact dates of the attacks, the peak time of worry and anxiety; and during the ensuing years he could watch progress. His observations might be of great comfort to the family, to whom the whole event is not merely a medical problem but a personal tragedy; for, having traced the correspondence between the planetary situation in relation to the natal chart at the time of the onset of symptoms (and this of course is far easier to do than to predict with accuracy), he could graph the course of the malady in future months or years.

To explain further what I mean: study of the progressed chart of the above case (known personally to me) showed that at birth the planets Uranus (suddenness, disruption) and Mars (heat, excitement) were closely conjoined in Aries, which according to tradition is the Sign associated with the head. Sun and Mercury were also in the same Sign, giving much impulse and excitement. The whole group of planets was in the section of the chart concerned with mentality or education. Progression for the relevant year showed that Uranus had come to the exact degree of the natal Mars, indicating that this would be the maximum period of tension or excitement. It also coincided with the age when the girl would be taking school-leaving examinations. Here I might say that I do not believe that any astrologer, unless possessed of psychic powers, would hit on epilepsy on the strength of such indications; but it is certain that *no* astrologer would fail to observe in this set-up a time of danger through sudden events, possibly involving overstrain of the brain or injury to the head.

In actual fact, this child's head suffered damage from forceps at birth and she suffered several accidents to the head during childhood. There was no history of epilepsy in the family. The sudden onset of this condition ties up very neatly with the fact that the conjunction (or mingling of forces) of Uranus and Mars matured, as it were, in the year of their coming to *exactitude* by progression.

As I do not practise medical astrology, my knowledge of the subject is limited to observations on my own chart and those of my family;

although I come across many instances of acute emotional trouble or psychological upheaval among my clients. The foregoing remarks are based strictly on my own views and experience and I am fully aware that much has been written on the subject suggesting that every variety of disease can be traced through the chart. I would agree that *in retrospect* this is true, but most definitely astrology should not be used for prediction of illness. Apart from the harm that could be done in creating fear in the mind, a lot of nonsense can be talked. I have known twins with identical charts and progressions. When bad patches come, the one may be affected through ill health while the other works off the difficulties in a different way. To give a crude example, one might have a headache while the other hits someone else over the head. The same astrological setup worked off passively or actively. One of the greatest difficulties in considering a chart is to form any idea just *how* a particular aspect will manifest. *Any* affliction *may* externalise in a health condition, but this is by no means certain. All that is certain is that two Planets in affliction will test the native in some way appropriate to the nature and placing of those two Planets in his chart. Even when health conditions seem involved, as it would be the case in the chart of a doctor or nurse, it would be rash to jump to the conclusion that it is the native or subject of the chart who is going to suffer.

What then are my views on the use of astrology in medicine? I hope that in the future astrology will be so generally taught that any doctor will be able to interpret a chart and that a new patient will automatically produce his chart for inspection. The doctor would not employ astrological techniques where clinical methods are more efficient, but to fill in the gaps. One glance at a personal chart will obviate much enquiry, making it clear, for example, whether the patient before him is a fixed, retentive, constipated or rheumatic type or a nervous, volatile hysteric.

It is not only the psychiatrist who should hold this key to the personality but any responsible person dealing with health or welfare matters, to whom a quick and true understanding of a personal problem is vital.

3. PHILOSOPHICAL QUESTIONS
I : EVIL

Planets in affliction associated with criminality, depravity, violence and cruelty are Mars, Saturn, Uranus and Neptune. But don't run away with the idea that a native of Aries or Scorpio, both of which have Mars as ruling planet, is more potentially evil than the next man. What could be true is that, if either of them decided to be wicked or violent, he might be so with more application than many. This also applies to Capricorns, who are ruled by Saturn. These, if they really try, can be coldly ambitious and calculating, which in a criminal can be very unpleasant. But just as the Mars energy factor for one person can manifest in courage and initiative and for another in aggression or a sort of bull-dozing violence, so Saturn for one person may be a serious, steadying factor and for another it may be coldly restrictive or cruel. The civilised man will have evolved beyond the stage of using a powerful planetary energy in killing or violence, but an excessive energy will still seek outlets that may be provided by the circumstances with which he has to cope . . . which leads us to consider *bad aspects*, as they still get called. But this term needs looking into.

Judges, lawyers, surgeons and all who deal with violence or its aftermath have the ingredients for violence in their patterns. So it cannot be stressed too strongly that the description of a bad aspect is really of some trait to be worked on during the present life. The unconscious holds a memory – or in many cases a phobia – relative to aspects that could be, according to evolution, a potential for evil deeds.

This must be so. For there are only the same signs and planets for everyone, in varying inter-relationships to describe saint or sinner. The spiral of soul progress is the differentiating factor.

"What aspects indicate cruelty or evil?" you may ask. The answer is, "None." For it is only misuse of available energy that produces evil, cruelty and violence. A 90° angle between Mars and Saturn used to be described in old-fashioned astrology books as a 'cruelty aspect'. This is perfectly rational . . . for the energy and potential aggression of Mars is at its most dangerous when directed to evil in combination with the cold or ruthless qualities of Saturn. At its worst, this combination can manifest in a calculated misuse of strength.

Some Examples of 'Bad' Aspects

Many years ago I had a visit from a gentle little old lady in whose map was this Mars/Saturn aspect. Mars was in the part of the chart to do with home (4th House) and Saturn in the 7th House which has to do with partners. I thought to myself, "This one doesn't look as if she's been sticking knives into her husband." And I wondered how I could find out how this 'potential cruelty' pattern had manifested in her life. I asked her straight, "In what way has cruelty figured in your life?" She looked at me with her gentle expression, "Oh, that's quite easy to answer. My first husband beat me till the blood came." "Blow me down," I thought, "we've got to the root of that one." But clearly it was not she in her present life who was being actively cruel. So what, one wonders, had she got up to in some earlier life to build that aspect into her birth pattern? For build it in she *had*, as her own statement showed.

Another case involved a seer friend of mine whom I knew very well. I asked her casually, "Did you ever kill anyone in a past life that you can remember?" "Goodness! yes, didn't I ever tell you? I was a highwayman." She remembered a great deal of that life, and was a keen horsewoman in this life too.

At one time the female half of a pair of twins was my client. They were middle-aged, and she suffered severe back trouble which I took to be karmic, so, as a matter of interest, I asked, "What's your twin doing now? Is he having pains and aches too?" "Him! No! He's just lording it over everyone as usual and being beastly to his wife!" I made further enquiries and found out that he was a cruel man and a selfish employer, so the inference was that he was less evolved than his sister and therefore working out actively the identical aspect that was working out in her by means of dorsal pain and mental suffering.

While it would be faulty thinking to put all cases of suffering down to some karmic reason, it would seem that we have a measure of choice between active or passive outworking of our aspects. People often wonder why saints have sometimes come to such horrible ends. Indeed this is a good question. On the rack, in the flames, executed or dying of painful diseases – and yet there they are . . . saints. One can only imagine that they have evolved through the active outworking of trouble and learned by crime or cruelty that this sort of action is not a good idea. Having learned this, the only thing that can happen in the working off of the residue of misdeeds is that they themselves experience some physical ill.

According to individual soul progress or regress, we travel upward or downward on our particular spiral. This means that we meet the same type of testing at intervals. In other words, the same 'bad' aspect can be activated more than once in a lifetime, but the YOU who faces the recurring test is not the same as formerly. As a result of earlier testing you may be more courageous and so able to face life at a higher level of response; or you may have gone downhill into supine cowardice.

One client had a particular sordid aspect that I longed to ask about, but she shut up like a clam when I suggested that something pretty sensational or sordid could have happened when a close Mars/Neptune aspect right across her chart from 12th to 6th Houses was activated. Only after her death did I learn that she had, in fact, contracted venereal disease. The same aspect was activated not long before she died. I asked her what was going on and was she working on anything sensational? "You could say that, I think. My present book is about vice in Harlem." That certainly filled the bill, but in fact her health also suffered a set-back at the same time. This illustrates how, if you live your life fully and use your talent, even the sordid aspects can be roped in to constructive use. The secret is to *use* your energies.

An actress with horrific aspects in a given year may be acting Lady Macbeth or Medea. This I have actually seen, for I have been astrologer to many well-known actresses. Sometimes we worried that a difficult aspect ahead might be dangerous or sorrowful. Of course sometimes the difficulties were personal or involved health, but the work in hand or the role being portrayed was, in many instances, enough to channel the difficulties.

I have said how a judge, lawyer or surgeon will of necessity have violent aspects in his pattern. So inevitably will policemen. Here then is the answer to those who wonder if violent *events* are in store if these appear in the chart. No! They are not. But what is inevitable is that the owner of the chart will be faced with the opportunity to work out his or her pattern for better or worse.

To someone who had read that Capricorn men could be 'cold, self-contained, calculating and selfish', and asked how I would reconcile this with the birth of Christ at Christmas? I reminded her that in England the monarch's birthday is celebrated on a traditional holiday which is not in fact the date of birth. The time of Christmas, at the traditional Winter Solstice holiday time is the same sort of thing. But saints or criminals can be born in any month. The saint would be using and the sinner misusing his energies.

Many are born with the same aspects as criminals without sinking to crime, just as many born on the same day as a genius fail to attain to fame. Circumstances may be out of our control, but we can, for instance, choose whether to go out in the rain or mope indoors. I would never say to anyone, "You have this or that aspect, therefore you *are* cruel or deceitful," or whatever negative outworking the aspect might suggest.

I am not saying that violent aspects are easy to turn to positive use. The owner of a violent, aggressive chart, if unevolved, may be too quick with the knife or even enjoy killing. In this case the urge for violence is active and unrepressed. In the evolved soul the same energy could be harnessed quite differently. The first may be a thug, the second a hero.

I have known exactly this in the case of a brilliant surgeon who was parachuted into France to join the Resistance Movement in World War II. He had Mars opposite Uranus – a violent, sudden, cutting potential. What was his work? Coping with crises in wartime casualty stations; using the knife to heal – to mend wounds rather than carelessly to inflict them, as possibly he had done in a former life to build up such a potential.

I have not studied the charts of many criminals, but once a client of mine who had had several abortive love affairs wrote to ask me to do the chart of a man she had recently met. She thought she might marry him.

I did his chart and saw an aspect which worried me on her behalf. Mars (energy and sex potential) and Neptune, which at its worst has to do with illusion and escapism, were in the same degree, and this combination of energies was isolated from his other planets – split off in a positively schizoid rift. The rest of the chart was rather pleasant, as if he could be attractive in half of his nature, and yet, goodness me! what would he get up to with the other side? It was a real Jekyll and Hyde situation. My mind ran through horrific possibilities, especially when I turned to my client's chart and saw to my dismay that this dangerous conjunction fell in the exact degree of her Moon.

What did I think? With the secrecy and illusion of Neptune activated by Mars, I thought he would be hiding something. It might not have mattered with most people. After all, most of us have some skeleton in the cupboard. But whereas with other people the skeleton might never have emerged, with this girl it was only too probable that she would suffer in her emotional and feminine life, as represented by her Moon. But how? I thought in turn of crime, deception, madness, religious mania, venereal disease. Oh, no! What to do about it? I wrote to her that I quite saw why she had been charmed by Mr. X . . . "So much of his nature seems attractive and agreeable . . . But! I have a feeling he may be hiding something from you and my advice is to try and find out a bit more about him. . . ."

The rest of the story is that before my letter reached her, the police had caught up with him. He had a criminal charge against him.

This illustrates how the comparison of two charts can show very reliably whether the worst side of one person involves the other party or not.

A man whose wife had left him remarked to me at the finish of a consultation that he could now see from what I had said about both their charts that she had suffered too. This seemed to surprise him as he was preoccupied with his own emotions. I agreed and suggested he had been rather cruel to her and no wonder she had walked out. "She always said I was cruel." "Well, look at your pattern. You have the capacity for cruelty – mental cruelty." I explained the planetary set-up again, which seemed to help him considerably.

This possibility of looking at yourself and your partner in diagrammatic form instead of flesh and blood can be enormously revealing. Often the client goes away feeling that the situation has been thoroughly understood, which is indeed possible by means of astrological analysis. He may feel too that he has been helped to free himself from some imprisonment of his own ego. For a brief moment he has stepped outside himself and taken a good look.

Textbook interpretations of bad aspects cannot be true for everyone with a particular aspect. There are so many forms of evil. I never found out all about the Mars/Neptune conjunction case – exactly what he had got up to – but in other cases I have known Mars energising Neptune to correspond to imaginative depravity. Inspired depravity, one could say. And the old black magicians who seem to have thought up some quite unspeakable malpractices have certainly combined the inspiration of Neptune with the lowest carnal capers that Mars can indulge in.

I was puzzled once to find what looked like the cold villainy of Saturn in the chart of a teen-age daughter of a friend of mine. With the exception of this afflicted Saturn, the chart showed charm, talent and normality. I said to the mother, "I can't understand this. I wonder if she has been the over-zealous head of some institution in a past life or has imprisoned people?" Saturn was in the 12th House, which has to do with prisons and other institutions – and Saturn here could correspond to a coldly stern attitude. Later on I was fascinated to learn that when the girl married and had children, her idea of suitable punishment for any naughtiness was to lock them in cupboards.

Far from increasing condemnation, knowledge of the chart pattern increases my sympathy. I look at the pattern of a violent criminal and think, "With all that, it's a wonder he wasn't worse!" When someone is behaving abominably and friends and neighbours are quick with criticism, a glimpse, by means of the astrological chart, into the probable karma leading to the conduct may throw a quite different light on the moral aspect of the problem. A girl who seems to have no moral principles may have chosen (or been advised) to incarnate with a strong sexual nature so as to atone for a life as, say, an over-strict Abbess of a convent – the type who would have walled up some poor erring novice with her baby. Many prudishly oriented types congratulate themselves that *they* aren't bothered with these disgusting sex urges. They just have no idea of what a temptation such urges can be. One girl I know who was born into a body which was, in effect, just a beautiful 'sex-box' used her sex appeal with more enthusiasm than wisdom. It is certain that *she* will never incarnate to judge those who succumb to sexual temptations.

Difficult aspects often correspond to some character trait in ourselves which, in the long run, attracts the experiences we need to undergo in order to learn a particular thing. But no honest astrologer will pretend to be able to judge precisely *how* a particular aspect will manifest. Indeed, when such aspects work out passively, perhaps in violence *to or attack on* the native, he or she is presumably having to learn the disadvantages of being at the receiving end of violence or misdeeds that in a former life they have handed out. The comfort of such a process is that presumably we don't have to learn the same lesson twice once the penny has dropped. It is pointless to waste time in useless resentment, hatred or non-acceptance. This only results in a sort of ding-dong karma. You kill me, I kill you . . . which gets no one very far.

It is my opinion that the wise and mature use of astrological analysis with psychological knowledge, the practice of which is on the increase, I am happy to state, can be of considerable help in studying criminals or psychopaths. Light can be thrown on motivation, and it can be seen when times of maximum stress and tension will arise in the future. This could be of value in making decisions as to the safety of freeing certain criminals.

It could also be used as a means of picking out a criminal from other suspects in connection with a particular crime. The time factor could show which man was under powerful stimulus at the relevant moment.

At the time of the notorious Moor murders, astrologers became familiar with the charts of the murderers. I had a distinguished client at that time whose chart had striking similarities to that of Ian Brady. In both charts there was strong emphasis on certain degrees of the zodiac. It is obvious, I trust, that if, in a chart, four or five planets of strong energy are in, say 9° of any Sign, that when a forceful planet in the sky (a transitting planet is the technical term) hovers in 9° of any Sign, your pattern is going to be touched off . . . over-stimulated or activated one way or another. This was the case for both Ian Brady and his girl-friend, Myra. A particularly strong activation was evidently too powerful for them to handle sanely or wisely.

In the case of my client with a similar configuration – I remember in his case that Mars, Uranus and Saturn were all in the same degree of different Signs – I asked him, "Was the year of this activation a time of danger, violence or cruelty? Or was it just another routine year?" He replied that the year was memorable. An attempt on his life was made at a time when he was involved in quelling a riot.

Here is yet again an instance of people at different levels of evolution reacting differently. The murderers were using the activated strengths of the same planets in active cruelty. My Ambassador client narrowly escaped being the *victim of violence*. These instances illustrate why I hotly dispute the claim of some astrologers to be able to see the precise outcome of a particular aspect. In this case the younger souls had not yet learned that primitive action and lack of self-control are undesirable traits and lead to trouble or punishment.

Most of us find it easy to identify wrong or evil in others . . . outside our own characters, in neighbours, in mob violence, in the news. Yet what rings the loudest bell for each of us in the actions of others is what resonates to a latent tendency in our own pattern. It triggers off some suppressed energy factor in ourselves, or some phobia.

To spread fear is evil. The wrong or tactless description by the astrologer of alarming aspects can do this. It is helpful, however, to illustrate the transformed image of what could be evil or negative. Imagination is needed. When one sees a potentially evil aspect, it compares with when the patient of a psychologist has an evil dream or a disturbing psychic experience. By some means this must be accepted, digested and understood.

It is generally agreed that criminals should be restrained. Yet, however tiresome it may be to the community, the criminal is at a necessary stage for his own development – one when he is demonstrating or 'living' his worst aspects actively. He is using his energies selfishly. At a later stage – perhaps many lives later – the wheel will turn and he will experience passively or helplessly the ills that he has done to others. There is no hurry. All eternity is there for each in turn to learn that crime and separateness don't pay in the end.

You may be getting bored with my representation of evil as a misuse of strength, but this is just what it is. I don't suggest that it is easy to switch one's energies once a bad habit has been formed, and some temperaments are more oriented to gloom, selfishness, suspicion, mistrust and self-pity than others. If only the wrongdoer could wake up to the fact that he is sowing the seeds for self-punishment, he would realise that *he* is the one who needs sympathy.

Does blame attach to criminals if, as it seems, they can't help their difficult potentials? It must be remembered that the birth pattern represents only the starting point of a developing pattern. Development can be positive or negative and lead the individual upward or downward. We all face tests of a nature indicated in the planetary birth pattern. Free-will, in so far as it exists, lies in our response to events or circumstances.

The chart of Saint Bernadette (Soubirous), as might be expected from her many difficulties, was one that might equally well have been the chart of a sinner, had the incarnating entity or spirit animated it at a low or selfish level.

My advice to young or inexperienced astrologers is to give people the benefit of the doubt and tell them of the possibilities of their charts at the highest level the practitioner can visualise. The reverse policy was indulged in with huge gusto by the astrologers of the last century. I will quote from the *Grammar of Astrology* written by Zadkiel the Seer, published in 1833. In many ways if read with a pinch of salt, this is a valuable and thoughtful book, but it is, I think you will agree, over-realistic in its gloom. I quote . . .

"The nature of Saturn is far more evil than that of Uranus: he is called the Greater Infortune; and he is undoubtedly the cause (Subservient to the will of Providence) of the greater portion of human suffering. When he is rising or setting at birth, the person born will suffer much lingering sickness, and be very subject to blows and falls. If he be on the meridian, he causes perpetual trouble and disgrace; all the native's affairs go wrong, and unless there be some very strong aspects of other planets to counteract this evil position, the native is the complete child of misfortune. If Saturn be in the opposite situation, that is, near the north meridian or cusp of the 4th House, his effects are nearly as evil. Persons born under his influence are nervous, fearful, bashful, cowardly, melancholy, and given to shed tears. They suffer from chronic diseases and are liable to mental infirmities. Their dispositions are thoughtful, malicious and reserved, and they are firm and obstinate in their opinions, and adhere strongly to their attachments."

But cheer up, all you who have strongly placed Saturns. I chose that particular passage about Saturn being 'evil' when near the Midheaven or angular on purpose because in Monsieur Gauquelin's exhaustive researches he found that Saturn figures significantly when angular in the charts of eminent scientists and doctors.

All this simply illustrates how, in the old days, astrologers tended to harp on death and disaster and criminal potentialities. Yet no amount of difficult aspects *necessarily* corresponds to evil or crime, or with ill-health either. What must be sought is the right outlet for dangerous energies. Suppression should be replaced by the encouragement of a constructive energy expression. Faults need to be studied more than virtues, as these give the key as to which strengths are in need of outlet.

Hate and Resentment

If you feel hate or resentment for someone else, the answer very often is that you don't hate them at all. What you hate is yourself. You hate being reminded, even unconsciously, of the horrible things you have incarnated to adjust. And this is well worth remembering in our lives and feelings. For when we feel resentful, as often as not it is because we are reminded of a fault in ourselves. We hate *what we are or what we have been* at our worst. For the time being we feel we hate the person who revives a latent sense of guilt in us.

Astrologically speaking, the capacity for hate can be studied primarily as a lack of love. Hate is negative and so cannot be found as a positive quality.

Having written this, I looked in the late Charles Carter's *Encyclopaedia* *of Psychological Astrology** and to my delight I find he agrees with me in the following sentence: "In maps of those capable of nourishing hatred and revenge the benefics are usually obscurely placed."

One would expect to find Mars and Saturn in negative application.

The other day I re-read an old but excellent thriller called *Hide my Eyes* by Marjorie Allingham (Chatto, 1958). In it the young criminal gives his recipe for criminal efficiency. Briefly it is to live without love. "Any kind of affection is a solvent. It melts and adulterates the subject and by indulging it he loses his identity and hence his efficiency."

By losing 'identity', this young criminal meant in fact that he was in fear (should he indulge in affection) of losing the separateness that stills the sneaking doubt, latent in even this hardened type, that he belongs to the world and therefore has responsibility for it and for other people.

* Theosophical Publishing House, 1924.

4. PHILOSOPHICAL QUESTIONS II: SEPARATENESS AND WHOLENESS

It is no small problem to pass the idea of wholeness to those who are riddled with the fear resultant from being bogged down in separatism.

We can remind the individual that his or her complicated birth pattern is just as valuable a segment of the Cosmos as another's. Indeed more so. For to the one who has to develop and make something of an ill-balanced, tense set of energies, the challenge is all the greater. Certainly the achievement of bringing a damaged or unevenly loaded craft safe into port is greater than is the easy docking of a liner or warship.

It is separateness that endangers the functioning of any whole. The body cannot function if it lacks a vital organ. Imbalance of the planetary pattern brings an echoing imbalance throughout the universe.

Being an astrologer is conducive to humility, for the work implies a correlation with the heavens and the earth – a very 'with-it' occupation in these space-exploring times. But the main lesson is not of man's separateness from the Cosmos and his need to visit other parts of it – but of his unity with it. One cannot think of separateness without thinking of its opposite – the wholeness of life. Man, even to his tiniest cell; earth to its minutest atom; all are microcosms to the greater pattern, the incredibly orderly pattern of space. There is nothing haphazard in the movements of the solar system. Were it so, calculations for space travel could not be made. We can find out so much about the outward orderliness by looking inward at the star pattern set up from the date demanded by astrologers, namely the time, date and place of the birth or beginning of an individual or of an idea.

In the New Age we are now entering it is especially important to study the wholeness and integration of it all. In the study of a birth-chart, if the pattern is seen to split or divide, there must be some sort of schizophrenia; a division or separation of one energy force from the rest of the chart. For instance, two planets may be related by aspect one to another and to nothing else, so that it is like a pair of energies or forces, as it were, talking in the side-lines and not helping or cooperating with the rest of the team. This lack of integration can happen in the chart (or horoscope) of the individual. Is this sort of pattern meant to teach a particular lesson? And how can a person with such a pattern learn what it is meant to teach? My feeling is that in the study of such an individual, the astrologer will have to wait for a major activation of an isolated planet or pair of planets and see what comes about – or what events, circumstances or changed attitude of the subject will show. There is no doubt that the same planets mean different things for different people, and if the activation is repeated the outcome can be changed.

I see as a New Age concept a fuller and more total participation in the life of the Whole. This demands our full attention. If we succeed in this participation, boredom is out. Loneliness is out, for separativeness and the feeling of being separate from life lead to a terrible deadness and finally to destruction. The astrologer whose work is based on this concept of the larger Cosmic pattern being reflected right down into trivialities, while operative at all levels simultaneously, can help his fellows to see all life as one. To live in consciousness of a universal, containing pattern is a prime necessity. Increased knowledge and awareness have their own dangers when they develop separately, and every kind of guidance is needed if a man is to become responsibly integrated into the growth of the Whole.

What is involved in this growth of the Whole? Just as we personally and individually evolve, so does the planet Earth, and whatever we think, say or do cannot but affect the Whole; and what we achieve, we achieve for mankind.

Arrogance and separateness in man can be likened to the stage in a child's life when he starts discovering his power as an individual and breaks out in disobedience. This is very natural in a child. In evolved men this 'separateness' is transcended in wiser acceptance of his part in the total plan.

It is not easy, of course, to develop our individual pattern, or ego, and yet NOT to the point of separation from – or competition with – the Whole. Paradoxically it is only in separate consciousness that we *can* develop or expand to the stage where we glimpse and finally reunite with the Cosmic Whole.

Astrology, studied in depth, can furnish a blueprint of ingredients that go to make up any whole – not only human characters – and I mean any whole that relates in its beginnings to a moment in space and time.

Understanding of this blueprint takes years of study. Given full knowledge of the ingredients – the signs and planets – the natural cleavage lines of the circle are only known when the rising degree and resultant 'angles' are known, and only as fitting in to the framework of this precisely calculated 'cross' can the functioning of an individual circle, with its ingredients, be read.

If one regards evolution itself as a great Circle or Cycle, one can imagine that in ancient times man was still close enough to his source to sense a unity. In recent times the world has reached, let us hope, a maximum degree of separateness and, at least in certain quarters, there is a movement towards a more conscious unity and identification with Cosmic life. I believe the tide has turned and an important battle in the fight of Light against Dark has been won. Man has descended into utter materialism and the vanguard of a New Age is coming up the far side . . . on the return home.

It is not surprising, perhaps, that in a maximum stage of darkness and separateness followed a period rich in world teachers. To mention a few, think only of Gautama Buddha, Lao-Tze, Zoroaster, Pythagoras and Plato. It is possible that the world is still recovering from indigestion from these teachings, not to mention those of Jesus the Christ. Realisation of his own individuality gives immature man an idea of his own importance, and when this takes too great a hold he loses touch with the Cosmos. Dane Rudhyar (see Recommended Reading, p. 251) has described this stage of development as the psycho-mental jungle.

I am not, of course, suggesting that the world teachers *taught* separatism, but that the first result of knowledge and philosophy is to increase the ability of man to think for himself. With this increased independence and self-importance he turns his back on the Macrocosm. This is no doubt a salutary and necessary stage of development, as it is a weaning process; but strength lies in unity and integration, and only in a return (which through experience becomes a *conscious* return), to the Whole can man attain to his highest potential.

Astrology of the Future

The Astrology of the future, which is rapidly coming under the control of educated and responsible bodies, will comprise, as astrology has always done, the study of the correlation of the planetary pattern with world or personal events. Such study will be a conscious elaboration of the primitive, instinctive knowledge that man lives in unity with the heavenly order.

This ultimate feeling of unity will develop a sense of purpose and brotherhood when each individual realises that birth is a descent of spirit into matter and that he is part of the Divine plan to further the evolution of the Earth planet.

Suffering is born of separateness, which is no more than an exaggerated reference to self. Of course there is a sense in which the individual is of enormous importance, since progress is only possible if each individual puts his own house in order. All life is one and the thinking astrologer never writes as though 'something up there' influences us from outside. It is the Whole of which we are a part that is *experiencing* the quadratic aspect tension or triune harmony, to which each of us responds via the filter of the individual birth pattern.

As thinking parts of a Whole, we cannot arbitrarily discard bits we don't like. It is natural for the young of each generation to burst their bonds, but they will eventually discover the usefulness of the 'whole' set-up. Saturnian discipline is old-fashioned, but as individuals we can no more discard Saturn than we can put our cars on the road with no brakes.

Wholeness doesn't mean that we are put through a mincer or liquidiser and blended into an amorphous mass. Each one of us is a microcosmic whole. Each cell, each gland, each organ has its specific function within the ultimate Wholeness of the Macrocosm. Whether we think of God and all His Angels or the Solar Logos and the planets – whatever our terminology may be, all live and have their being in the body of the Whole as its necessary organs.

Separateness and imbalance bring an echoing imbalance throughout the universe. Each of us has a responsibility to maintain total harmony, for we are inescapably a part of it. Only when men realise this can they emerge from the plaintive "Why should this happen to me?" attitude. Indeed the answer to this is contained in the framework of totality. We are each like a cell in the body of our Creator who is not to be thought of as some long-ago, static Father-figure. With every moment that passes, the pattern of Creation is changing, so we can think of our birth moment as something to be taken on and *developed*. And do you see how this makes us necessary to the Whole? We can harm the Whole just as one drop of our blood, if infected, can be fatal to us.

The kind of 'pop' astrology that divided mankind into twelve tribes is primitive. Each man is part of the totality which contains all the twelve signs and all the planets, and it is this sense of belonging that is so up-lifting. It is not a healthy concept for man to feel that he is a helpless pawn in some 'state' that owes him a living. He is an individual in the entirety of Cosmos. It matters if he succeeds or fails, since failure affects the health of the whole as does a diseased cell in any living body.

In the astrological concept of a team of planetary energies, therefore, each man is a whole in the sense that a team is a whole. In the body, his heart is not the same as his liver or kidneys, yet all are he . . . and necessary to proper functioning. Neither does Saturn do the work of Mars nor Venus replace Mercury. The art of life is to combine and educate our energies to operate as a useful team.

Our aim, then, is for unity. A person who has successfully attained a sense of being part of the Whole has, in the deepest sense, discovered the divine spark in himself. We have suggested that separateness is an overactivity of the ego. Often a man's whole incarnation seems to take him down through maximum separation and up the other side into a conscius wholeness. Astrology at its best brings clarification of the path an individual can follow to become a conscious part of the universe he inhabits.

Yes, the basic truth behind astrology is that all life is one. The 'Star' pattern (a moment of it, that is to say) is your pattern . . . the pattern of your soul's progress. The popular idea that astrology is only of interest if oriented towards prediction should be replaced by the knowledge that it can be employed in the study of personal evolution. While I do not deny that the study of trends – forwards or backwards – is fascinating and revealing, it is surely the inner progress of the soul that is of prime importance. Events and circumstances are both secondary to this, for as we progress towards achieving control of our various planetary energies, we can ensure that events and circumstances in our lives move up, as it were, to a more desirable evolutionary level.

You are YOU! Like a stick of seaside rock, a lettered candy with the name of the place visible at whatever place you break it, you are always yourself, with your individual talents or prejudices, responding in your individual way to circumstance. Only by knowing yourself profoundly – and your astrological analysis helps with this self-knowledge – can you become more self-governing – more able to use your strengths wisely and by this means compensate for your weaknesses. Man should never be ruled by his stars. Rather should he steer his ship with their aid.

New Age astrology must shake itself free of fatalism and superstition. It is already, in the reputable teaching bodies and associations, becoming a study of correspondences rather that than that of 'fated' compulsions. Man should be free to shape his own destiny, knowing that he has the power to react well or ill to each challenge. Knowledge of his individual microcosmic pattern in the Cosmic macrocosm by means of his astrological chart can help him to know his place as part of the 'whole' of Creation.

Astrology above everything demonstrates the law of cause and effect – 'What we sow, we reap'. At the turn of the century, the Theosophists channelled a wealth of information, and this was echoed in the astrological writings of Alan Leo. Although accepted at that time by an élite minority, the pill of reincarnation acted like any indigestible substance and was largely rejected. Now, over three-quarters way through the century, the tide has turned and this knowledge is accepted as truth by many.

Although evolved souls incarnate bearing the potential of past inner development, it is seldom that harmonious aspects correspond to achievement. I imagine that this is because an inborn talent needs no proving. The soul is tranquil in the knowledge that the talent is there. This may be why it is common to find the so-called 'bad' aspects (the quadratica) in the charts of famous musicians, stage personalities and, perhaps less surprisingly, politicians. It could be that all these have incarnated to meet a challenge.

For those who accept that they have a soul, therefore, I suggest that the astrological chart can show them the pattern into which the soul or Higher Self has chosen to place a fresh 'persona'. In the case of some less evolved souls, perhaps *pitchforked* would be a truer way of stating the case. In either case the pattern selected is that best fitted to further development of the paying off of karmic debts outstanding from former lives. And not to be forgotten is that this pattern is part of the containing pattern of world evolution in which major world events, inventions or calamities are portrayed.

Where does the astrologer come in? Some don't! For not all believe in reincarnation. But whether or no he thinks this way, there is no doubt at all that he or she can see if you have incarnated with a special talent or difficulty. This chart of yours cannot represent anything you have created *since* birth since it depends on the birth moment. I have set out the charts for my own family the moment the telegram announcing the birth gave me the necessary data. Thereafter I am fascinated to watch each child manifesting the faults or the charm – the talents or inhibitions – of the chart set out in the first week of his or her life.

While there is no question of foretelling exact events, it can be foreseen *when* the karmic difficulties or rewards will be activated. By this means I have overwhleming evidence that the chart applies to the individual, for, as a consultant since the end of 1952, I have watched babies whose charts I analysed growing up to develop the potentials I described. They come, saying, "This is what you wrote about me at birth. Now let me tell you my life-story!" And always the main outlines of character and potential prove correct. Not, I would stress, events, for the very good reason that I make no attempt to forecast these.

Can former lives be read by the stars? When asked to attempt such a thing I have always said that I don't undertake this. Not because I don't believe in former lives, but because it depends on the level of evolution of the individual whether they can 'take' the full implication of what might emerge. The chart is that of a moment and nothing more. An evolved child or one of a litter of puppies may be born at the same moment in the same house. You would certainly not agree that a dog was the reincarnation of the same type of being as your son.

I have found the odd educated guess to be right on target. But I would not feel it right to go further than to suggest somewhat along the following lines. "It would seem that you blotted your copy-book in the field of business – or property – or relationships (whichever field of activity is adversely emphasised) – otherwise you would not be having troubles now in this particular field."

It would seem that, numerically, human incarnations run into thousands rather than hundreds. The progress of the soul is a slow descent through many lives until a stage of maximum materialism is reached. I don't mean that we are more wicked if more materialistic as this is as necessary a stage to be reached as when a tree puts down its final roots. Once we are through the rock bottom stage, the stage that I have heard termed the 'nuts and bolts' level, we start coming up, and in each successive life we animate our new body (and individual pattern) at the level of evolution and of material or spiritual interests to which we have attained. The ultimate goal is a return to Spirit. But whereas we started out in innocence or ignorance, the rejoining with our Source – with the Light – will be in full consciousness.

And so the opportunity for the incarnating soul, each with her or his individual pattern, is to bring back something to enrich the Soul-self, which is the Self which holds the memory of all the successive descents into Earth-life.

Astrological knowledge can be illuminating in this connexion; for in the chart, the aspects which have to be dealt with in the present life have relevance to a series of past lives. Idle peering into past lives by astrological or psychic means is not advisable. When the right moment comes for the individual to be aware of a particular past life, one finds that in one way or another it surfaces. It is usual to find that a particular incarnation such as our present one (if especially eventful or 'karmic') resonates to two or three former lives, and is typified in the present-day chart by a particular group or groups of aspects. It is not unequally the case that the life immediately before the present one shows up. The thread is not necessarily through consecutive lives and it is erroneous to think of each life falling neatly into sequence with the next one or the previous one. The wheel symbolism comes nearer to the complex truth, with the hub of the wheel holding the connexion between any two lives, however widely separated by time.

The present-life astrological chart shows very clearly the type of karma to be tackled. A seer with the necessary vision to see former lives connected with your particular problem would almost certainly 'key' the life that is most karmically involved in the testing aspects of your present-day chart. This chart can give, not the whole picture but certainly a pattern which indicates the purpose of the present life and the potentials (helpful and otherwise) of the planetary energies at our disposal for coping with what our Higher Self or Soul knows to be our 'portion'.

Progress along these lines does not lie in what we *do*; whether we are successful or clever. It depends on how we cope with the tasks which are put in our path. As the astrologer knows only too well, two people born on the same day can have the pattern (by minutely different orientation, due to a short passage of time) for two very different life styles.

Each person's pattern is different, so what passes for a retrograde life may not be so at all. Indeed what is judged as a failure or even as immorality may be the necessary outworking of a particular pattern. It is unwise to judge. I have analysed many young people whose charts seem to show emotional chaos. But in these cases, the chaos can be traced (by means of the progressed chart) and seen to endure only as long as emotional or high-tension factors are activated. That person, in fact, is going through exactly what he or she has incarnated to tackle, and if the astrologer can put this point across, it will help that individual through a difficult patch. We all learn the hard way, and to see it mirrored diagrammatically in the natal and progressed charts can help us to use a set of alarming energy patterns or potentials constructively, instead of being swung around by them.

So, instead of holding up hands in pious horror, it may be that we should allow for the fact that certain misdeeds may constitute – as I said earlier when writing about evil – the precise experience needed by the individual to teach him to be more tolerant of others who succumb to the same temptation. The point I want to make is that very different values apply when it is the progress of the soul that is involved, consciously, and not mere conformation to society's rules and mores.

I recall the first time I linked an astrological chart with reincarnation. The chart was for a friend of mine who is an 'old soul' if ever there was one, but I had no idea that she had recall of past lives. When analysing certain difficult aspects, and sure that she was not using them destructively, I went on the assumption that they had bearing on past lives. In three separate instances, instead of trying to analyse present trials or misdemeanours, I told her of the *type* of actions and circumstances appropriate to the various groupings of planets and their placements. I suggested certain relevant misdeeds which I reckoned could have necessitated the experiences for readjustment and soul growth she was obviously going through in her current difficulties. To my intense surprise she wrote that I had described incidents and even crimes from two of her remembered former lives with some accuracy. I had no confidence that this semi-guesswork could hit the nail on the head like this; I had merely used the chart with its aspect patterns and emphasised fields of activity and made educated guesses as to what, in other lives, might have set in train this or that arrangement of testing aspects for her present life.

This portrayal of difficult aspects is not meant to imply that the individual has nothing further to do about them, or that they are just a mirror of past lives set out to entertain them. On the contrary, my suggestion is that there must be something to adjust during the present life in order to wipe the slate clean of former mistakes.

We all create, with every word or deed, the pattern that has to be lived tomorrow and tomorrow. It is thus obvious that there is every point in creating the type of future we want. It would be foolish to employ our negative potential to produce the kind of environment that we would hate to inhabit. Good fortune is created by ourselves through kindly, constructive action, hard work and dedication. It is in our hands to create what we *will*. If we perfect some skill or talent it is thereafter built into the soul pattern. A musician whose talent stems from a series of lives as a musician, will be born again with an instinctive love or talent for music; perhaps with perfect pitch. But good aspects do not give the individual the urge to prove himself. I stress this point because I meet so many people who shrink at the thought of difficult aspects and tests. Yet they may be the needed spur to achievement.

Reincarnation and Human Potential

. . . If 'music has charms to soothe a savage breast', it can as easily arouse primitive emotions. There are two sides to almost everything. In this connection, so long as man has the Mars energy unregenerate in him, he will fight. How can war cease while there are souls in incarnation who actually love fighting? On the other hand, there are souls on the way out of incarnation who are far beyond misusing their Mars energy in deeds of violence; they have transmuted it.

How long will this go on? This is hard to answer. Madame Blavatsky, one of the world's great seers and sensitives, wrote of an immensely long cycle as the 'inbreathing and outbreathing of Brahm'; which suggested that at a certain stage souls would stop coming into incarnation on Earth. Is this, perhaps, the same as a Cosmic Day which, I read, is four hundred thousand years long? Any change could be expected after such a punctuation mark in world progress. It would seem at the moment that there are still plenty of souls coming in with a keen enjoyment of violent exercise of their Mars energy. But if it is not in your individual pattern to meet them, you won't do so.

As we evolve spiritually, we use our violent aspects more constructively. We don't lash out or give way to cruelty, aggression and dramatic outbursts. But this transformation of human potential doesn't occur overnight. A mistake made by world reformers sometimes seems to be that they proceed as though all mankind evolves together, or from some neatly lined-up start. It is surely reassuring that it is not so. At the present time, for example, there are many beginners on the evolutionary path who have to learn the lessons that more advanced souls have learned long ago. In short, there are always people at the end of the need for reincarnation and others at varying stages along the long road.

The astrologer should take the stage of evolution of his client into account. Both he and his client should be aware of the fact that neither can understand the other at a level above his own ceiling of consciousness. A diploma in astrology is no warrant of advanced evolutionary status!

I do not want to give the impression that past lives can be keyed by anyone who knows how to set out a birth-chart. The chart should be thought of as illustrating what you, between lives, have agreed should be dealt with. Life can then become a constructive process; in effect, *progress*, for the soul. However I would be the first to agree that not many people, astrologers or clients, even want to know about *soul* progress.

The consultant astrologer must play along very gently with someone who has a life of frustration and hardship and remind him that he can count himself lucky to have progressed beyond the stage of wounding others, mentally or physically, since he is now at the receiving end of trouble.

I don't advocate any astrologer to use this technique of analysis unless he finds it comes naturally. World evolution into the New Age (or can it be into a new Cosmic Day?) is proceeding at such a pace that, whereas in my early days as a practitioner Alan Leo's turn of the century acceptance of reincarnation was derided except by Theosophists, the opposite is now the case, and clients are more prepared to learn about their pattern in greater depth.

Prophecies of the Aquarian Age refer to the 'changes' to come. As I see it, Earth itself, which evolves as we do, is rising to what might be termed level X. I intuitively feel we are nearing this time, and one explanation of the population explosion could be that souls have rushed, and are rushing, into incarnation wherever they can find a point of entry. My theory, and it may be fantastic, is that when the moment arrives that Earth evolves above level X, the entry, as it might be called, will be limited to those evolved enough to stand the vibrations of Earth at its more spiritual, 'X-plus' level.

The full participation of man in the life of the Cosmic 'Whole' is important, for if our participation is faulty, can those of us living on Earth at this period of change, count on being raised in consciousness by changing circumstances? Like the fleas on a dog that go where the dog goes? It might be an error to assume this. If the average person thinks about it at all, he might well think that mere existence on Earth qualifies him for continued participation in the life of Earth. Is this rational? Qualification for New Age living involves waking up. The planet Uranus has been called the 'Awakener' by Alan Leo and later by more esoterically oriented astrologers. Since its discovery man has responded in invention and technological progress: from horse-bus to space travel in a single life-span.

Man is helped to participate more fully in the life of the 'Whole' by knowing himself more fully. A thinking man or woman would not tolerate the use of astrology except for 'keying' the path of the soul. The potential of any individual soul depends on its present 'persona', the 'you' or the 'me' at present animating it. And as I have tried to illustrate, this chart can tell us something of the former pattern to which we are resonating in the present life.

When thinking in terms of the soul, it is helpful to remember that man is a spirit/soul with many bodies. It is at the higher, soul level, that there is continuity and memory, although mercifully in most cases the memory of past lives is blotted out from down-here consciousness. The very fact that the natal chart is such an accurate diagram of the individual's characteristics supports the premise that the individual has, at some time, created this pattern. Only as a man evolves can he really take control of the forces (or planetary energies) at his disposal. Once he determines to do so, he can become self-governing within the framework to which he is born.

Nothing in life stands still. It would be a living death to think, "I am born this way, therefore I cannot help my faults or deficiencies". The astrological birth-chart shows us a starting pattern, a blueprint for life which can go into successful or faulty production. And it is this production which contributes to or detracts from the progress of the soul.

There are many who object that reincarnation isn't fair because *we* – you and I, get punished for things we never did. This of course is true if you don't accept the long-term picture, that you are suffering for what was built in to your Soul in a former existence.

All of life presupposes that 'something' has gone before. The seed of a plant as well as the plant itself is not something new, but the product of an earlier plant. It is not disputed in nature that we reap what we sow. Recent reports from hypnotists who obtain from patients details of lives lived centuries ago have aroused interest even among those who doubt the reality of a future, let alone a past experience. It must be hard for astrologers who do not believe in reincarnation when faced with clients in grave trouble who ask "Why should this happen to me?" Do they seriously blame it on a stellar influence? Whereas if we accept that each life involves karma, good and bad debts, it is not surprising that we get put through the hoops from time to time.

There are valid objections to the expression 'Transmigration of souls' which seems to suggest that on death the soul hops, as it were, into some waiting body, even perhaps that of a pig! There is a truer picture in nature. The tree appears in leaf or blossom every year always as a tree, not suddenly as a cabbage. So with humans. Each life is a separate thing and yet it is part of the experiences of its controlling entity or Soul-self. Each present life contributes to its controlling entity for better or for worse.

The astrological chart is of use in showing the type of experience necessary for the individual. Some children are born with everything: kind parents with the means to educate them; natural beauty and brains, magnetism or personal charm. Good luck to them! They have built up this potential in past lives. Others have built different patterns. The world will be a happier place when people come alive to the fact that each person creates his own future, not only by actions but by thoughts and words.

In recent years there has been a strong reaction against the thought of Hell and eternal punishment. But pendulums are apt to swing too far. Reason demands that each man pays his *just* debts, no more and no less. To incarnate into a punishing pattern is not seen as unjust by the person who accepts that life is what he makes it, whether by means of quick karma in the course of a single life or stemming from some whopping misdeed or misuse of power in the perhaps far past.

While reincarnation fits very neatly into astrology's conceptual frame, it is by no means necessary to hold this or any other belief in order to enjoy its study. Dane Rudhyar describes astrology as an 'algebra' which can be applied at will to a variety of problems. It is worthy of application at the highest levels as a means of guiding humanity; showing man to himself; pointing the way to more perfect integration of his component energies. The chart, for those who have eyes to see, shows clearly that each incarnate soul is an individual who cannot be wholly indoctrinated by education or whatever means. He cannot be made into what he is not. "Do men gather grapes of thorns, or figs of thistles?" (St Matthew vii;16).

This expresses very neatly what is seen in the chart. We all have a starting pattern of our own out of which we cannot step. It is essential, however, to remember that it is only the starting pattern – the material on which we can work.

Man has free-will within the pattern of his abilities and his own dis-crimination. It is not good to live in bondage to some starry pattern and to conform automatically. Life should be an inspired response to the pattern of the 'now'.

When astrology is ready to blossom once again in the minds of leaders of thought, as it has done in the past, there will be no stopping it. Victor Hugo wrote: "There is one thing stronger than all the armies of the world, and that is an idea whose time has come."

Man himself has misused astrology and brought it to unworthy levels. I try to rid people's minds of the notion that astrology could or should be accurate fortune-telling. To force limitations of this sort on to astrologers is unacceptable to any who think. We are dealing with Cosmic forces and patterns so vast that it is an impertinence to tailor them down to small, ridiculous, personal problems. In fact the more *exact* in prediction that astrologers try to be, the more they bring ridicule on the subject.

What then is the correspondence to be read from the starry pattern? Without doubt there *is* one. If we could rise in consciousness and take a God's-eye view of life as a whole, what would we learn? Mystics have it in perspective when they talk of 'the God in whom we live and move'. This God is not separate from us, for we are part of His life. In astrology this is exactly portrayed by the ever-changing Cosmic pattern; the planetary pattern within and against the ring of the zodiac which can be likened to the all-comprehensive, ever-evolving wholeness of the Creator. What we study when we look at a chart is a moment, isolated, as the camera in the hands of a photographer isolates and crystallises a moment. When we grasp the immensity of the subject, we know that in effect our birth moment portrays our link with the Whole, with the Cosmos. The descent of Spirit into matter is enacted with every individual birth. As part of the Whole we contain the living spark of divinity in us and there is no man, however unevolved, who is not a representative of the Whole or of his God.

What a responsibility, once we realise it, falls on each one of us. The responsibility to represent a moment in God-time; to incarnate in physical life a fragment of the Almighty. Just as light becomes visible only when it has something on which to reflect itself, so the Almighty relies on us, as particles of dust, to reflect His light. And our possibilities to reflect it are readable in the chart of our birth moment, which is a chart of a single moment of the Cosmic pattern.

The link with the Source is never broken. Each one of us has his pattern, different from the pattern of another, which reacts in individual fashion to the stimulus of the ever-changing daily pattern of Cosmos. Have you sometimes wondered why in a moment of danger you have escaped? Or why you were the only member of a crowd who got hurt? What is a critical moment for one is not for another.

Man is a complex being, formed not only of his physical but of his subtler bodies. He can interact with the world-totality through his etheric body, his emotional body, his mental body and ultimately his Soul or Higher Self. The realisation that the astrological chart can provide a key to the progress of the soul is a momentous one which adds in no small measure to mankind's dramatic New Age progress into Fourth Dimensional living.

CONCLUSION

What is the most striking result of our examination of life and the birth-chart taken together? Is it not perhaps that the worth-while lives are those lived in defiance of circumstances; or, better, in a confident and determined collaboration with them? Man may have less in the way of free-will than he likes to suppose; but he has the decisive power to reject and perish or to accept and create.

It is fatal to think of 'the Stars' as determinants. We must not turn them into inexorable or malignant gods. This is altogether to mistake their power and to misunderstand the function of astrology; which should be to give us a glimpse of a cosmic purpose with which we should strive to harmonise. A man imprisoned in Saturn's dungeons may find real freedom in himself whilst the chaos and disillusion of Neptune may drive him inwards until he finds the secret of his own integrity. Hard times may turn him into a walking Complaint or he may learn to enjoy freedom from possessions. There is no difficult condition that courage cannot turn to good use.

APPENDIX

RECOMMENDED READING –
STUDY COURSES –
SOCIETIES AND JOURNALS

If, as may be tested by investigation, birth-chart equals life-pattern, complete with character and potential, this is knowledge that should be used by people of sound sense and not exploited behind bead curtains or debased into fortune-telling.

It is important to follow a course of study that gives comprehensive and unbiased instruction in the technique of astrology pure and simple. Many astrologers develop leanings in different directions according to their beliefs and interests. Some, like myself, while making no claim to be a trained psychologist stick to this side of the work. Others, mathematically minded, delight in such exact data as are afforded by earthquakes and large-scale disasters, and spend their time perfecting or inventing methods of correlating world events. Yet others relate their activities to spiritual or occult matters. But whatever line or branch of astrology appeals, little progress will be made without thorough knowledge of the rudiments. This can only be obtained by systematic study, subsequent application of what has been learned through strict observation of 'live' cases with a view to confirmation that the basic theory *really does work* and that characterisations *do apply*.

Time and effort are saved by following a reputable course and concentrating on this for the first year while basic principles are digested. In the second year, reading should widen to include as many standard works as possible, as by this time there is less likelihood of confusion through controversial statements in books or journals which cut right across basic teaching. People are entitled to their own opinions; but some astrologers in their enthusiasm write up elaborate theories on the strength of a limited number of cases and the student is advised to be well grounded in his subject in order to judge what he reads on its real merit rather than at the stated value.

The courses reommended at the end of this section are not for the dabbler. They entail hard work and the examiners look for a high standard, so don't spend your money unless you have time and determination.

Serious astrological journals, such as those mentioned below, are definitely not for the beginner and what I said earlier about digesting basic knowledge before embarking on wider reading applies especially to these. For the advanced astrologer, however, they are a means of keeping in touch with astrological thought in other parts of the world; but even he may find himself out of his depth when reading some abstruse idea that has been hatching for long years in the brain of an occult-minded and highly technical colleague.

It is wiser not to buy textbooks before embarking on your choice of available courses, as each course may have a different list of works which they wish students to study. I will not, therefore, recommend textbooks other than all the works of C. E. O. Carter, late President Emeritus both of the Faculty of Astrological Studies and of the Astrological Lodge of London and for many years editor of their quarterly magazine *Astrology*. His books give information on many branches of astrological research and one feels privileged to share the thoughts of this erudite and experienced astrologer.

Further Recommended Reading
Students who wish to extend their knowledge could profit by exploring the pages of the following books, all by reputable authors, but they represent only a small selection from what is now available to meet the needs of a growing astrological public.

Whereas I am only mentioning one work for each of the following authors, it must be said that this is to give the reader an introduction to a few of my favourite authors, some of whom have many works to their credit.

Addey, J. M.: *Harmonics in Astrology* (Fowler).
Arroyo, S.: *Astrology, Psychology, and the Four Elements* (C.R.C.S.).
Davison, R. C.: *Technique of Prediction, The* (Fowler).
Dobyns, Z. P.: *Finding the Person in the Horoscope* (T.I.A.).
Ebertin, R.: *Combination of Stellar Influences* (A.F.A.).
Greene, L.: *Relating* (Coventure).
Hone, M. E.: *Applied Astrology* (Fowler).
Oken, A.: *Alan Oken's Complete Astrology* (Bantam).
Rudhyar, D.: *Astrology of Personality* (Doubleday).

Among useful 'tools of the trade' I would certainly include:
American Ephemeris for the Twentieth Century, Michelsen (Astro-Computing Services).
Encyclopaedia of Astrology, de Vore (Littlefield, Adams).
Fowler's Compendium of Nativities, Harrison (Fowler).
Time Changes in the World, Doane (A.F.A.).

For those whose interest in astrology is inseparable from their interest in religion, reincarnation and spiritual unfoldment, I recommend *Wisdom in the Stars; Astrology, the Sacred Science; and Planetary Harmonies*, all by Joan Hodgson (White Eagle Publishing Trust, Liss, Hants).

Correspondence Courses

The following teaching schools are known to me personally:

1. THE FACULTY OF ASTROLOGICAL STUDIES

Patrons: John M. Addey, M.A., A.F.Astrol.S.
Ingrid Lind, D.F.Astrol.S.
Dane Rudhyar, Hon. D.F.Astrol.S.

The Faculty was founded in London in 1948 as a non-profit-making Educational Body by a group of far-sighted astrologers, including the late Charles E. O. Carter and the late Margaret E. Hone. Their aim was to raise the standard of astrological technique and practice by provision of adequate training and by yearly Examinations, culminating in the award of a Diploma which would be recognised as a status of efficiency and integrity the world over and be held in public respect.

This work has continued faithfully, and thousands of students from all over the world have learnt the groundwork of their subject through the Faculty's Correspondence Courses. After a year's work or thereabouts a Certificate of Merit can be gained by writing an Examination. The demand is ever-increasing and many each year now seek the full professional qualification of the Diploma. This takes at least two full years study.

The Faculty is a unique institution, and is now administered by a democratically elected President and Council, who give their services. A dedicated and experienced staff provide personal tuition by means of Correspondences Courses, Classes and Seminars. All courses are under constant revision to keep pace with new developments in astrological thought and research; and the latest Diploma Course is the most comprehensive available, with contributions from many well-known experts in various fields.

The Examinations are held yearly in May, and are open to all schools or individuals.

Prospectus available from:

The Registrar
Hook Cottage
Vines Cross
Heathfield, Sussex, TN21 9EN
ENGLAND

2. THE MAYO SCHOOL OF ASTROLOGY

This is a comparable correspondence course, leading to a recognised qualification. It is run by Jeff Mayo, author of several excellent textbooks. I have known Jeff since the days when we were fellow students. His school provides Courses for beginners and for more advanced students. Those who complete the Beginners' Course are awarded a Certificate of Proficiency. Advanced students may take an Internal Examination to gain the School's Diploma.

Details for this course from:

> The Mayo School of Astrology
> 8, Stoggy Lane
> Plympton, Plymouth
> Devon, PL7 3DL
> ENGLAND

3. THE WHITE EAGLE SCHOOL OF ASTROLOGY

This Course is especially suitable for those who seek in astrology a key to man's spiritual evolution. Instruction is by Correspondence Course prepared by Joan Hodgson and there are regular meetings and lectures in London and in Liss, Hampshire. The three courses are designed to guide the student from the earliest stages to become a professionally qualified astrologer, and culminate in a Diploma examination.

In addition to the Beginners' Course and the Advanced Course which speak for themselves, there is an Intermediate Course for students who already know how to calculate a chart. Six lessons take such students to the point where they are ready to embark on the Advanced Course.

All necessary material is supplied with the lessons, and each student receives individual tuition.

Details may be had from:

> The White Eagle School of Astrology
> New Lands
> Liss
> Hampshire, GU33 7HY
> ENGLAND

Societies and Journals

Societies in London that may be joined, where meetings are held and books may be borrowed by members, include:

The Astrological Lodge of the Theosophical Society, 50 Gloucester Place, London W.1.

The Astrological Association. Information from:

> The Membership Secretary,
> D. Llewellyn,
> Bay Villa,
> Plymouth Road,
> Totnes,
> Devon,
> ENGLAND.

Membership of both the above societies includes the quarterly issues of each: respectively *Astrology* (editor, R. C. Davison) and *The Astrological Journal* (editor, Zach Matthews). Both journals are available on subscription to non-members.

Finally it is useful to know that most astrological requirements can be obtained from my publishers in their capacity as Mail Order booksellers. Write for their catalogue to L. N. Fowler & Co. Ltd., 1201/3 High Road, Chadwell Heath, ROMFORD, Essex RM6 4DH

GLOSSARY

This glossary suggests definitions, some technical some not, of terms used in astrology. It incorporates the list of definitions given to students of the Faculty of Astrological Studies (with kind permission of the late Mrs. M. E. Hone, Principal and author of *A Modern Text-Book of Astrology*).

This list of definitions is more comprehensive than is necessary for the understanding of the foregoing pages and it is hoped that it will be of use for purposes of quick reference to students and readers of astrological works.

Angles   When astrologers refer to the angles of the chart, they are not referring to the angular relationship between Planets and Earth (*see* **Aspects**) but to the cross formed by a line drawn from the Ascendant or Rising degree to a point opposite known as the Descendant and another line drawn between the degree of the Midheaven or M.C. and its opposite point, the I.C. (Immum Coeli).

 The degrees cut by these lines are sensitive points, and planets close to them whether natally, by transit or progression, take on an added importance.

Arc   Part of the circumference of a circle.

Ascendant   The degree of the Ecliptic ascending above the eastern horizon at any moment.

 The whole of the Sign or the whole of the 1st House of a chart is referred to as the Ascendant. (*See* **Rising-Sign**.)

Aspects   Astronomically, aspects are measured by the angle made between a line drawn from one planet to the centre of the Earth and a line joining it here from another. This angle is measurable in celestial longitude. Thus if your Sun is 90° distant from your Moon by celestial longitude they are said to be in 'square' aspect. Where they 120° apart they would be in 'trine' aspect. These and other angular relationships have astrological significance. Such aspects are termed geocentric. The astrologer, like the navigator, is concerned with angles to the Earth on which he lives. (*See* Table of Aspects, Part II, Chapter 7, p. 116.)

Birth Data   Necessary data for calculation of a personal chart is time, date and place of birth. It is not the name of the place but the latitude and longitude that is vital; a fact to be remembered if a child is born at sea or in the air.

Campanian House System   (Space System)
 That by which one half of Prime Vertical is divided equally into six; lunes

255

being made between house circles through these points of division, passing through north and south points of horizon and the other half of Prime Vertical. House circles then pass through degrees of Ecliptic, which define cuspal boundaries, forming almost equal houses at Equator, but becoming more unequal as latitude increases.

Biographical Note. **Giovanni Campano**, died about 1297. Italian. Chaplain and physician to a succession of Popes. Mathematician.

Celestial Equator (*See* **Equator**.)

Celestial Latitude Just as terrestrial latitude is used to state the distance, in degrees, of any place north or south of the Earth's Equator, so Celestial Latitude is used to state the distance of any Planet or star north or south of the Ecliptic. For clarity, the Ecliptic may be imagined as the while line down the middle of the broad road of the Zodiac.

Celestial Longitude This is the distance of a heavenly body from 0° Aries. If the Zodiac is thought of as a circular road round the Earth, Celestial Longitude indicates how far along the road the Planet is while Celestial Latitude indicates if it is in the middle or to right or left of the road.

Celestial Sphere The visible heavens.

Circles of Position These are the Great Circles (whose planes pass through the centre of the Earth) running at right angles to another Great Circle to form the house positions of whatever house system is used. (In Equal House these would be at right angles to the Ecliptic.)

Constellations Groups of stars in all parts of the heavens. Zodiacal constellations are those which overlap the plane of the Ecliptic. These bear the familiar names of Aries, Taurus, etc., but it must be remembered that this Aries does not coincide in position with the point of the Vernal Equinox known as 0° Aries except once in every twenty-five thousand years, due to the precession of the Equinoctial Points.

Culminating Degree Just as the Ascendant is the same thing as the Rising Degree, so the Midheaven is the same as the culminating degree. (*See* **Midheaven**.)

Culmination The transit of a degree or body across the upper meridian. The opposite is referred to as the transit of the lower meridian.

Cusps (House) Cusps are the points of division between the houses, or more precisely the degrees of ecliptic cut by the house circles. (As these vary with varying house systems it is inadvisable to place reliance on them as sensitive points.)

Day

Solar Day The time between two successive passings of the Sun over a fixed point of observation. As the Earth moves at a variable speed, so the Sun *appears* to move more or less than 1° a day; thus the Solar Day is variable.

Mean Day Because of the above variation the mean or average is taken.

Sidereal Day The time between the moment when a certain fixed star is seen at exactly due south and the moment when it is there again. This day is nearly 4 minutes shorter than the average, mean or clock day. Sidereal clocks are set at 0° when 0° Aries is culminating on the meridian of the place.

Declination A measure up and down (north and south) from the Celestial Equator. Compare Celestial Latitude, which is a measure north and south of the *Ecliptic*.

Degrees   Signs of the Zodiac are measured in degrees of longitude along the Ecliptic, 30° to each Sign. Planetary positions for noon of every day can be found in Raphael's Ephemeris for the year where the noon position in degrees of longitude is given for each day.
Sensitive Degrees in a chart are those occupied by a planet or cut by an angle of the chart. Mid-points between planets are also significant.

Descendant   The point on the chart (or on the Ecliptic) exactly opposite or 180° from the Ascendant.

Ecliptic   The great circle around which the Sun appears to travel in a year. (*See also* **Celestial Latitude**.)
Plane of the Ecliptic   The level on which the circle of the Ecliptic lies, projected to infinity. (Planes in general are the extension in space of any of the Great Circles.)

Elongation   The furthest distance of an inferior Planet from the Sun *as seen from Earth*. Elongations of Venus and Mercury are listed among the phenomena for the year in the current Ephemeris.

Equal House System   The 360° of the Ecliptic are divided into twelve equal sections analogous to the twelve Signs. These *can* begin from any degree of importance such as that of the horizon (rising degree), Meridian, Sun or other planet. The usual starting point is that of the horizon. Houses of 30° each are bounded by secondaries of the Ecliptic, passing through these degrees, meeting at the poles of the Ecliptic. Degrees of upper and lower Meridian (M.C. and I.C.) are charted but will not necessarily correspond with the degrees on cusps 10 and 4.
   Note on Ascendants in High Latitudes. In high latitudes, many degrees are circumpolar, the number increasing with the height of the latitude (north or south). It follows that only those degrees which *do* cross the horizon can be used as Ascendant. In such latitudes, the Equal House system is the only one by which a reasonable charting can be made, since twelve equal houses can always follow in natural sequence from whichever degree rises, until the actual pole itself is reached when 0° Aries and 0° Libra forever circle round the horizon.

Equation of Time   The addition or subtraction to be made daily if it is required to convert Solar into Mean time.

Equator   (Terrestrial and Celestial)
The Terrestrial Equator is a great circle passing round the middle of the globe and equidistant from the North and South Poles.
The Celestial Equator is the Terrestrial Equator projected to infinity.

Equinox   (*See* **Seasons** and **Vernal Equinoctial Points**.)

Extra-Saturnian Planets   These are the planets further from the Sun than Saturn, namely Uranus, Neptune and Pluto. To make their journey through the twelve Signs (as observed geocentrically) the time is as follows:

Uranus about 84 years	. .	7 years in a Sign
Neptune about 165 years	. .	14 years in a Sign
Pluto about 248 years	. .	21 years in a Sign

Fixed Stars   The fixed stars are so called because they are so far distant from Earth that they maintain their relative positions and so form recognisable constellations or groups of stars. The whole group may appear to rise or set owing to the rotation of the Earth on its own axis. The further the group is from the Ecliptic the less it appears to move, until (in Northern Hemisphere) the Pole Star remains as a fixed point and can be thought of as the hub of the Earth's rotatory movement.

Geocentric Considered as viewed from the Earth's centre. Compare Heliocentric, as viewed from centre of the Sun.

Great Circle Any circle, the plane of which passes through the centre of the Earth.

Compare Small Circle: any smaller circle, the plane of which does not pass through the cente of the Earth, e.g., the circle of the visible horizon.

Greenwich Mean Time or G.M.T. (*See* **Time.**)

Heliocentric As viewed from the centre of the Sun.

High Latitude Charts (*See* **Equal House** and **Placidus.**)

Horizon

Visible Horizon is that normally seen. This is a Small Circle whose plane does not pass through the centre of the Earth and is the line formed by the apparent meeting of Earth and sky.

Rational Horizon A Great Circle parallel to the Visible Horizon and extended to meet the heavens.

House Home of a Planet, originally applied to its Sign or Signs. Astrologically speaking, the house of the horoscopic chart is a section of the whole circle of Signs, having interpretative application in terms of human experience.

Mundane House Section formed by the calculation of the trisection of the quadrant in various ways.

Zodiacal or *Ecliptical House* Section formed by division of Ecliptic following conventional Sign division into twelve. (*See* **Equal House System.**)

House Circles (*See* **Circles of Position.**)

Houses These are divisions of the astrological chart arrived at by calculation from the birth data. There are twelve divisions corresponding in character with the twelve Signs of the Zodiac, so that the First House will stand for personal primary 'Arien' matters, even though any of the twelve Signs may be occupying the house.

House Systems (*See* **Campanian, Equal House, Placidus** and **Regiomontanus.**) Other systems include Colin Evans' **Natural Gradation and Topocentric.**

I.C. or Immum Coeli, opposite of M.C. or Medium Coeli.

Inferior Conjunctions The terms inferior and superior conjunctions only apply to the Inferior Planets. When either of these (Mercury or Venus) come between Earth and Sun so that viewed from Earth both occupy the same degree of Celestial Longitude it is known as an Inferior Conjunction.

A Superior Conjunction is when one of these planets is in the same degree of Celestial Longitude as the Sun but on the *far* side of it and therefore millions of miles further from Earth.

Inferior Planets Venus and Mercury are known as Inferior Planets, being nearer the Sun than the Earth is.

Latitude *Terrestrial* The measurement of distance of any place north or south of the Earth's Equator.

Celestial The measurement of distance of any planet or star north or south of the Ecliptic.

Longitude   *Terrestrial*   Distance east or west of a given meridian.
Celestial   Distance along Ecliptic from 0° Aries.
Lunes   Portions of a sphere (moon-shaped) contained between two great semi-circles.
Mean Day   (*See* **Day.**)
Mean Time   (*See* **Greenwich Mean Time.**)
Meridian   An imaginary Great Circle passing through the Poles of the heavens (celestial) and the Zenith and Nadir of the observer. The Sun crosses the Meridian of *any* place at midday local time.
A *Meridian of Longitude* (terrestrial) is an imaginary Great Circle passing through the poles of the Equator, north and south at any given place.
Midheaven (or degree of the M.C. or Medium Coeli).
The degree of the Ecliptic which is culminating at a given time in a given place. Differently worded, it is the degree of ecliptic through which the meridian passes.
Nadir   Opposite of zenith (not to be confused with I.C.).
Nutation   In 25,000 years the Pole of the Earth completes a circle. This motion can be compared to the motion of the point of a top which describes a slow, observable circle while spinning at high speed. It is this slower swinging movement that is called Nutation.
Pole Star   5,000 years ago the polar star was in the constellation Dragon. It was called Thubin. Now it is Polaris. In 1,400 years it will be Vega.
Occultation   An occultation is the same thing in principle as an eclipse, but it is the correct term to use when the Moon occupies the same longitude and latitude as a Planet, or when one Planet passes in front of another so that the light of the Planet is occulted (or cut off from view) as the other body passes in front.
Placidus   *Placidean System of House Division* (Time System.) That by which the *times* (in Right Ascension) taken for each degree of the Ecliptic to rise (on its own parallel of latitude) from lower meridian to horizon (nocturnal semi-arc) and from horizon to upper meridian (diurnal semi-arc) are trisected.
At any moment of time, one degree of the 360 will have completed one-third of its own nocturnal semi-arc and will be in the position to be that on the cusp of the 3rd House; at the same moment, another will have completed two-thirds of its own nocturnal semi-arc and will be in the position to be that on the cusp of the 2nd House. At the same moment, another degree will have completed its nocturnal semi-arc and will be on the horizon (cusp of 1st House); another will have completed one-third of its diurnal semi-arc (cusp 12); another two-thirds of its diurnal semi-arc (cusp 11); another will have completed its diurnal semi-arc and will have culminated at the upper meridian (cusp 10). Their opposites will provide cusps 9, 8, 7, 6, 5, and 4.
The essential factor of this system is that there should be semi-arcs to trisect. It is obvious that in latitudes where many degrees are circumpolar (never touching the horizon), these will have no separate diurnal and nocturnal arcs, their whole position being *either* diurnal *or* nocturnal. Since there are no semi-arcs to trisect, the requirement of the system is missing. Certain degrees can therefore never form house cusps or be included in houses. Sun, Moon, and Planets in those degrees at that time *cannot appear* in any charting attempted by this system and so must also be omitted. In other words, no

complete chart can be made. *Biographical Note:* **Placidus de Tito**. Born about 1590, Italian. Professor of mathematics.

Plane   The extension in space of any Great Circle.

Plane of the Ecliptic   (*See* **Ecliptic**.)

Planet   A heavenly body which moves in its own orbit round the Sun. (For names, size, movement, and position *see* **Solar System**.)

Polar Elevation   The height of the Pole above the horizon. This measurement in degrees equals the latitude of the place. When studying a celestial globe for any particular place, the correct polar elevation is obtained by setting the Pole to the elevation equivalent to the latitude.

Polarity   Signs or houses in opposition are said to be in polarity.

Pole Star   (*See* **Nutation**.)

Pole   One of the ends of the axis of a sphere.

Poles   Two opposite points on a Great Circle. The Earth rotates round the two opposite points known as the North and South Poles.

Precession of Vernal Equinoctial Point   Owing to the unequal gravitational pull of the Sun and Moon on the Earth's equatorial bulge there is a slow change in the position towards which the pole points. (*See* **Nutation**.) This movement also accounts for the fact that each year the point of the Vernal Equinox (the point in space where the Sun in spring crosses the Equator into Northern declination, after which the days lengthen in the Northern hemisphere) is seen each year from Earth in a position a little *behind* that of the preceding year. This Vernal Equinoctial Point is known as 0° Aries and provides the starting point for the *Signs* of the zodiac as opposed to the Constellations, which only exactly coincide with the Signs once in every 25,800 years.

Prime Vertical   (*See* **Vertical**.)

Progressions   The setting up of a progressed chart requires a further calculation on the basis of the natal chart to enable the astrologer to discuss the trends of a given year.

For this purpose most astrologers base their work on what are technically called *Secondary Directions*, where for no very clear reason the planetary set-up for a given number of *days* after birth corresponds with the trends in the individual life the equivalent number of *years* after birth. Other methods of directions such as Primary and Tertiary Directions are also employed, but the whole question is technical and for the casual reader it can be taken that 'progressions' or the progressed chart has to do with future trends rather than natal characteristics.

Quadrant   The earliest division of the heavens was into four parts or quadrants made by an imaginary line from the stationary point of the North Pole to its opposite Southern point, crossing an east/west line (or parallel of latitude) at an angle of 90°.

Quadruplicities   A division under four headings of the twelve Signs:

Fire	*Earth*	*Air*	*Water*
Aries	Taurus	Gemini	Cancer
Leo	Virgo	Libra	Scorpio
Sagittarius	Capricorn	Aquarius	Pisces

Rational Horizon (*See* **Horizon.**)

Regiomontanus House System   (Space System.)
This is a house system by which the equator is equally divided into twelve, lunes being made between house circles passing through these points of division and the north and south points of the horizon. These pass through degrees of ecliptic which define cuspal boundaries forming almost equal houses at the equator, but becoming more unequal as latitude increases. *Biographical Note:* This system invented by **Johann Muller**, a German mathematician, who died in 1476. He translated *Ptolemy* from Greek to Latin. He was a professor of astronomy and had his own observatory and printing press in Nuremburg.

Right Ascension   A measure in time.
This is a measure of longitude along the Celestial Equator. Compare **Celestial Longitude**, which measures along the Ecliptic. Both measures start from 0° Aries.

> Example: Right Ascension of 0° Aries = 0 hours
> Right Ascension of 0° Cancer = 6 hours
> i.e. 2 hours = 30°, or 2 hours to a Sign.

N.B.–With Right Ascension the Latitude measurement is known as Declination and gives height in sky. Positions of planets in Nautical Almanacs are given in this measure.

Rising-Sign   Owing to the rotation of the Earth the Sun *appears* to rise. In, shall we say, February, the Sun is in the Sign Aquarius, so whenever we look at the Sun we are also looking at the section of the Zodiac known as Aquarius, and at sunrise in February Aquarius will be rising. Roughly two hours later, although unmarked by a luminary, the Sign of Pisces will be coming up over the eastern horizon, and in another two hours Aries and so on at slightly varying intervals throughout the twenty-four hours. It needs calculation to arrive at the exact degree rising when a child is born, but very roughly, if we know the time we can limit the field to two or three possible Signs. For instance, in February when Sun is in Aquarius, a child born at *sunset* would have the opposite Sign to Aquarius rising, namely Leo.

Astrologically speaking, the exact degree of zodiac rising over the horizon at the time and place of birth provides the most personal indication of the chart. It gives, as it were, the precision of the second hand on the watch.

Ruler   Every Sign has a Planet that is in affinity with it. This planet is known as the ruler of the Sign.

Ruling Planet   The Ruling Planet is the Planet which rules the Rising Sign. To give an example: At your birth 12° Taurus was rising. Venus rules Taurus. Venus is your ruling planet.

Sun-ruler   Unless born at sunrise the Sun will be in another sign than the Rising-Sign. Let us say it is in Aries. Mars is then your Sun-ruler. Both Mars and Venus will be of added significance in your chart by virtue of their rulership.

Seasons   In Northern latitudes
Spring begins 21st March, Vernal Equinox (day and night equal the world over).
Summer begins 21st June, Summer Solstice (longest day).

Autumn begins 23rd September, Autumnal Equinox (equal day and night)
Winter begins 22nd December, Winter Solstice (shortest day).

The amount of heat received from the Sun does not depend on the distance between Earth and Sun at various times of year, but on the time it remains above the horizon and the altitude it reaches during the day.

Sidereal Day   (*See* **Day**.)

Sidereal Zodiac   This is a zodiac of the constellations, 0° Aries coinciding with the beginning of the constellation Aries, but thereafter following an arbitrary division into 30° per constellation regardless of the actual size or overlapping of these groups of stars.

This is the zodiac against which the Precession of the Equinoctial Points is viewed, so that at the time of writing 0° Aries of the Signs (as opposed to the constellations) is seen against the background of Aquarius.

Interrpetation by means of the Sidereal Zodiac   Much work was done by such astrologers as Cyril Fagin, Brigadier R. C. Firebrace, Rupert Gleadow and others to prove the validity of the 'zodiac of the constellations'. Nothing I have heard to date has persuaded me to use this method for personal characterisation, but I have seen evidence that it may be of value in plotting exact areas of world events or disasters. It is used widely in Hindu astrology.

Signs of the Zodiac   (*See* **Zodiac**.)

Small Circle   (*See* **Great Circle**.)

Solar Day   (*See* **Day**.)

Solar System

The Sun   Centre of the Solar System. It is self-luminous. The other Planets in the system shine in the reflected light of the Sun.

Diameter, 109 times that of Earth (865,400 miles).

Mass, 333,000 times that of Earth.

It rotates on its axis once in about 25 days.

The Moon   A satellite of Earth. Its light, like that of the Planets, is reflected from the Sun.

Diameter, 2,160 miles.

Revolution round Earth, just over 27 days.

Rotation, once in every revolution, so that the same face is nearly always presented to the Earth.

Mercury   Nearest Planet to the Sun (36m. miles).

Diameter, 3,000 miles.

Mass, 1/27th that of Earth.

Revolution round Sun, 88 days.

Rotation, only once in its circling of the Sun so that it always (or nearly) presents the same face to the Sun, as the Moon does to the Earth.

Venus   67m. miles from Sun.

Slightly smaller than Earth.

Revolution round Sun, 225 days.

Rotation period unknown with certainty.

Mars   142m. miles from Sun.

Diameter, half that of Earth (4,216 miles).

Mass, 1/9th that of Earth.

Revolution round Sun, 687 days.

Rotation period, $24\frac{1}{2}$ hours.

It has two moons.
Jupiter 483m. miles from Sun.
Diameter, 87,000 miles.
Mass, 316 times that of Earth.
Revolution round Sun, 12 years.
Rotation, a little less than 10 hours.
It has thirteen satellites or moons, some as distant from it as 20m. miles. Two of these revolve in the opposite direction to the rest.
Saturn 886m. miles from Sun.
Diameter, 75,000 miles.
Mass, 95 times that of Earth.
Revolution round Sun, 29½ years.
Rotation, 10 hours.
Saturn has three rings composed of small particles. These lie in a plane inclined to the Ecliptic at about 28°. There are ten moons outside the rings, one of which is very small and moving in an opposite direction to the rest.
Uranus 1,782m. miles from Sun.
Diameter, 30,900 miles.
Mass, 15 times that of Earth.
Revolution round Sun, 84 years.
Rotation, 11 hours.
Uranus was discovered in 1781 by the astronomer Herschel. It has five satellites, four of which revolve in a plane perpendicular to the Ecliptic and in a retrograde direction.
Neptune 2,793m. miles from Sun.
Diameter, 32,000 miles.
Mass, 17 times that of Earth.
Revolution round Sun, about 165 years.
Rotation, 16 hours.
Neptune was discovered by Adams and Verrier in 1846. It has two satellites, one of which moves in a retrograde direction.
Pluto About 3,670m. miles from Sun.
Diameter, about the same as Mars.
Revolution round Sun, 248 years.
Discovered in 1930 by the Lowell Observatory in Arizona.
Solstice (Latin: solsitium. Sol, the Sun; Sistere, to make stand.)
Summer solstice, approximately 21st June, when Sun enters the Sign of Cancer. Hence Tropic of Cancer, the demarcating line of the northernmost point on Earth where the Sun can be seen directly overhead. On or near 22nd December is the Winter solstice, when the Sun is directly overhead on the line of the Tropic of Capricorn and on this date Sun enters Capricorn. At these dates the Sun is at its farthest point from the Equator, or maximum declination, and we have the longest or shortest day according to hemisphere.
Superior Conjunction (*See* **Inferior Conjunction**.)
Terrestrial Latitude (*See* **Latitude**.)
Terrestrial Longitude (*See* **Longitude**.)
Terrestrial Sphere The Earth.
Time *G.M.T.*, or *Greenwich Mean Time*, is the zone or standard time used in Great Britain.

Zone Standard Time is the clock time used in most countries to avoid having varying times for the exact moon of each place.

Sidereal Time (See **Day**, SIDEREAL.)

Transit Dictionary meaning: a passing over or through; conveyance; the passing of an inferior planet across the Sun's disc; the passage of a heavenly body across the meridian of a place. (For full discussion on Transits in their astrological significance *see* Part II, Chapter 6.)

Astrologically speaking a planet 'transits' any sensitive degree in the personal chart, or chart under consideration, when it reaches such a degree in its movement through the heavens.

Triplicities A division under three headings of the Signs of the Zodiac:

Cardinal	Fixed	Mutable
Aries	Taurus	Gemini
Cancer	Leo	Virgo
Libra	Scorpio	Sagittarius
Capricorn	Aquarius	Pisces

Vernal Equinoctial Point Known as 0° Aries. This is the point that starts the Signs of the Zodiac (not the constellations of the same name).

Vernal Equinox 21 March, when the Sun in its apparent path appears directly above the Equator, thereafter crossing into Northern Declination so that days begin to lengthen in the Northern Hemisphere.

Its opposite, the **Autumnal Equinox**, occurs six months later when the Sun is once again over the Equator and day and night are of equal length all over the world. (*See* **Precession**.)

Vertical Circle A Great Circle rising vertically from the horizon and passing through Zenith and Nadir.

Prime Vertical The vertical circle which passes through the prime or East point of the horizon.

Visible Horizon (*See* **Horizon**.)

Zenith A point in the heavens immediately overhead at any given time or place.

Nadir Exactly opposite point to Zenith. The point in the heavens directly below our feet.

Zodiac A band of sky which extends to about 8° on each side of the Ecliptic (Sun's apparent path).

Sign of the Zodiac A division of 30°. Twelve of these complete the circle and starting from 0° Aries they bear the same names as the Constellations lying in the band of the zodiac with which they coincide once in every 25,000 years.

Zodiacal Longitude The distance in degrees along the Ecliptic.

Zone Standard Time (*See* **Time**.)

THE KEYWORD SYSTEM OF INTERPRETATION

(included by kind permission of the late Margaret E. Hone)

The Planets and their Principles

Sun	Power; Vitality; Self-expression.
Moon	Response; Fluctuation.
Mercury	Communication (mentally and by transport).
Venus	Harmony; Unison; Relatedness.
Mars	Energy; Heat; Activation.
Jupiter	Expansion; Preservation.
Saturn	Limitation; Cold.
Uranus	Change (Revolutionary; Disruptive; Dictatorial).
Neptune	Nebulousness; Impressionability.
Pluto	Elimination; Renewal; Regeneration.

The Signs as Customarily Grouped

(a) *The Triplicities*

Fire	Ardent; Keen.
Earth	Practical; Cautious.
Air	Intellectual; Communicative.
Water	Emotional; Unstable; Sensitive.

(b) *The Quadruplicities*

Cardinal	Outgoing.
Fixed	Reluctant to change.
Mutable	Adaptable.

(c) *Positivity and Negativity*

Positive	Self-expressive.
Negative	Self-repressive, receptive.

The Signs and their Modes of Planetary Expression

(A planet in a Sign will show its own principle, urge or drive, but it will do so in the mode of that Sign.)

In Aries	Assertively.
Taurus	Possessively.
Gemini	Communicatively, with alert versatility.
Cancer	Sensitively, protectively.
Leo	Creatively, joyfully.
Virgo	Critically, detailedly.
Libra	Harmoniously, unitedly.
Scorpio	Passionately, secretively, penetratingly.
Sagittarius	Widely, deeply, free-ranging.
Capricorn	Prudently, coolly, aspiringly.
Aquarius	Detachedly, scientifically.
Pisces	With appreciation of intangibles, or confusedly.

The Houses and their meanings
(A planet in a house will show its own principle, urge or drive according to the sphere of activity of that house.)

1–6
Personal

1. The Person.
2. Possessions and feelings of the persons.
3. Short communications. Mental interests. Nearest relations, such as brothers and sisters. Neighbours.
4. Home (basic matters).
5. Creativity, risks, pleasures, love, children.
6. Service. Health. Welfare.

7–12
Wider Expression

7. Others in close association.
8. Possession of or from others. Legacies, shared feelings. Life-force in birth, sex and after-life.
9. Longer communications. Far travel. Profound mental interests.
10. Matters outside the home. Public standing. Career. Attainment.
11. More detached contacts, such as friendships. Objectives.
12. More secluded service. Retirement; escape; sacrifice; hidden life of the unconscious.

(The two sets of houses are arranged in parallel columns so that it may be observed that there is an extension of expression from each in the first six to that one which is connected to it by polarity in the other six.)

Interpretation of Planet in Sign and House
Refer to keywords. Put their meanings together in what will be stilted language. Then expand the meaning in a phrase.
Example 1. Sun in Aries in 9th House.
By keywords: Your *power and vitality* are used *assertively* in matters of *travel* and *deeper study*.
Fuller interpretation: You are a busy, forceful, energetic person, keen to get about, see other countries and use your brain for serious study.
Example 2. Uranus in Aquarius in 7th House.

By keywords: Your urge to be *disruptive* is used *detachedly* when dealing with others in close *connection*.

Fuller interpretation: You have a strong tendency to split from anyone linked with you in close partnership. You will do this coolly and in an independent spirit.